W9-BEJ-704

Aces and Pilots
of the
US 8th/9th Air Forces

Jerry Scutts

Ian Allan
PUBLISHING

Front cover: Crew Chief Bill Gertzen adjusting the Merlin engine of Capt Robert Woody's P-51B-5 (42-6520/WR-W) of the 354th FS, 355th FG at Steeple Morden, probably in May 1944. Despite the 12 kills marked, Woody was officially credited with seven victories before being transferred to 8th AF headquarters. His Mustang, named 'Woody's Maytag', was lost to flak on 4 June 1944 while being flown by F/O Henry W. Davis. *Alexander C. Sloan*

Back cover: Virgil K. Meroney back from another successful mission. The five kills chalked up made him the first ace of the 352nd Group at Bodney. The aircraft is his personal P-47D-5, 42-8473. *Sam Sox*

Previous page:
Another Eighth Air Force 'deadly duo', although they flew in different groups, was Walker Mahurin of the 56th and Walt Beckham of the 353rd Group. On 3 February 1944 Beckham was congratulated on achieving his 17th and 18th victories. *Imperial War Museum*

ACKNOWLEDGEMENTS

Once again, my thanks to a number of individuals and organisations that helped make this project happen, mainly on the photographic side: Jim Bivens; Ian Carter; Jim Crow; John Hamlin; Imperial War Museum; Jack Lambert; Merle Olmsted; Sam Sox; United States Air Force and Richard L. Ward.

First published 2001

ISBN 0 7110 2895 8

All rights reserved. No part of this book may be reproduced or transmitted in any form or by any means, electronic or mechanical, including photocopying, recording or by any information storage and retrieval system, without permission from the Publisher in writing.

© Jerry Scutts 2001

Published by Ian Allan Publishing

an imprint of Ian Allan Publishing Ltd, Hersham, Surrey KT12 4RG.
Printed by Ian Allan Printing Ltd, Hersham, Surrey KT12 4RG.

Code: 0112/B

Worldwide distribution (except North America):
Ian Allan Publishing Ltd
Riverdene Business Park
Hersham
Surrey
KT12 4RG
Tel: 01923 266600   Fax: 01932 266601
e-mail: info@ianallanpub.co.uk

North American trade distribution:
Specialty Press Publishers & Wholesalers Inc
11605 Kost Dam Road, North Branch, MN55056
Tel: 651 583 3239   Fax: 651 583 2023
Toll free telephone: 800 895 4585

Contents

Bibliography

Bodie, Warren M.: *The Lockheed P-38 Lightning*; Widewing Publications, North Carolina, 1991

Caine, Philip D.: *American Pilots in the RAF*; Brasseys (US), Virginia, 1993

Franks, Norman: *The Battle of the Airfields*; William Kimber, London, 1982

Freeman, Roger A.: *Mighty Eighth War Diary*; Jane's, London 1981

Freeman, Roger A.: *Mighty Eighth War Manual*; Jane's, London, 1984

Freeman, Roger A.: *Thunderbolt; A documentary history*; Macdonald and Jane's, London 1978

Freeman, Roger A.: *The Ninth Air Force in Colour*; Arms and Armour Press, London, 1995

Fry, Garry L.: *Eagles of Duxford: the 78th Fighter Group in WWII*; Phalanx Publishing, Minnesota, 1991

Fry, Garry L. and Ethell, Jeffrey L.: *Escort to Berlin – the 4th Fighter Group in World War II*; Arco Publishing, New York, 1980

Gray, John M.: *The 55th Fighter Group vs The Luftwaffe*; Specialty Press, North Branch, Minnesota, 1998

Hammel, Eric: *Air War Europa Chronology 1942–45*; Pacifica Press, California, 1994

Hess, W. N. and Rust, K. C.: *The Slybird Group*; Aero Publishers, California, 1968

Infield, Glenn B.: *The Poltava Affair*; Robert Hale & Company, London, 1974

Ivie, Tom: *Aerial Reconnaissance – The 10th Photo Recon Group in WWII*; Aero Publishers, California, 1981

Keller, Isham G.: *The 474th Fighter Group in World War II*; Roma Associates, Minneapolis, 1988

Kucera, Dennis C.: *In a Now Forgotten Sky: the 31st Fighter Group in World War 2*; Flying Machines Press, Connecticut, 1997

Ludwig, Paul and Laird, Malcolm: *American Spitfire Camouflage and Markings* (Vols 1 & 2); Ventura Publishing, Wellington, New Zealand, 1998 and 1999

Maurer, Maurer: *Air Force Combat Units of World War II*; Franklin Watts, New York, 1963

Maurer, Maurer: *Combat Squadrons of the Air Force*; USAF Historical Division, Washington, DC, 1969

McLaren, David R.: *Beware the Thunderbolt! – The 56th Fighter Group In World War II*; Schiffer Military History, Atglen, Philadelphia, 1994

Miller, Kent D.: *Jigger Tinplate & Redcross*; Academy Publishing, Indiana, 1987

Miller, Kent D.: *Seven Months over Europe – the 363rd Fighter Group in WW II*; Kent Miller, Ohio, 1989

Noah, Joe and Sox, Samuel L., Jr: *George Preddy Top Mustang Ace*; Motorbooks International, California, 1991

Olynyk, Frank: *Stars & Bars – A Tribute to the American Fighter Ace 1920–1973*; Grubb Street, London, 1995

Powell, Robert H., Jr: *The Bluenosed Bastards of Bodney*; Taylor Publishing, Dallas, Texas, 1990

Rust, Kenn C.: *Eighth Air Force Story*; Historical Aviation Album, California, 1978

Rust, Kenn C.: *Ninth Air Force Story*; Historical Aviation Album, California, 1982

Scutts, Jerry: *P-47 Thunderbolt Aces of the 9th and 15th Air Forces*; Osprey Publishing, Oxford, 1999

Steinko, John Truman: *The "Geyser" Gang – the 428th Fighter Squadron in WWII*; Roma Associates, Minneapolis, 1986

Wagner, Ray: *Mustang Designer: Edgar Schmued and the P-51*; Smithsonian Institution Press, Washington, DC, 1990

Weatherill, David: *Aces, Pilots & Aircraft of the 9th, 12th and 15th USAAF*; Kookaburra Technical Publications, Melbourne, 1978

Glossary

ALG: Advanced Landing Ground

Bluie West One (and Eight): Bases in Greenland which served as stopovers for US aircraft flying the North Atlantic ferry route to Europe

Box Score: Combined score by all squadrons of a single fighter group or several groups

BS: Bomber Squadron.

Circus: RAF operational codename for heavy fighter escort for groups of bombers designed to draw the enemy into battle

Debden Eagles: 4th Fighter Group nickname – derived from RAF Eagle Squadrons

Eagles: Short form of the above

FC: Fighter Command

FG: Fighter Group

FS: Fighter Squadron

F/O: Flying Officer; RAF rank occasionally perpetuated by American pilots serving with the USAAF

JG: Jagdgeschwader (fighter wing)

'Jubilee': Codename for the Dieppe operation on 19 August 1942

KG: Kampfgeschwader (bomber wing)

NACA: National Advisory Council for Aeronautics (later NASA)

P-70: Night-fighter version of the Douglas A-20 Havoc

Pioneer Mustang Group: Nickname of 354th Fighter Group, first in USAAF to operate the P-51B

Pioneers: Short form of the above

P/O: Pilot Officer; RAF rank occasionally perpetuated by American pilots serving with the USAAF

Ramrod: RAF operational codename for fighter escort to bombers

Rodeo: RAF operational codename for fighter sweep designed to destroy enemy aircraft

Rhubarb: RAF operational codename for fighters attacking ground targets, often in poor weather conditions

TAC: Tactical Air Command

TDY: Temporary duty

T/O: Target(s) of opportunity

TRG: Tactical Reconnaissance Group

TRS: Tactical Reconnaissance Squadron

Wolfpack: 56th Fighter Group nickname

ZG: Zerstörergeschwader (heavy fighter wing)

Introduction

In many quarters the aerial side of World War 2 began with the premise that the bomber would be the decisive weapon, but as the conflict widened across Europe it encompassed numerous operations by fighter aircraft. It was quickly realised that the key to air superiority lay not in bombers but in the quality and quantity of fighters. These developments were observed by commanders of the United States Army Air Corps, as their country was slowly drawn into another 'foreign war', although the pursuit aircraft or fighter, the 'pea shooter' of popular journalese, was not very highly regarded as a primary weapon. The eventual deployment of pursuit planes was definitely seen as being of a secondary, 'support' nature, very much an adjunct to bomber operations. Fighters, it was imagined, would probably be deployed to defend American cities in the event of enemy air attacks, to 'support troops in the field', fly interception sorties to protect ground installations, carry out one or two useful additional duties such as a limited amount of photographic reconnaissance and even drop the odd bomb or two on tactical targets. A definite policy of using fighters to escort bombers over long ranges did not exist, nor was there a suitable type to fulfil such a role.

Notwithstanding the success of the three Eagle Squadrons serving with the RAF in England, the focus remained firmly upon the deployment of bombers, a situation that prevailed even as the USA declared war on the European Axis on 11 December 1941. Aircraft such as the B-17 Flying Fortress and B-24 Liberator had been developed to the point where they were believed to be virtually self-protecting with their awesome defensive armament of heavy machine guns. Daylight precision bombing by aircraft able to defend themselves was the plan of the Eighth Air Force in England which embarked on its mighty crusade in August 1942.

Short-range fighter escort was available in England, but as the American bombers pushed ahead to their ultimate goal of hitting the industrial heartland of Germany, they flew beyond friendly fighter range — and the Luftwaffe pounced. Many gruelling months of learning lay ahead for the crews as they proved that the concept of the 'self-defending' formation was fatally flawed.

If the offensive was to be maintained, the only answer was to provide escort to the bombers all the way through to the most distant targets. Fortunately, back in 1940 Britain had commissioned North American Aviation to build a new fighter for the RAF, and, as subsequently modified, the P-51 Mustang proved more than capable of meeting the range challenge. Thus by the end of 1943 the brutal tutorial had all but ended and during the next 14 months or so the vague prewar doctrines *vis-à-vis* the deployment of fighters were turned completely upside down; long-range fighters, exemplified by the Mustang, could now fly from England to Russia, a hitherto undreamed of distance for single-engined aircraft. In addition, the P-38 and particularly the P-47 became outstanding fighter-bombers able to support ground forces more effectively than any other aircraft type. Lightnings and Mustangs also carved their indispensable niche as photo-reconnaissance aircraft.

In the course of escorting their bombers, American fighter pilots steadily wore down the cream of the German Jagdwaffe to the point where it was unable to defend even its own airfields. Decimated by the sheer scale of operations that defending the Reich demanded, the enemy lost hundreds of pilots and aircraft to the point where the Luftwaffe fighter force, the former hunters of Europe's skies, increasingly became the hunted.

In the European Theatre of Operations (ETO) those hunters rode cockpits of Mustangs, Thunderbolts and Lightnings and wore the patch of the Eighth and Ninth Fighter Commands. They succeeded in carrying the air war to the enemy in a way that had never before been possible. By so doing, numerous American pilots became air aces with a baseline five confirmed victories. A substantial number stopped at that point, the USAAF rotation system ensuring that many such men were rested from combat for long periods or were sent home, their duty done. Others who volunteered for additional tours of combat flying managed to boost their victory tallies way beyond the average — but in a conflict where numbers counted, everyone contributed to the final victory over the Axis, even those individuals who flew missions without ever having a brush with the Luftwaffe. It is to all frontline fighter pilots in the ETO, whether or not they achieved the coveted status of an ace, that this volume is respectfully dedicated.

Jerry Scutts
London, 2001

1 RAF Classroom

From the British standpoint the Battle of Britain was judged to have officially ended on 31 October 1940. Foremost among the mass of statistics compiled on the campaign were records of all participating pilots, by nationality. Among them were 11 Americans[1] who had contributed to the victory gained by the pilots of RAF Fighter Command. All of them were operating with the British in an entirely unofficial capacity; they had volunteered of their own free will and had joined Hurricane squadrons to cut their combat teeth in what later came to be termed by their compatriots as the European Theatre of Operations (ETO).

These fighter pilot pioneers from the other side of the Atlantic were soon followed by many more of their countrymen. Their imagination fired by Britain's David and Goliath struggle against the German Luftwaffe, they were eager to 'do their bit'. Some had decided to duck the over-stringent recruitment requirements of their own Air Corps, while others had refused to accept the arbitrary stamp of failure during basic training. It

was often the case that even civilian-qualified pilots were routinely 'washed out' of military flight training schools in their own country if they did not measure up to the established doctrine. With the admirable self-confidence of youth, they set out, most often via Canada, with the aim of joining the RAF and flying a fighter, preferably the fabled Spitfire.

Although the larger part of the epic struggle to save Britain from a German invasion had been in the capable hands of Hurricane squadrons, it was the 'Spit' which garnered the publicity, not least because of its highly apt name. And as many pilots came to appreciate, the Supermarine fighter was, with some small reservations, the best there was, anywhere. But the 'glamour factor' aside, it would be some time before the Americans who arrived in Britain in late 1940 and early 1941 would be considered well enough trained to fly the Spitfire. Most were obliged to spend time at Operational Training Units and, in the main, to fly Hurricanes. They came to appreciate that, while it was an older design compared to the Spitfire, the Hurricane was an

unrivalled gun platform, rock steady and tough, and that, when well flown, it could out-turn most enemy aircraft with ease.

There was much the Americans needed to learn — formation flying, gunnery and air combat tactics. Bad weather flying was a particular source of anxiety (many pilots were amazed at how low the visibility had to be to ground the RAF) as those who hailed from the sunnier states often had little experience of it. They also knew that in the US all flying would have been cancelled in conditions far superior to those they were regularly exposed to in England.

One major stumbling block to their quickly becoming a valuable part of an organisation that emphasised teamwork above most other attributes, was that most of the American volunteers lacked much in the way of military discipline. Their antics sometimes amazed the more strait-laced British officers charged with welding them into a fighting force, who feared that they faced an uphill struggle. As things turned out, there were few problems and only one pilot ever had to be sent home.

As the number of Americans (and other nationalities) in Britain increased, it

Above: Hawker Hurricane Mk Is of No 71 Eagle Squadron scrambling from Kirton-in-Lindsey on 18 March 1941. All three US-manned units were initially equipped with the Hawker fighter. *Imperial War Museum*

seemed logical to form squadrons almost entirely staffed, both operationally and administratively, by foreign nationals, the one proviso being that these squadrons were led by experienced RAF officers. Accordingly No 71, the first American Eagle Squadron, was established at Church Fenton in Yorkshire on 19 September 1940. The original cadre of pilots came from No 609 Squadron: Pilot Officers Andrew B. Mamedoff, Eugene Q. 'Red' Tobin and Vernon C. 'Shorty' Keough. The first CO of No 71 was Squadron Leader Walter M. Churchill, a name that could hardly have been more appropriate in the circumstances!

On formation, No 71 had no aircraft apart from a single Miles Master for training. Frustration began to set in among the pilots when fighters failed to materialise. Then someone apparently had the bright idea that Americans might prefer to fly a fighter designed and built in the USA. Several Brewster F2A-2s (Buffalo Mk Is) duly arrived at Church Fenton on 24 October and a number of evaluation flights were made. These soon confirmed that the Buffalo was totally inferior not only to the Hurricane but to contemporary German fighters and even

contemplating its use was questionable. Something had to be done.[2]

Squadron Leader Churchill turned a blind eye when three Buffaloes flown by Red Tobin, Andrew Mamedoff and Royce Wilkinson touched down after a training flight — and all of them ground looped with disastrous results. This was due to the tailwheel being 'down but unlocked', which usually induced the aircraft to whip around uncontrollably on touchdown, a fact known both to the pilots and the CO. Nobody let on that this desperate act of vandalism was to force the RAF hierarchy into giving No 71 something combat-worthy to fight with. The ruse paid off and when the unit moved to Kirton-in-Lindsey, Lincolnshire, on 23 November, it took with it Hurricanes.

In the spotlight
Pleased to have something to fight with, No 71 became hot news. Used to publicity at home, some individual members of the unit were nevertheless unprepared for the barrage of press and radio interviews focused on the squadron. Journalists and photographers swarmed to gather what was undeniably a good story but one that the

American pilots could not yet endorse with any tales of combat. That did not stop some members of the press corps from giving the impression that their mere presence in England meant that the war was as good as won. Such irresponsible journalism embarrassed Americans and British alike, and a brake was eventually put on the wild stories. While Americans were recruited in the US they were not free to travel abroad to fight, as their country was not at war; a guarded approach was therefore taken in officially heralding the fact that a neutral country was openly siding with one of the combatants. Some news on the Eagles was held back from general release until after America entered the war.

January 1941
Flying sorties that were more of an operational training nature to build up pilot hours and experience, the Eagles came to grips with flying high performance aircraft in formation, often in poor weather conditions. Cloud, rain and low visibility always harboured the spectre of collision and on 5 January 1941 No 71 Squadron experienced the loss of Philip Leckrone, one of the original members of the unit.

Above: A practice scramble for the press carried out by pilots of No 71 Sqn at Kirton. Publicity surrounded the Eagles to the point of frustration at times.
Imperial War Museum

Flying a training sortie, Leckrone's aircraft was at 20,000 feet when it hit the Hurricane being flown by Ed Orbison, who managed to land safely, despite damage. As the stricken Hurricane dived, Shorty Keough followed it down, calling in vain for Leckrone to bail out.

This sobering event was made worse for No 71 by the departure of their popular leader when Churchill was taken ill during January and replaced by Squadron Leader William E. G. Taylor. The appalling weather which sometimes prevented flying for days on end got on everyone's nerves, but a significant raising of spirits accompanied the late January announcement that the squadron was operational in 12 Group, Fighter Command.

First ops
Records indicate that the first operational mission for No 71 Squadron was undertaken on 5 February. Numerous patrols to provide an escort for convoys sailing off the English coast followed, but the unit had to wait weeks before firing its guns in anger. As dull as these overwater patrols could often be, they still held hazards for the unwary by inducing a highly dangerous sense of disorientation, when sky and sea blended into a grey mass without reference points. On 9 February Ed Orbison apparently succumbed to this phenomenon when he spun into the sea from 4,000 feet altitude.

Having to come to terms with the loss of another pilot in a situation remote from any form of enemy action was hard, but the US airmen at least took comfort from the fact that they were ready for more ambitious operational sorties as and when these came along. Soon afterwards, on the 15th, Keough also went into the sea — and this third accident indirectly resulted in No 71 being moved from 12 Group to join 11 Group in the south, where everyone knew the real action was.

Army Air Corps chief Henry H. 'Hap' Arnold had a hand in the move as he wanted the American fighters to see some real combat action as soon as possible. If they could not do so, he recommended that the pilots be sent home. Consequently, No 71 was on the move again on 9 April when it took up residence at Martlesham Heath, Suffolk. The action craved by the American pilots almost materialised on the 13th in the form of a Ju88 which dived away with four Hurricanes in hot pursuit. While No 71's pilots impatiently waited for some confirmed aerial victories, William Taylor handed over the CO's reins to Henry de C. A. 'Paddy' Woodhouse.

Second squadron
Meanwhile – and attended by far less publicity than had surrounded No 71 — the second Eagle Squadron was formed on 14 May 1941. No 121 Squadron was also equipped with Hurricanes and was established at the original unit's aerodrome at Kirton-in-Lindsey. Its rise to operational status proceeded much faster than its sister unit's, due in no small part to the transfer of some of No 71's experienced pilots and the choice of the RAF officer to lead it, in this case Squadron Leader Peter R. Powell. Along with fellow Battle of Britain veteran Hugh C. Kennard and Royce C. Wilkinson of No 71 who were his flight commanders, Powell helped No 121 to prosper; that the leadership choices were sound was shown by the fact that the second Eagle Squadron was cleared as operational just over two months after forming, on 21 July.

A peripheral event during May was the official change of the US 'pursuit' category of aircraft to that of 'fighter' — which did not mean that the former description was dropped. It continued to crop up in documents, newspaper reports and the like — and especially amongst the pilots themselves. Another more fundamental change came on 20 June when the US Army Air Corps (USAAC) became the US Army Air Force (USAAF) — and once again the old 'Air Corps' terminology took a long time to die out.

No 71 Squadron had moved to North Weald in Essex during June and still a confirmed kill eluded it. Then on 2 July the squadron's Hurricanes drew an escort mission for a raid by some Blenheims. Taking the bomber bait, the Luftwaffe jumped the RAF formations, up to 30 Bf109s being reported. As the opposing fighters manoeuvred for advantage, Paddy Woodhouse drew first blood, his victim going into the sea trailing smoke. Gus Daymond was credited with another Bf109E for his first confirmed victory when the German pilot was seen to abandon an aircraft that looked to be uncontrollable, presumably through combat damage. It, too, was seen heading down, trailing smoke. Elsewhere in the mêlée, Bill Hall came off worst in combat and took to his parachute to make a landfall in France and become the first

Eagle to become a PoW. Despite this loss, the collective pleasure felt by men of the premier Eagle Squadron when a telegram arrived from 11 Group congratulating the pilots on their success, can be readily appreciated.

July 1941
Further action on 6 July enabled Daymond to obtain his second victory, a Bf109E shot down west of Lille, while Bill Dunn's probable victory over a Bf109E netted him a quarter share. In a busy month compared to the dearth of contact with the Luftwaffe in previous weeks, No 71 clashed with the new Messerschmitt Bf109F on 21 July and while it was strongly rumoured that this improved sub-type of the famous German fighter was superior to the Hurricane IIB, that did not inhibit Dunn's aim. He received a credit for destroying a single 'Friedrich' west of Lille.

Last of the trio
On 1 August 1941 No 133, the third Eagle Squadron, was formed at Coltishall in Norfolk under the command of Squadron Leader George A. Brown. Working up began immediately and the squadron was declared operational on Hurricane IIBs on 29 September. A familiar round of convoy patrols, practice Rodeos and diversionary sweeps followed, with the aim of building up theatre experience as soon as possible. Again the new unit was helped by the transfer of experienced American pilots from the other Eagle Squadrons. Bill Dunn, who remained with No 71, got another Bf109F on 9 August to give him 3.5 confirmed.

Spits at last!
During August 1941 No 71 Squadron passed another milestone when it converted to the Mk IIA version of the Spitfire, the first Eagle Squadron to do so. On the 17th the first Spitfire mission was flown and before the month ended, more potent, cannon-armed Mk VBs had arrived. No 121 would similarly start to relinquish its Hurricanes during October, as would No 133; all three Eagle Squadrons were fully equipped with Spitfires by the end of 1941.

Flying a Spitfire IIA on 27 August, Dunn shot down two Bf109Fs off the French coast near Ambleteuse to bring his score to five plus the earlier half share. This turned out to be his last operational flight as a member of the RAF, as he was

Above: A photo dated 27 November 1941 showing Jim Daley of No 121 Sqn strapping into a Spitfire, probably for yet another routine convoy patrol. *Imperial War Museum*

wounded during a dogfight that day and hospitalised. Back in England as a USAAF captain in 1944, Dunn joined the 406th Fighter Group of the Ninth Air Force to claim one more victory to give him a wartime total of six confirmed.

September 1941

The first Spitfire victory for Gus Daymond of No 71 Squadron was on 4 September when he shot down a Bf109F for his fourth kill. Further contact with this same German fighter type on the 19th recorded Daymond's fifth, plus a damaged. A Bf109E fell to Red McColpin on the 21st for his first victory. October was an even more successful month for McColpin as he destroyed four Bf109Es and an Hs 126 to give him six, which by American criteria now made him, Bill Dunn and Gus Daymond aces.

As serving pilot officers in the RAF, McColpin and Daymond were recommended for the DFC and, although the British did not officially recognise aces, aerial victories by Eagle pilots did not do No 71 Squadron's reputation any harm at all. With Dunn out of the fight, the autumn air combat successes of Daymond and McColpin helped put their unit in the lead,

ahead of all Fighter Command squadrons in terms of enemy aircraft destroyed for October 1941. Although No 71's aggregate of nine confirmed was commendable, the figure reflected the paucity of German fighter reaction to the many 'live bait' raids laid on by the RAF primarily to tempt the Jagdwaffe into battle.

The other side of the coin for the Eagles was the steadily rising number of pilots lost in accidents as well as combat, which would reach double figures by the end of the year. They were by no means all fatal casualties, but a pilot who was wounded or, even worse, became a PoW, was still a blow to a squadron in terms of valuable experience lost. Two changes of CO brought Squadron Leader Stanley T. Meares to take the helm of No 71 during October.

November continued the typical mix of triumph and tragedy, Meares being killed in a mid-air collision with Ross Scarborough's aircraft during a training flight. Again the squadron was in the lead in terms of Fighter Command victories for the second consecutive month.

After the death of Meares, members of

the first Eagle Squadron appreciated the considerable honour of being given an American commanding officer. The previous policy of having only an experienced RAF pilot in command had paid off handsomely, but now, as Squadron Leader Chesley G. Peterson prepared to take over No 71, every member of the squadron knew the American fighter units in England had come of age.

December 1941

Overshadowing most other events in a world already on a war footing was the Japanese attack on Pearl Harbor on 7 December. America was now at war and for many pilots of the Eagle Squadrons, a change of emphasis appeared to be imminent; their country would, they assumed, want them all back home to fight the Japanese. Their willingness to do so was communicated to the highest levels of the US military and the government, but while the pilots' spirited response to the crisis was acknowledged, nothing much changed and the Eagles stayed put.

In planning its cross-Channel fighter offensive, the RAF had expanded the wing system whereby three or more squadrons were grouped together on the same aerodrome and/or located on several nearby satellite stations. Wings could concentrate a substantial number of aircraft on a given operation and maintain a cohesion in combat tactics and mutual support. RAF wings initially took their names from the major fighter aerodromes, most of which were in southeastern England and came under 11 Group control for offensive operations. It was considered an honour to be part of such groups of fighters, as it was usually only the top performing squadrons that were given the chance to join, although units were regularly rotated within each wing, depending on operational commitments.

Having overcome another frustrating period of winter weather, the Eagles anticipated increased action during 1942, but weather and an at times very elusive enemy would combine to deny the Americans the large scale aerial combat they sought. The early months of the year saw more tedious convoy patrols and weather reconnaissance flights and the

monotony was too much for some pilots, who volunteered to be posted away. Almost in desperation, several took up the option of a transfer to Malta. That was where real action was to be found, albeit in a hectic and dangerous corner of the world. Those that remained in Britain were rewarded with much the same fare as before; there was hardly any contact with the Luftwaffe, which of course had no need to intercept British fighters looking for combat.

Not until 26 April did enemy fighters deign to enter combat with No 133 Squadron — and promptly paid the price of an Fw190 shot down by Red McColpin, who had been posted from No 71 during the previous winter to become one of No 133's flight commanders. Contact with enemy fighters on the 27th led to claims of two probables against Focke-Wulfs, but one US pilot failed to return. More probables accrued to Eagle Squadron pilots in a third consecutive day of action on 28 April, Pilot Officer Don Blakeslee, then flying with No 401 Squadron RAF, claiming hits on two Fw190s. Having but one confirmed and no less than five damaged

was getting a little tiresome for Blakeslee, but in due course things would improve for this outstanding fighter pilot.

'Big league'

On 3 May 1942 pilots of No 133 Squadron were delighted to make a move to Kent to become part of the Biggin Hill Wing on that most famous of RAF aerodromes. The station history recorded that the American pilots serving at that time represented no less than 13 states of the union and that their exuberant behaviour, ripe language and bawdy songs over the R/T, plus sheer eagerness to get to grips with the Luftwaffe, were well in keeping with Biggin's traditions! No 133 flew its first sweep on 7 May, but it was to be another 10 days before one of the pilots achieved a confirmed kill. This fell to Red McColpin in the shape of a Bf109F during a sweep to Le Tréport on the 17th.

Fighters for the Eighth

Under US war policy that had, contrary to some expectations, put the defeat of Germany before that of the Japanese, moves were made formally to establish numbered air forces overseas. Each was

Above: A picture that says it all — Old Glory fluttering below a fine echelon of Spitfires of No 121 Squadron over Kirton on 22 November 1941. *Imperial War Museum*

originally intended to have heavy and medium bomber, fighter, transport and support groups, which would vary in number depending on the perceived importance of the theatre of war.

When the Eighth Air Force was established in England under Major General Carl 'Tooey' Spaatz in April 1942, Brigadier General Frank O'Dell 'Monk' Hunter was appointed to command six attached fighter groups, none of which was to continue that assignment much beyond the end of 1942. The initial strength of VIII Fighter Command was the 1st, 14th, 31st, 52nd, 82nd and 350th Groups. Of these, the 31st and 52nd arrived in England without aircraft and were re-equipped with Spitfires and the 350th brought its P-39 Airacobras across the Atlantic. The other three came equipped with P-38G and H model Lightnings and retained their aircraft.

Led by Colonel John R. Hawkins and based at Atcham in Shropshire with nearby High Ercall as a satellite base, it fell to the 31st Fighter Group's Spitfire Mk Vs to undertake VIII Fighter Command's first mission of the war, on 26 July 1942. Six US-manned Spitfires accompanied RAF Spitfires for a sweep of the Abbeville and St Omer areas, notorious as the lair of JG 26's

Above: A lucky hand of cards and dice painted on the fuselage band of his Spitfire Vb (AV-M) did not prevent P/O Richard Fuller Patterson of No 121 Sqn being lost, on 7 December 1941. *Imperial War Museum*

Above: Pilots of the 307th Fighter Squadron at readiness (*left to right*) are Capt Louis Zimlick and Lieutenants James A. Cooper, Vincent Dusan, Beryl Hawkins, Vincent Baher and Merlin P. Mitchell. Several American pilots, like Hawkins, had what the British would have considered as strictly female first names, which must have raised a smile or two. Spitfire Mk V MX-U is visible in the background. *Imperial War Museum*

Messerschmitts. Greeted over France not by the 'Abbeville Kids' but flak, the aircraft piloted by Lieutenant Colonel Albert P. 'Red' Clark, the group executive officer, was hit during a strafing run. Obliged to bail out, Clark thus gained the dubious distinction of becoming the first USAAF fighter pilot to be captured in the European theatre. The sweep took place a matter of weeks after the 15th BS (L) had flown the inaugural VIII Bomber Command bombing mission in borrowed RAF Bostons on 4 July. While the 31st was not destined to remain long in the Eighth, its effort was to be the most active, with a total of 1,286 operational sorties logged before it left for North Africa.

This was a period when a considerable degree of reshuffling of units took place while AAF operational plans were still being formulated. The composition of the Eighth's fighter element had not been decided and, in this respect, things took months to settle down. Before that happened, there would be a major upheaval to meet commitments for the American part in Operation 'Torch', the invasion of French North Africa in November 1942.

Early VIII FC operations carried no numerical Field Order designation, a situation that prevailed until May 1943; before that date fighter missions were alternatively identified under the RAF system of numbered Rodeo and Circus operations. On those occasions when such were flown and involved American squadrons, they simply went into the records under borrowed RAF terminology.

During the last week of July 1942 more P-38s arrived in England in the hands of the 1st Fighter Group, commanded by Colonel John Stone. These Lightnings were the 'advance guard' from the group's headquarters flight, the component 27th, 71st and 94th Squadrons having become badly strung out along the north Atlantic ferry route even though single-seat fighters flying to Europe warranted the assistance of a bomber 'escort' to handle the navigation. The route was to become familiar in succeeding months, taking in as it did Goose Bay, Labrador, Bluie West One or Eight in Greenland then Reykjavik, Iceland, and finally Scotland. The Lightning was the one fighter in the Allied inventory at that time which appeared able to escort heavy bombers over a considerable range — but the impending requirements of 'Torch' were to deny the UK strategic

bomber force its own P-38 groups for some months to come.

Fortunately for the future of the Eighth, one of the pilots who flew a 1st Group Lightning to England was to remain. He was Major Cass Hough, whose expertise as head of the Eighth Air Force Service Command organisation gave the fighter and bomber groups in England an outstanding 'behind the scenes' service of technical troubleshooting and innovation in numerous areas.

August 1942

Pilots flying early fighter patrols from England in 31st Group Spitfires were, in common with the Eagle Squadrons, to find combat with the Luftwaffe elusive. But on 9 August, tenacity was rewarded when John Hawkins was credited with an Fw190 damaged. It wasn't much, but it was a start.

On 14 August AAF pilots found somewhat easier prey *en route* to England from Iceland; on stopover at Keflavik, Captain John Weltman and Lieutenant Elza E. Shahan of the 27th FS, 1st Fighter Group, were alerted to the fact that two P-40Cs of the 33rd Squadron had been scrambled to intercept a prowling Fw200 reconnaissance bomber which was regularly seen over Icelandic territory.[3] Weltman and Shahan, who had along with the rest of the 27th been ordered to remain in Iceland for the time being, took off in their P-38Fs to see if they could catch the German aircraft. They knew that Keflavik-based P-40s and P-39s had had little success in the past, but on this occasion one P-40C did catch up with the Condor and opened fire on it.

Boring up through the broken overcast Weltman spotted the Condor in the clear and he and Shahan attacked. The German gunners returned the fire and Weltman's aircraft suffered some damage. Drawing off, the Lightning pilots saw that the Condor, reportedly from I./KG 40 and flown by Fritz Kuhn, appeared to be damaged. Telling Shahan to carry on the attack while he landed to get another P-38, Weltman left the scene. His wingman, fearing that the quarry would escape, then fired at point-blank range until the Focke-Wulf blew up. That the American pilots were a little inexperienced was shown by the fact that the body of one of the German crewmen recovered from the sea was literally riddled with bullets. For his contribution, Shahan was credited with

half the kill as was Joseph Shaffer of the 33rd FS. The Condor was confirmed as the first enemy aircraft to be shot down by US Army aircraft in the ETO.

On 19 August the 31st Group was to have been joined in combat by P-38s of the 82nd Group, the first occasion when fighter units were dispatched under direct VIII Fighter Command operational control. In the event the 82nd did fly, but it was held back and never allowed near enough to enemy aircraft to trade fire. It too departed for North Africa without seeing any action while based in England and did not log any missions as part of the Eighth Air Force.

Bombing debut

August 1942 was a momentous month for US air operations in Europe for on the 17th, all 12 B-17E Fortresses dispatched by the 97th Bomb Group from Grafton Underwood in Northamptonshire returned from their first mission to bomb the marshalling yards at Rouen-Sotteville in occupied France. Everyone involved especially Spaatz, Ira C. Eaker, head of VIII Bomber Command, and the C-in-C RAF Bomber Command, Air Chief Marshal Arthur Harris — not to mention Hap Arnold and Winston Churchill — was greatly relieved that a US strategic heavy bomber offensive had thus begun.

Although there was no direct fighter support to the Flying Fortresses on their debut mission in the ETO, subsequent operations were to have both direct escort and indirect support by Spitfire squadrons. The latter usually consisted of attacks on enemy aerodromes along the route taken by the bombers into and out of the target area as a diversion to draw Luftwaffe fighters away. Using Spitfires it was not possible to cover the bombers very far into Europe. Although the early Eighth Air Force bomber missions were mostly to targets in occupied Europe, not at very long range, the Spitfire pilots could accompany the B-17s, the 'big friends', only as far as an operational radius stretching into northwestern France and bisecting Paris. The bomber crews were nevertheless highly appreciative of the support given by their Allies and it became a wartime truism that they were always glad to see their own fighters, however short the duration of the escort's stay may have been.

As Eighth Air Force bomber missions continued at a modest rate, so the 31st Group built experience in more diversions,

Above and below: Many photos of US fighter pilots were released in England on 28 August 1942, some showing the aftermath of the Dieppe raid on the 19th. Here, Lt Merlin Mitchell of the 307th FS surveys several holes apparently inflicted by cannon fire in his Spitfire Mk V, MX-X. *Imperial War Museum*

air-sea rescue (ASR) patrols and the occasional sweep over enemy territory. Considerably more excitement was anticipated by the American pilots of the 31st Group and all three Eagle Squadrons on 19 August when the RAF laid on massive air support for Operation 'Jubilee', an invasion rehearsal on the other side of the Channel in the Pas de Calais.

Dieppe

Bitching mightily at a rumoured intention to leave them out of the action to support Operation 'Jubilee', the predominantly Canadian landings at Dieppe, pilots of the 307th Squadron, 31st Group got

their way — they would be part of the Biggin Hill Wing for the 'big show'. Leading the American Spitfire squadron was Major Marvin L. McNickle. The wing then comprised Nos 133 (Eagle), 401 (Canadian), 222 and 602 Squadrons. No 133 and the Canadian squadron operated from Biggin's satellite at Lympne. The 31st Group's other two squadrons were based respectively at Kenley under Major Fred M. Dean (308th FS) and at Westhampnett (309th FS) led by Major Harrison R. Thyng. These American squadrons each contributed up to four Spitfires to the Dieppe operation, the Eagle Squadron

element being led respectively by Squadron Leader Chesley Peterson (No 71 — four aircraft from Gravesend); Squadron Leader W. Dudley Williams (acting CO of No 121 — three aircraft from Southend) and Flight Lieutenant Donald J.M. Blakeslee, acting CO of No 133, which put up four Spitfires from Lympne.

The American pilots were but a small part of a force of 750 aircraft that included no less than 48 squadrons of Spitfires, the largest contingent of the total of 63 fighter squadrons marshalled for the operation. Air cover for Dieppe was the largest the RAF had put up since the height of the Battle of Britain — in fact there were more squadrons available than had been on hand for the entire decisive air battle in 1940. Under Air Vice-Marshal Trafford Leigh-Mallory, AOC 11 Group Fighter Command, the RAF flew nearly 3,000 sorties during the day.

By contrast, the six Luftwaffe fighter Gruppen of JG 2 and 26 based within range of Dieppe had a combined total of 115 serviceable Fw190As and Bf109Fs, both of which were superior to the Spitfire V with a competent pilot at the controls. Spitfire Mk IXs were flown by four of the participating RAF squadrons, this much improved variant, in its turn, enjoying an edge over the German fighters. As the Allied armada swept in, the German fighters mounted the first of a series of patrols that would last throughout the day to nullify any advantage their opposite numbers believed that they enjoyed. There were numerous combats as the Germans parried the continuous RAF sorties into the battle area.

Initially flying a defensive patrol to search for enemy aircraft reported off Northern Ireland, some of the total of 23 US-manned Spits airborne for 'Jubilee' intercepted enemy aircraft, and pilots of the 31st claimed two downed. Only one, an Fw190A, was confirmed, the victor being 2nd Lieutenant Samuel F. Junkin, Jr, of the 309th FS. Leading the squadron, Major Thyng was credited with an Fw190 damaged.

No 71 Squadron was credited with a Ju88 destroyed by Chesley Peterson plus a damaged claim against a second. Peterson's victory over Dieppe gave him a total of six confirmed; he had become an ace on 1 June. P/O Selden Edner of No 121 Sqn shot down an Fw190 to make him an ace with 5.5 victories. No 133 had the most

Above: Taken on 19 August 1942 during the Dieppe operation, Spitfire V coded HL-U of the 308th Fighter Squadron is refuelled. *Imperial War Museum*

Above: Taxying Spitfire Mk VBs of the 307th Fighter Squadron with EN799 in the foreground bearing the squadron badge below the cockpit. *Imperial War Museum*

Above: Maj Harrison Thyng, CO of the 309th Fighter Squadron, in his Spitfire V 'Mary and James' (the names of his wife and son) on 28 August 1942. Coded WZ-A, the serial was EP179. *Imperial War Museum*

success, with Don Blakeslee being credited with one of KG 2's Do217s north of Dieppe, Richard L. Alexander a second Do217 and Don Gentile an Fw190 and a Ju88 for the first two of his eventual 21-plus victories. Alexander was additionally credited with probably destroying an Fw190 and damaging a third. Blakeslee, who led all four of the squadron's patrols during the day, inadvertently continued his run of damaged and probable claims, with the three Fw190s he fired at being placed in these categories.

The Luftwaffe fighters fought well and, on the debit side for the Allies, the 31st group lost six Spitfires and had four pilots listed as missing in action (MIA), two of whom survived. The price paid by the three USAAF and three Eagle Squadrons was not extraordinarily high on that black day for Fighter Command, which lost a total of 106 aircraft. Of the seven American-manned Eagle Squadron Spitfires that failed to return, only one pilot was killed. All the others, three each from Nos 71 and 121, bailed out, one of

whom was captured. All the 31st Group aircraft fell to the guns of 4./ JG 26's Fw190s, 7./ and 8./ Staffeln doing the damage among No 121's element.

Oberleutnant Rolf Hermichen of 3./JG 26 claimed an Airacobra as well as a Spitfire, a far from unique case of mistaken identity. It was thought that the white star marking on a Spitfire created an instant association of an American aircraft type in the German pilot's mind. In the wild mêlée of battle there was a considerable amount of over-claiming on the Allied side also — certainly none of the American pilots had ever seen anything like the mass of aircraft milling around over the contested beach below.

RAF fighters were presented with plum targets such as the Do217s and Ju88s which were thrown into the battle, primarily to prevent warships evacuating troops. Well planned screening by German fighters actually made bomber

interception quite hazardous, the defenders reacting strongly and inflicting severe casualties among the Allied air and ground forces. Much may have been learned from Dieppe (as is always claimed) about the challenges involved in amphibious operations, but the RAF's lesson was bought at high cost.

Undaunted by the events of the 19th, the 31st Fighter Group sent out 49 Spitfires the following day to complete a number of patrols, usually in squadron strength of 12 aircraft. Escort to B-17s was provided for the first time and three uneventful diversionary sweeps were flown, one to Cherbourg. Two Spitfires were also dispatched to escort an RAF Lysander carrying out ASR duties.

In the meantime it had been decided to form the Eagle Squadrons into a wing based at Debden, with Colonel Edward W. Anderson in administrative command. Wing Commander Raymond M. B.

Above: Pastoral scene on 28 August 1942 showing a 309th Squadron Spitfire Mk V during a press visit to several aerodromes used by AAF Spitfire squadrons in Britain. *Imperial War Museum*

Duke-Woolley remained as wing commander, flying. He was to oversee the transition of the RAF squadrons into a USAAF group and continued to lead the 4th until November when Chesley Peterson (with the equivalent US rank of colonel) took over.

Eagles into the Army

On 22 August 1942 the 4th Fighter Group, Eighth United States Army Air Force, was formally established by absorbing the Eagle Squadrons: No 71 became the 334th Fighter Squadron, No 121 the 335th and No 133 the 336th. Officially there was no mention of the origins of the units in the US documentation which accompanied the activation, this being, incidentally, 'backdated' to 1 July 1942.

Part of a brief ETO combat period for two more American Spitfire V squadrons (the 2nd and 4th) of the 52nd Fighter Group began on 27 August. Under the expert eye of Battle of Britain ace Squadron Leader Jamie Rankin, the newcomers were posted to Biggin Hill for further training prior to their combat debut on 7 September. The remaining squadron of the group, the 5th FS, took no part in operations and remained at Goxhill in Lincolnshire for theatre training.

September 1942

On 1 September the P-38Fs of the 1st Fighter Group went operational from Ibsley in Hampshire. These Lightnings flew a dozen shakedown missions under VIII Fighter Command direction without seeing any air action before they departed for North Africa. No combat missions were logged as such in the ETO.

On the 4th the 336th FS, then technically still No 133 Squadron, took delivery of enough Spitfire Mk IXs to replace its Mk Vs. No combat operations were scheduled before the unit became fully occupied with the details of the transfer from one air force to another which involved personnel making trips to London in small groups to be sworn into the AAF.

In the meantime the 52nd Group prepared for its combat initiation. Having aborted a mission on 7 September due to radio silence preventing remedial action being taken when pilots confused the departure point at the English coast, the mission was rescheduled for the following day. The 'screw up' was much derided by Jamie Rankin, but on the 8th 12 Spitfires reached the French coast and popped inland to take a look at St Omer and

Abbeville before beating a retreat for Dover's white cliffs. The pilots learned later that Tooey Spaatz and Monk Hunter had forbidden the 52nd to engage in combat in a move undoubtedly designed to preserve the full strength of those groups destined for 'Torch'.

The 2nd FS — which incidentally adopted the tongue-in-cheek nickname 'American Beagle Squadron' — flew three more missions up to 13 September before being posted to Goxhill for further training. Command of the 2nd passed to Captain James Coward, his unit then being reunited with the 4th and 5th Squadrons. With only 13 of its original pilots still in the group, the 52nd had welcomed a number of transferees, including eight from the Eagle Squadrons. Rosters were made up by other pilot transfers between the squadrons, and on or about 14 October the 52nd began moving out to Gibraltar, its 12 pilots being accompanied by 12 from the 31st Group. By the 19th the group's Spitfires were also moving out, the two squadrons of the 52nd having by then completed 83 sorties.

With US fighter pilots leaving *en masse* for Africa, the composition of an enlarged

Above: A transitional marking for US Spitfires from October 1942 was to highlight the original plain blue fuselage circle with a yellow ring, as demonstrated by these 307th FS Mk Vs. *Imperial War Museum*

VIII Fighter Command was delayed pending the arrival of new groups from the States. When the Eagle Squadrons became the 4th Fighter Group they continued to operate much as they had done while under RAF control; as an AAF three squadron group was equivalent to an RAF wing, official records understandably tended to refer to them as the Debden Wing.

On 23 September No 133 Squadron was ordered to move to Great Sampford, Duxford's satellite base in Essex, to prepare for the ceremony of handover on the 29th. Apprehensive about leaving his command in other hands, Red McColpin had not then been sworn into the AAF, but on the 25th he was ordered to London. Command of No 133 passed to Flight Lieutenant Edward Brettell and on the morning of the 26th he led 11 Spitfire IXs to Bolt Head where pilots were briefed for a routine escort to 26 B-17s that were scheduled to bomb Cherbourg/Maupertus and Morlaix/ Poujean aerodromes. Very strong winds at altitude began blowing the fighters way off course, the upshot being that they missed the rendezvous and the bombers abandoned the mission. Being blown towards Spain, the Spits lost contact with ground control, found some B-17s and

escorted them south. Brettell dived to verify their position and the squadron followed him down. Horrified to find themselves not over England but the deadly flak hotspot of Brest, the pilots took evasive action in vain. Six Spitfires were shot down, all the pilots becoming prisoners. Their presence over France now detected by the Luftwaffe, Fw190s of JG 2 intercepted and reportedly shot down one or two of the four that crashed fatally after running out of fuel in the Morlaix area. Marion E. Jackson claimed an Fw190 destroyed before going down, Robert Smith bailed out and evaded capture and Richard Beaty made it back to England and was injured in the crash-landing. All the Eagle PoWs survived except Brettell, who was shot for his part in the 'Great Escape' from Stalag Luft III in 1944.

The Morlaix débâcle had some far-reaching effects; Mk IX Spitfires were then in very short supply and the loss of almost a squadron of them meant that the 4th Group would initially revert to the less capable Mk V. Only a handful of ex-No 133 Squadron Mk IXs were taken over by the 4th, which soldiered on with

the earlier mark, plus some Mk IIs, until the type was replaced by the P-47.

Nomadic squadrons

Up to the point where they were absorbed by the USAAF, all three Eagle Squadrons had led a nomadic existence: No 71 had served on six stations, ending up appropriately enough at Debden, its new home; No 121 had served on four including Debden where it had arrived on 23 September; and No 133 had flown from eight different aerodromes including Great Sampford. By then personnel had already been sworn in as members of the USAAF and more than a few were relieved to find that the physical fitness standards they had failed to meet in the US were somewhat more relaxed in a war zone overseas. Having passed the required tests, the majority of officers 'signed up' for service in the AAF.

The handover of the Eagle Squadrons was made official on 29 September, the rain falling steadily on the parade ground at Debden making everyone feel quite at home. There was a genuine sense of loss by the British as the three squadron commanders, Gus Daymond of No 71,

Jim Daley of No 121 and Red McColpin of No 133, marched onto the parade ground as RAF squadron leaders and marched off as USAAF majors.

Despite raising a new American unit in the UK, the planners had no new aircraft for it to fly at its inception. There was little choice but for the 4th to retain its Spitfires, pending deliveries of an American fighter to re-equip the group at a later date. Few of the Debden pilots argued against retaining this continuity; in fact the move was much to the relief of almost everyone who opted to make the transfer. The 4th thus remained an RAF fighter unit in most respects: in traditions, operational doctrine and aircraft.

Tempted by being paid three times what they had received in the RAF, a notable improvement in the food and in some cases a correspondingly higher rank than they had previously held, most individual pilots made the transition without qualms. The change did not meet with everyone's approval, however, and some American pilots chose to stay in the RAF or opted for a different military career. Nobody was forced to make the transition; Eagle Squadron pilots had agreed to serve with the British force for the duration of the war and some preferred that option.

For the Eagle Squadrons *per se*, the sorties they had flown, the different aerodromes they had operated from, the weather conditions they had met and the sheer time they had put in as part of the RAF's fighter organisation, plus combat operations, had provided all pilots with invaluable experience. Up to the point of being absorbed by the USAAF, the 244 US and 16 British pilots who had served as Eagles had achieved a collective score of 74.5 aerial victories. Of these, 41 were claimed by the oldest unit, No 71 Squadron, No 121 had 19 and No 133 had 14.5. The ratio of victories to losses had been narrow — 77 American pilots and 5 Britons had been killed as a result of flying training and combat operations; 16 US pilots were prisoners of war at the time of the transition and others had been posted to RAF squadrons overseas. In subsequent years 31 former Eagles died whilst serving in American units.

Back to business

The 4th Fighter Group wasted little time in mounting its first offensive patrol with Spitfires, its Mark Vs taking off for Circus 221 on 2 October. It was a diversionary sweep to take the heat off the bomber escort mounted by the 334th and 335th Squadrons that found the most action. Led by Wing Commander Duke-Woolley, affectionately known to his pilots as 'the Dook', the Spitfires clashed with Fw190s at 24,000 feet over Calais and claimed four shot down. Duke-Woolley shared half an Fw190 kill with James A. Clark and the group was officially credited with a box score of 3.5.

On 2 October the 14th Fighter Group also flew its debut mission. Flying the P-38F, the group remained based at Atcham, but again a Lightning group would depart England (in November) without recording any operational activity of note — in fact despite putting up many sorties, no P-38 group clashed with the enemy during the pre-North African period of service in England. The only other similarly equipped group to come into the area before departing for warmer desert climes was the 82nd. This unit was not actually based in England but trained in Northern Ireland before transferring to the Twelfth Air Force in January 1943.

While the Eighth's fighter force was being established on a small scale, its early heavy bomber missions with the Boeing B-17 Flying Fortress and Consolidated B-24 Liberator continued to be marked with sporadic German reaction. Crews soon began to realise that the enemy had ample anti-aircraft guns to defend important targets, and flak in varying degrees of accuracy and concentration came to be expected on every occasion. In this, the crews were rarely disappointed. On the ground US crew chiefs and specialist repair teams assigned to the bomber bases embarked on what would soon become a very familiar duty in the Eighth Air Force. Patching up the bombers' torn skins, at times replacing surprisingly large areas of airframe that the aircrew had been obliged to leave on the Continent, repairing shattered engines — and clearing up the gruesome results when crewmen had been killed or wounded by shrapnel exploding inside the bombers — were some of the multitude of tasks handled by a burgeoning ground organisation.

The first heavy bomber losses to enemy fighters did not occur until November 1942, after which the number of interceptions gradually increased and the bomber crews quickly came to realise another fact of the air war in the ETO: that Messerschmitt Bf109s and Focke-Wulf 190s could be far more deadly than any amount of flak.

As 1942 came to a close the 4th Group bade farewell to Duke-Woolley who left to become a fighter liaison officer at HQ, Eighth Bomber Command. The Eagles of Debden had, in retrospect, put the first few months of their existence as an Army Air Force group down to experience as in return for 8.5 victories, the unit had lost 14 pilots. The ground crews were then training to maintain a new US single-seat fighter scheduled to re-equip the unit, the Republic P-47 Thunderbolt.

Notes

1 One of the early US volunteers, Billy Fiske was killed in a No 601 Squadron Hurricane on 16 August 1940 and was honoured by a memorial unveiled in St Paul's Cathedral on 4 July 1941.

2 Three or four Buffalo Mk Is have been quoted as being delivered to and briefly taken on charge by No 71 Squadron. They included W8131, W8132 and AS414, apparently those deliberately wrecked at Church Fenton, but a fourth aircraft may also have been involved. The exact number delivered to the squadron is unknown.

3 This was reportedly WNr 0125/ F8-BB believed based at Trondheim-Vaernes in Norway for convoy surveillance duties at the time of its destruction.

Above: 'Seven ton milk bottles' – P-47s – being unloaded from a ship in England *circa* early 1942. Deck cargo-type transit across the Atlantic required some protection of delicate parts, particularly engines. *Imperial War Museum*

2 Thunderbolts and Lightnings

Under Air War Plans Division-1 (APD-1) which governed much of US early war policy, no provision had been made to provide a fighter suitable for the long-range escort of heavy bombers. Suggestions had been put forward for such an aircraft as early as 1940 but nothing had been done; plans instead centred on an escort in the shape of a heavy bomber carrying not high explosive but guns. This idea, later made tangible in the YB-40, the 'escort' version of the B-17, was not a success.

As Eighth Air Force bomber losses began to rise during early 1943 a belated search for an effective escort fighter continued. There was little that could be done quickly but an interim measure was to deploy the P-47 Thunderbolt to England. This large and heavy fighter could at least take the bombers further than the Spitfire and would have to cope pending something better. There was really no alternative: the early demands of Operation 'Torch' and the North African campaign had stripped the Eighth of all the P-38 units that would otherwise have been assigned to it, but plans were put in hand to add a number of new Lightning groups to the ETO order of battle as soon as sufficient aircraft were available and enough pilots had been trained.

There was a very widespread belief that the Lightning could repeat its success in other theatres if only enough could be made available for groups in the ETO. That only a twin-engined fighter could meet the range problem was the view of many, one that prevailed even when the Mustang had showed its mettle. But in the first part of 1943 Lockheed production simply could not meet demand and it was not lost on the Eighth's planners that their dire situation occurred primarily because the Mediterranean forces had acquired 'their' B-17s and B-24s and were escorting them with 'their' fighter groups in another theatre of war!

In the meantime the 4th Group continued to fly its Spitfire Vs on RAF-derived Ramrod, Circus and Rodeo sorties from Debden, weather permitting and the group that had originally flown the Thunderbolt in the US and done much to prepare it for combat, completed its training.

Above: Spitfires were still going strong, pending replacement by P-47s, with the 4th Group at Duxford until the spring of 1943. This 30 March photo shows Lt-Col Chesley Peterson (in cockpit) with members of his flight aboard a Jeep. The Spitfire was probably Mk Vb W3627. *Imperial War Museum*

Thunderbolt champions

The 56th Fighter Group, which had begun shipping out, bound for the ETO in December 1942, was established at Kings Cliffe in Northamptonshire by January 1943. Its three component squadrons, the 61st, 62nd and 63rd, were under the overall command of Colonel Hubert A. Zemke.

The Thunderbolt and Spitfire could not have been more different. While the sleek British fighter was a small and light dogfighter, the P-47 was huge. Having originally been designed as a high altitude interceptor powered by an in-line liquid-cooled engine, the P-47 had gone through various design modifications to result in a very large single-seater with a radial engine. This latter was powerful for the standards of the day and at 2,000hp the Pratt & Whitney R-2800 was capable of hauling the 15,000lb weight — including a supercharger — of the fighter and endow it with a good performance. To fighter pilots, the P-47's most notable feature had to be its enormous firepower; eight 0.50in machine guns were roughly equivalent in terms of weight per burst of a couple of 20mm cannon. With a substantial 'bullet spread' the Thunderbolt could rip apart anything on wings if the fire was concentrated in a vital spot.

As might be appreciated for a fighter that weighed nearly as much as two Bf109s, the P-47's outstanding forte was the dive. Few aircraft anywhere could catch the aircraft as it dropped out of the sky at high speed — a fact that numerous Luftwaffe pilots were to learn to their cost. But in a superficial, purely visual appraisal the P-47 did indeed seem cumbersome; the atmosphere of apprehension prevailing at Debden when the P-47 was later presented

Above: Press demonstration for a P-47C-2 (41-6264) with temporary fuselage numbers providing a rudimentary form of air-to-air recognition. *Imperial War Museum*

Above: P-47Cs with two-digit fuselage numbers were used by the 4th Group for training purposes similar to this example with a recognition band and some damage to the cowling lip. *Imperial War Museum*

to the 4th Fighter Group as its future combat aircraft can be readily appreciated. From the Spitfire — to that?

If a similar reaction to the dimensions of Republic's brainchild had been felt in the ranks of the 56th when it was based on Long Island, it was soon dispelled. Taking the big fighter by the scruff of the neck, the 56th's pilots proceeded to wring it out to the point that they had full confidence in its capability as a combat aircraft by the time they moved to England. A few of the bolder pilots had bought experience at the cost of their lives when flying a P-47 to its limits. In a high speed dive the aircraft could enter the aeronautical realm of compressibility and become uncontrollable before diving straight into the ground. Warning notices were posted in all cockpits to limit diving speed as, without dive brakes, which had not been included in the design, there was little else that could be done. It remained true that the P-47 could not climb as fast as other contemporary fighters, but at altitude it could manoeuvre with the best, which offset any disadvantages its bulk may have appeared to represent.

Several examples of the P-47 had been shipped to England as deck cargo and when RAF observers and liaison officers, who assisted the Americans in numerous ways, had a chance to examine it they shared the reaction of the Debden pilots. First suicidal daylight bombing — and now a huge, cumbersome-looking fighter that surely stood no chance against the agile Focke-Wulfs and Messerschmitts. Had the Yanks taken leave of their senses? Such comments angered and embarrassed the men of the 56th, who as yet, had no proof that what they said in defence of the P-47 had any basis in fact. As with the Eagles before them, they could hardly wait until the day they went operational — the reasons were different, but the sense of anticipation was very similar.

Single group

In operational terms the 4th remained the sole first line group in VIII Fighter Command for the first few weeks of 1943 and, although its pilots flew numerous sorties, things remained at quite a low key. The Jagdwaffe, uncertain as to its most effective response to AAF bombers attacking targets in the occupied territories, avoided combat whenever it might be put at a dangerous disadvantage. Interspersed with operations that at least held the

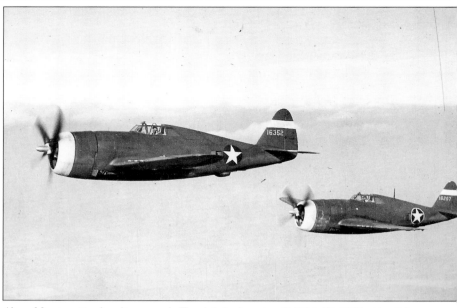

Above: More transitional markings on early Thunderbolts shown by a P-47C-5 (41-6352) with a C-2 (41-6267) following. The white recognition bands were applied before any combat operations were undertaken. *Imperial War Museum*

potential excitement of dogfights with the enemy, the American pilots completed convoy patrols, ASR flights and training sorties, putting a substantial number of hours on their Mk VB and VC Spitfires.

In Debden's case the pilots' off duty hours offered considerable diversion from operational flying as the station became one of the most popular venues for the press, the top brass and a long list of VIPs and dignitaries. The 4th's social calendar was as full as its pilot rosters, and everyone accepted the hazards of parties with alacrity when the cloud base was down to zero feet.

When the overcast lifted a little, the boys were out over the Channel, emulating the time-honoured tactical doctrine of the RAF. Rhubarbs particularly appealed to the more adventurous, individualistic pilots, although Don Blakeslee, who led the 335th Squadron from 22 November 1942, continually preached caution and the vital teamwork of the leader-wingman combination. Highly respected for his common sense and flying skill, Blakeslee was not a man to trifle with when it came to the conduct of air operations. Having the kind of analytical mind that made for an outstanding fighter leader, he was often stretched to keep his wild young men from killing themselves by taking undue risks. That said, pilots who believed that antics such as low level buzzing of the airfield were part of the

fighter pilot's creed tended to modify their views if 'the boss' witnessed such recklessness. With Blakeslee, one transgression was usually enough.

In line with the offensive policy of Fighter Command, the 4th regularly sent small sections of Spitfires out to keep the Germans off balance. They would often fly when the weather was less than ideal, race low over the Channel wavetops and climb in over the coast heard but unseen, to squirt a few cannon and machine gun rounds at choice targets — barges, staff cars, troops and locomotives — before heading for home, flat out. With constant repetition, such sorties ripped at the nerves of the German units based on the coast. Personnel were killed and wounded and valuable equipment was lost in these 'under the radar' sorties as the 4th's Spitfires managed on numerous occasions to surprise the Germans.

Unfortunately for the keener pilots, clashes with the Luftwaffe had been few and far between, a frustrating situation highlighted whenever men were lost in accidents. The 4th naturally preferred any replacements to be RAF-trained pilots as it continued to operate very much on British lines at that time. But as the weeks rolled by, ex-Eagle Squadron pilots who completed their tour rotated home or were posted and it was inevitable that in time the unit would change in character as the ratio of pilots with RAF experience

Above: As well as white bands, VIII Fighter Command's P-47s were given enlarged national insignia below each wing, as seen here on P-47C-2 (41-6209), which carried the temporary fuselage code '264'. *Imperial War Museum*

Above: The stars went under the port (left) wing to ensure nobody mistook the Thunderbolt (represented here by a P-47D-1 42-7922) for an FW190. *Author's collection*

Above:
It was vital that US bomber crews recognised their own fighters as 'little friends' in the air and visits to bomber stations helped the process. The 4th's P-47s visited Ridgewell, Essex home of the 381st Bomb Group's B-17s, on 10 July 1943. *USAF*

Right:
Lt-Col Harry J. Dayhuff talking about a (shared) victory over a Bf109 near Koblenz on 29 January 1944. P-47C-5 (41-6618/MX-Z) 'Mackie' was his personal aircraft. *Imperial War Museum*

Above: One of the great fighter leaders of the war, Hubert 'Hub' Zemke of the 56th admires some of the tools of his trade. *Imperial War Museum*

Above: As missions piled up there were visual records to be updated and painters were kept busy. Pilots like Lt Grant Turley of the 82nd FS at Duxford had his ranch logo, bomb log and enemy aircraft kills, not forgetting the girl of the moment, applied to P-47D-2 42-7998/MX-D. The swastikas did not, on subsequent analysis, always represent confirmed claims by one pilot. *Author's collection*

lessened in favour of USAAF trainees, but efforts were made to stave this off as long as was possible.

January 1943

Although training of 4th Group ground crews on the P-47 had been put in hand by the end of 1942, none of the Thunderbolts allocated to the unit had arrived by early January 1943 and the first 10 days of the month were spent on convoy patrols in Spitfires. Then on 13 January despite Chesley Peterson having to scrub an escort to some Bostons because of low visibility, the group flew three separate missions during the day. Peterson also led the last sorties during the afternoon, an uneventful withdrawal support mission for B-17s, the Spitfires patrolling between Furnes and Calais to rendezvous with their charges.

Action on 14 January resulted in claims for two Fw190s by Stan Anderson and Bob Boock of the 334th Squadron, while the 336th went out to shoot up locomotives and gun emplacements in France and Belgium. Two Spits came back to crash-land, their airframes shredded by shrapnel.

On the 15th the 334th was stood down from operations to begin pilot training on the P-47. Convoy and ASR patrols,

several scrambles against suspected enemy air raids and escorts to RAF medium bombers figured regularly in the rest of the group's calendar along with the usual cross-Channel operations against ground targets. Air combat with the Luftwaffe remained elusive as the last days of January came and went. A similar situation lasted well into February, but by mid-month several P-47s had arrived at Debden and, less two written off by a crash-landing Mosquito on the 18th, the 4th's pilots had enough of them to continue conversion training flights.

An order soon went forth to paint the big fighters with white nose and tail bands to prevent friendly but trigger-happy individuals on the ground as well as in the air from shooting at Thunderbolts in mistake for the Fw190. From head-on there was a superficial resemblance between the American and German fighters and the new paintwork was a cheap insurance against mistaken identity. To the same end the 4th filled in non-combat time by touring RAF airfields so

that as many Allied personnel as possible became familiar with the new fighter.

Ensuring that the P-47 was an effective combat aircraft in the ETO was a far from trouble-free exercise; oil fires, supercharger failures and particularly radio malfunctions were among a catalogue of woes that plagued the early examples. As far as the Eighth Air Force was concerned these were production versions from the P-47C-2 and C-5 batches onwards with the deep rear fuselage and faired canopy, later referred to as 'razorback' models.

Since some of the technical problems were serious enough to keep the P-47 off operations, they had to be attended to without delay. The top brass, the pilots and especially the ground crews, who had the job of keeping the radial-engined beasts in good order, wanted the aircraft in service and reliable. Ground echelons were given a list of modifications to complete before a pilot even thought of taking the type into combat. In one respect the P-47 was no different from other US aircraft coming to Britain which all required changes in their radio equipment to enable the pilots to communicate with British ground stations; all had to be compatible with British standards and operate on the correct wavelengths.

Technical problems with the aircraft were made more maddening as they often had absolutely nothing to do with enemy action. The first week of March brought the boredom level to screaming pitch for the Debden pilots, as the weather still allowed so few operations to be flown. Major Oscar Coen took over the 334th Squadron from Gus Daymond on 3 March.

Thunderbolt debut
Making its combat debut with the P-47 on 10 March, the 4th swept the Channel out to Walcheren Island and along the French coast. Numerous aircraft suffered from terrible radio interference, a fault traced to the engine electrical system. The P-47s were taken off operations to have their radio reception sorted out and further sweeps during March had to be flown in Spitfires. There was still very little action, but one blessing was that on 1 April the brass put a stop to convoy patrols, at least for the 4th Group.

In the meantime the inevitability of the P-47 fully replacing the Spitfire at Debden gained momentum and on 8 April, Lieutenant-Colonel 'Hub' Zemke, Major David Schilling, Captain John McClure and Captain Eugene O'Neill of the 56th Group arrived at Debden to fly a practice P-47 Circus operation. On only its second mission with the P-47, the 4th put up seven aircraft, while a third group, the 78th based at Duxford in Cambridgeshire, contributed four more. This was an established pattern in the Eighth and other air forces whereby groups with theatre experience loaned individual pilots who passed on their knowledge to the newcomer or 'freshman' groups.

Having moved south from the Eighth's theatre training airfield at Goxhill in Lincolnshire, the 78th was led by Colonel Arman Peterson. Its three squadrons were the 82nd, 83rd and 84th. On 13 April the 56th put up enough Thunderbolts to constitute a high squadron on Ramrod 50, an operation involving 56 aircraft. The bulk of the force was made up by aircraft of the 78th's 82nd and 83rd Squadrons, the mission marking the unit's first full operation in the ETO. And that afternoon the 56th flew what it deemed

to be its first mission in the theatre, 12 P-47s carrying out Rodeo 202 from its base at Halesworth in Suffolk. 'Hub' Zemke continued to command the unit at that time. The 'seven ton milk bottles' as the 4th's pilots somewhat disparagingly dubbed the P-47, were proliferating in England as the spring weather finally began to bring better flying conditions. With nine operational squadrons in three groups, a substantial fighter force was available to VIII Fighter Command.

At that time the establishment of a USAAF fighter squadron was 25 aircraft, a full group consisting of 75 machines, although this number invariably fluctuated in terms of serviceability and the number of reserve aircraft. Total personnel of a typical fighter group was 805 enlisted men and 144 assigned officers, about half of these being pilots.

All early model P-47s issued to the 4th, 56th and 78th Fighter Groups relied entirely on their internal fuel tankage of 305 US gallons (115 litres/253 Imperial gallons), there being no belly shackles or wing racks to take extra tanks, even had these been available in England. For the time being the P-47s would fly escort missions only on internal fuel.

Action for the Eighth's fighters during mid-April included three victories for the 4th Group on the 15th, enemy fighters being encountered during sweeps in the St Omer and Furnes areas. Two days later, all hell broke loose when 107 B-17s attacked Bremen. Intercepting German fighters shot down 16 Fortresses, the US escort being unable to intervene to protect the 'big friends' in the target area, which lay beyond their maximum permissible range. In the strongest Luftwaffe reaction to an Eighth Air Force bomber mission to date, this operation held grim portents for those who still maintained that the formations were able to protect themselves against enemy fighter attack. Clearly they could not.

What tended to confuse nearly everyone involved in planning bomber operations was the relatively small numbers of B-17s or B-24s actually shot down by fighters compared to the number dispatched, the totally unquantifiable reaction by the Luftwaffe to the American raids — and as ever, the weather. Given two or three days on the ground, the Eighth's bombers were repaired and available for the next mission, all losses on the previous raids seemingly made good. That was patently untrue in regard to crews, as any examination of the

records would reveal an otherwise greater but hidden loss in terms of experience. But the statisticians could be confounded when the next 'maximum effort' might be barely challenged by the Luftwaffe, or not at all. Over a period of months the sortie rate would always remain way ahead of the losses to fighters and flak in actual and, particularly, percentage terms. The term 'acceptable loss' began to be bandied around, much to the annoyance of the crews: to them losses were never viewed in that light, but they had to admit from the planners' viewpoint, the figures usually came out very much in favour of the Americans. And targets were being bombed.

The planners at VIII Fighter Command soon realised that bomber losses should reduce in proportion to the distance fighters could fly to protect them directly. Protection right through to the targets, particularly those deep inside Germany, was the ultimate goal but seemed an insurmountable challenge in the spring of 1943. There was also a fair degree of apathy among the bomber-dominated Eighth Air Force generals; many individuals with influence still clung to the notion that no fighter escort was really necessary, and Monk Hunter, though he understood fighter operations, appeared to lack the drive necessary to push for quick remedies to the range problem. Hunter was subsequently fired by Arnold who also perceived his fighter commander as in some way to blame for the technical shortcomings of the P-47.

The only practical answer to the fighter range problem was to carry extra fuel tanks, but steps to obtain enough of them to equip all the Eighth's P-47s went forward with frustrating slowness. Multiple hundreds of tanks were required for even one month's operations, amounting to thousands over a longer period. British and US industry was approached to supply drop tanks and although some progress was made, the sheer number required proved to be way beyond the resources of many manufacturing companies. Delivery of conventional tanks which were in limited production in the US proved agonisingly slow, not least because people actually questioned the need for them at all and, inevitably, the cost. An innovation that looked promising was a lightweight tank made of impregnated paper designed by the Bowater Company in the UK.

The pro-bomber lobby in Washington

remained divided and even clung to the notion that escort fighters were all but superfluous to the bombing campaign. Hap Arnold himself was a bomber man and had to sift numerous conflicting reports of the performance of the P-47, the attitude of the pilots and the indifference and vested interest of some of his generals and rival aircraft manufacturers.

Mustang progress

Since the first flight of the prototype in October 1940 the P-51 had gone from strength to strength, mainly in RAF service. The experimental installation of a Merlin engine had created the P-51B, flight test reports of which were highly encouraging. There was as yet little official US interest in the aircraft as it was after all a British project subject to priority deliveries to a foreign customer. Despite knowing the details of the re-engined P-51's potential, influential individuals pushed the P-38 as the only real answer to the bomber escort problem, even to the point of deliberately sidelining the P-51 because it was a better aircraft. After spending valuable time examining proposals for a completely new escort fighter, the AAF chief finally was persuaded that there really was nothing to touch the P-51 in respect of range. The primary reason was because the P-51B's wing was incredibly efficient; by reducing drag way below any comparable NACA fighter wing section, the Merlin Mustang was able to reduce fuel burn to an amazingly modest 68 gallons per hour which compared favourably with the 100 US gallons per hour (83.3 Imperial gallons) needed by the P-47. By making provision for substantial internal tankage and a pair of drop tanks, the projections were that P-51s based in England could reach Berlin and beyond, combat the enemy and get home with fuel to spare.

Making the aces

Despite the many problems surrounding the daylight bombing offensive, US fighter pilots had proved that their aircraft were quite capable of taking on and beating contemporary German single-seaters. Some individual pilots recalled the days when their reading matter had included the exploits of the pilots of World War 1. Most of the generation of pilots who fought in the second war had been born during the 1920s and their formative years coincided with the heyday of pulp fiction comics filled with the

exploits of the Lafayette Escadrille, Baron von Richthofen and American heroes such as Eddie Rickenbacker, the top-scoring American ace. Eighth Fighter Command was in tune with men in the cockpit of Thunderbolts when it intimated that it would be a great boost to the Allied air offensive if an American fighter pilot in the ETO could equal or surpass Rickenbacker's final score of 26.

The French-coined term of 'ace' to denote a pilot who had shot down five of the enemy in aerial combat was resurrected by the USAAF and other air arms in World War 2. Its value had never really been accepted by the RAF, but the AAF recognised the positive effect, both in public relations terms and as an inspiration to fighter pilots in general, that the air ace could have. People loved heroes and while fighter pilots were first and foremost serving their country, much had already been made of the many German pilots who had become aces or *Experten* in the early war campaigns. In creating their own, the Americans would merely be following a tradition.

Fostering healthy rivalry between pilots — and indeed whole units — had always helped create *esprit de corps* and brought positive results; the desire by the rank and file to emulate the most successful pilots would sharpen their reactions, increase confidence and hone the necessary 'killer instinct' all effective fighter pilots needed. Pride in belonging to what many believed was 'the best fighter outfit in the world' was ingrained; confidence in the rightness of America's cause against Nazi Germany and in getting the job done was there in abundance.

Viewed from Washington, the European air offensive certainly needed a boost. The personal scores of fighter pilots were accumulating far too slowly for some generals and senators, who made simplistic comparisons of the number of sweeps flown versus enemy losses. The plain fact was that the Germans were marshalling the bulk of their fighter force beyond escort fighter range and preparing to make the daylight bombing campaign as costly as possible.

May 1943

With the Eighth Air Force gradually increasing its strength with additional groups of B-17s, May began in terms of fighter action (albeit inconclusive) on the 4th when the 56th and 78th Groups dispatched 117 P-47s on the first Ramrod the two units had flown — although this

and other RAF terminology was soon dropped by VIII FC. The task of the 56th was withdrawal support for 54 1st Wing B-17s briefed to bomb the Ford Motor Co works at Antwerp. 'Hub' Zemke led 12 Thunderbolts each from the 62nd and 63rd Squadrons, the 61st bringing up the rear with 13 more. 'Gremlins' struck Zemke's aircraft and he was forced to relinquish the lead to Major Loren McCollom and return home. Four other pilots did the same. McCollom meanwhile rendezvoused with 40 of the B-17s north of Flushing and escorted them back as far as the Oxford area.

There was some contact with Fw190s by the 63rd Squadron and fire was exchanged without any victory claims. The day's only US fighter loss was a P-47 from the 4th Group which was hotly pursued out over the sea until it went 'into the drink'. The unfortunate pilot was lost.

Little further action ensued for the fighter pilots until 14 May, when the day's combats yielded some valuable lessons for the 56th and 78th groups, neither of which had yet met the Luftwaffe in force. That day's mission was a large scale, 118-ship escort to bombers sent against Antwerp docks. All three P-47 groups contributed to the force, the 63rd Squadron taking up station as top cover for 40 B-17s at around 12.45 hours. 'Hub' Zemke, as group leader for the day, called in enemy fighters approaching the bombers at 24,000 feet, some 5,000 feet below the Americans.

Making a 180° turn, Zemke cut into a *Rotte* (flight of two) of Fw190s and fired at one with no visible result. With a dozen of their colleagues behind them, the leading German pilots seemed intent on their bomber targets as Zemke switched his aim to a second *Rotte* of Focke-Wulfs. This time the future 56th ace felt sure he had hit one of the enemy machines, although he soon downgraded this to a probable. With fuel now low, Zemke led his flight home.

Red Flight had in the meantime dived on four Focke-Wulfs seen pursuing the bombers. Each AAF pilot took a shot at the enemy machines, but apart from a few pieces flying about as some bullets found their mark, the 56th could claim no definite results. A better showing by the 78th resulted in three down, the victorious pilots being Major James J. Stone, who claimed the first kill for the group, while future ace Captain Charles London was awarded a probable. In return for these milestone but yet modest victories, the group lost three P-47s. Don Blakeslee's skill and tenacity were rewarded with a confirmed Fw190 which gave him a total of six. He already had four kills from his RAF days and one from a 15 April P-47 mission which made him an ace.

Back at Halesworth, Zemke ran his gun camera film and viewed his combat in a more leisurely fashion — and sure enough the flickering monotone frames revealed little more than a 'damaged' assessment. Zemke's experience would be shared by hundreds more fighter pilots who had some doubts as to exactly what they had achieved in the heat and confusion of combat. Claims were carefully checked to ensure that the appropriate credit was given, a process that could often be confirmed by gun camera footage — if it had exposed correctly. Some pilots were denied such evidence as not all the early P-47s were fitted with cameras, a situation that was rectified as soon as possible. Such a detail would be noted and acted upon, as the Thunderbolt was the subject of a comprehensive programme of improvements which was greatly aided by feedback data on its performance in combat. As with other aircraft and engine manufacturers, Republic dispatched its field representatives to the Air Service Command and the frontline aerodromes to act as troubleshooters to operational units.

Eyewitness accounts of what happened to friend and foe alike were remarkably frequent and detailed considering the circumstances, but observation had often to be prematurely curtailed to execute a manoeuvre. Many times when that happened the witness never saw the outcome and could only partly describe the scene to the intelligence officer on return home. If it was a question of independent confirmation of a victory claim, a pilot eager to open or add to his score then had to hope that someone else had seen his victim crash. Some 'eager beavers' had to live with a downgraded credit when they were convinced of having made a sure kill because the necessary unbiased confirmation was lacking. There was the consolation of percentage share, a fraction of a kill shared with other pilots. This RAF practice, continued by the Eighth Air Force, was fair, although it could get a little complicated if pilots had to tot up four 'quarters' to make one 'whole' victory, as was quite common. Some pilots had also been awarded third shares and were

understandably unwilling to disregard what had already been credited to them.

Perhaps as there often remained an element of doubt in air combat claims, the Luftwaffe did not follow such a practice but credited a shared kill not to the pilots involved but to the unit, which in many ways appeared more realistic. That did, of course, leave the pilots who actually damaged enemy aircraft, probably on more than one occasion, out in the cold as regards their status as *Experten*.

More action

It was not unusual at certain periods of the war for one month's most intense air action to be compressed into several consecutive days; May 1943 was one such period. Having clashed with the Luftwaffe on the 14th after weeks of low-key flying, AAF fighter pilots saw the 16th positively light up when they made contact with 100 German fighters. But although there was much manoeuvring and tail chasing and trading of fire, the results were hardly spectacular. The 78th claimed three shot down for one P-47 lost.

Two days later Lieutenant Duane Beeson of the 334th Squadron shot down a Bf109 to begin a steady rate of scoring that would net him 12 victories before the group relinquished the P-47 in the spring of 1944. Beeson was one of the pilots in the 4th who managed to master the P-47 completely and use it to good effect. Those who knew Beeson reckoned he had the advantage of not comparing the Thunderbolt with the Spitfire as he had joined the group after the British fighter had been replaced.

It was unusual during May for the P-47 force to number less than 100 aircraft for escorts, sweeps and diversions, few of which stirred the enemy into any great effort. The Germans had no wish to waste valuable pilots, particularly as their perceived task was increasingly the destruction of US heavy bombers. Nevertheless, the USAAF maintained a fighter presence over France, Belgium (where they usually rendezvoused with the returning bombers) and Holland to the point where they could not be totally ignored by the Luftwaffe, which challenged those incursions and sweeps that appeared directly to threaten its own operations.

Invasion date

May 1943 also saw the Allied leaders at their Trident Conference officially

confirming that an invasion of northwest Europe would go ahead less than one year hence — on or about 1 May 1944. And on the 29th the Eighth flew the first YB-40 sorties in an attempt to provide a long-range escort to the bombers. The idea was flawed in a number of ways, not the least of which was persuading German fighter pilots to attack only these heavily armed B-17s rather than the conventional Fortresses they were there to protect. It was also found that the ammunition-packed B-17 escorts suffered in performance to the point where they lagged behind their charges. After only a few sorties the 'escort Fortress' idea was shelved.

June 1943

Moves to integrate the Eighth's daylight bomber offensive more closely with that of the RAF at night took shape in the form of the Combined Bomber Offensive (CBO) directive, issued on 10 June. By so doing, the chiefs of staff aimed to dovetail the attacks of the two commands to deny the enemy any respite for a full 24-hour period and this they achieved to some degree against selected targets. Listing bomber targets in order of priority, the CBO directive put U-boat bases first and foremost, on a par with the German aircraft industry, oil and ball-bearing production. Of secondary importance were facilities building military vehicles and plants producing synthetic rubber. An ambiguous section of the directive read: 'German fighter production must be considered an Intermediate Objective second to none in priority'. That last actually translated into a prolonged bombing campaign against the various Focke-Wulf and Messerschmitt fighter production centres and assembly plants, plus Germany's aero engine manufacturers.

Compliance with the CBO directive appeared to be taking immediate effect when the bombers went to Wilhelmshaven on 11 June to attack U-boat yards. The Germans all but foiled this intention by igniting a massive smokescreen to blanket the target which, combined with the effects of cloud, prevented half the bombardiers from identifying their aiming points. Fighter attacks resulted in the loss of eight B-17s in yet another indictment of the lack of an escort. The US fighters meanwhile swept the Ostend area without incident.

June continued with more action for the VIII FC fighters and on the 12th Captain Walter Cook opened the 56th Group's account with the Luftwaffe by destroying an Fw190. Catching the enemy fighter over Ypres, Cook's fire went into the 190's wing and touched off the ammunition, which blew part of its wing off. On the 13th 'Hub' Zemke shot down two Fw190s to open his personal score.

Unseasonably bad weather caused the Eighth to restrict its long-range missions in late June, although the fighters were able to stir up the occasional action. Many enemy aircraft were seen on such missions, but the Germans invariably continued to avoid contact with the P-47s, preferring to play a waiting game and pounce on the bombers when their protection had turned for home.

On 22 June Captain Charles London of the 78th shot down an Fw190 for his first confirmed kill, and by the 29th a pair of Fw190s had fallen to his guns and a third was claimed as damaged. On 26 June Lieutenant Robert S. Johnson of the 56th was attacked — 'terrorised' might be a more appropriate word — by an Fw190 of JG 26 seemingly determined to test fully the robustness of Republic's construction. Snapping at Johnson's heels, the German pilot played cat and mouse with the American, systematically shooting his P-47C to pieces around him. Wounded and unable to bail out because his canopy had been jammed shut, Johnson edged for home, bullets peppering his Thunderbolt like lethal hail. Finally abandoned by the German who, Johnson believed, could easily have ended the pursuit by blasting him out of the sky, the future ace brought his flying wreck in for an excellent 'no flaps' landing at Manston in Kent, the designated emergency airfield of the Eighth Air Force.

On 30 June 1943 the RAF formally relinquished control of all VIII FC units, but having officially 'regained' its fighters, the Eighth had lost all its 2nd Wing Liberators to the Ninth Air Force in North Africa to train for project Tidal Wave, the long-range bombing of the Ploesti oilfields in distant Romania. In June the first sorties had also been flown by B-17s fitted with the so-called 'Tokyo tanks' in the wings. The bombers could thus fly even further beyond the protective reach of their fighters and while such a move could hardly be viewed as counter-productive, events were soon going to make things look very much like that.

Examining the total of aerial victories achieved in the ETO up to late June and comparing them with the number of P-47s dispatched on escorts and sweeps, Hap Arnold and his staff experienced bitter disappointment. Even with the kills achieved in late 1942 added, the figure was less than 50 enemy aircraft destroyed in several hundred Thunderbolt sorties. Taken purely at face value, the ratio looked bad.

July

Bad weather disrupted the fighters on 4 July when the heavy bombers undertook a 'first anniversary' mission to aircraft industry targets in France. Another eight B-17s failed to return from the two separate missions they flew that day. On the 6th ships bearing the P-47s of the 352nd Fighter Group docked in England.

On the following day the Eighth's all-important photographic reconnaissance capability was streamlined when the 7th Photographic Reconnaissance (PR) Group assumed operational control over the previously independent 13th, 14th and 22nd Squadrons. Equipped with Spitfires and F-4 and F-5 Lightnings, the group had already carried out many hazardous target assessment sorties from its main base at Mount Farm in Oxfordshire, and which it would continue to do.

More short-range tactical-type attacks on German airfields occupied the bomber force, which was expanded with new groups fresh from the US during mid-July. A three-phase attack on French aerodromes on the 14th brought action to the fighter escort, which managed to cover only one element of the bomber force, that bound for Amiens/Glisy aerodrome. All 128 fighters involved from the 4th, 56th and 78th Groups ran into the Focke-Wulfs. Two enemy aircraft were destroyed for the loss of three P-47s.

During July the Eighth's 3rd Bomb Wing of B-26 Marauders began medium altitude operations, many of which would involve a fighter escort. Initially handled by the RAF, VIII FC would fly some of these missions, as required. In the meantime the fighters would mainly support the heavies.

In continuing to wage war on the Luftwaffe fighter force, half of which was then estimated to be tied down in defence of targets in the Reich and its occupied territories, the Eighth announced the start of 'Blitz Week' on 24 July. This campaign, which would involve seven major missions designed to tempt the German fighters up to do battle, began on the 25th. Bombers briefed to knock out a diesel engine factory in Hamburg lost 15 of their number to fighters and flak. Four more B-17s went down when a second raid of the day bombed Kiel shipyards. A further 22 were lost on 26 July, a day that saw another round of multiple missions, which, despite the losses, reflected the Eighth's growing strength at that time.

The P-47s drew a medium bomber escort mission to Tricqueville aerodrome on the 27th. Much more satisfying from the fighter pilots' perspective, in that they could cover the smaller bombers right through to their targets, these missions rarely attracted enemy fighter attack. It was over Germany that the US fighter leaders knew they had to be in order to do real damage to the Luftwaffe fighter force.

First belly tanks

At last there had been some practical steps towards supplying VIII Fighter Command with drop tanks for its P-47s and 28 July was something of a turning point in the air war in Europe. Fitted with cumbersome, 200 US gallon (166.6 Imp gal) unpressurised belly tanks made of fibreglass, the 4th Group's P-47s nevertheless penetrated German airspace and flew about 340 miles across the Continent to surprise elements of the Jagdwaffe over Utrecht. Exploiting the advantage external fuel tanks had given them, the AAF pilots were awarded nine victory credits. What the 4th Fighter Group called 'the first belly tank show in the ETO' had finally brought some air combat gains — which was not really surprising.

Duane Beeson of the 334th Squadron was among the pilots who were credited with confirmed victories, his single Bf109 making him an ace. With two Eagle Squadron kills, Beeson also had two earlier AAF claims. It was a memorable day for the 4th, the more so because the Thunderbolts succeeded in breaking the cohesion of a group of Bf110s fitted with underwing launchers for 21cm rockets. In the first recorded encounter with aircraft carrying this weapon, the US fighter pilots reported the loss of three B-17s from one such attack. Two more Fortresses were destroyed when a German crew crashed into a B-17 after their initial pass on a 385th Bomb Group formation had destroyed one aircraft. Flying wreckage took down a third Fort.

Although they were unguided, Wgr 21 rockets were lethal enough and they allowed the attacking aircraft to keep clear of the bombers' defensive guns. Each Bf110 carried up to four launchers, while the Bf109 and Fw190 were adapted to

Above: Belly tanks were the partial saviours of the US daylight bombing campaign. A 200-gal model fitted with an airflow buffer is seen on a P-47C being serviced under field conditions. *Imperial War Museum*

take two each. But from the German viewpoint any weight added to relatively slow aircraft like the Bf110 made it a deathtrap in daylight. On several occasions the Messerschmitt twins were shot to pieces by the US fighter escort, a fate generally shared by the similar Me410 and Ju88 if they were unlucky enough to be thrown against the American heavies and happened to be caught by fighters.

On 30 July the P-47s pushed through to Bocholz where the 78th Group shot down 16 of the enemy, bringing Charles London the accolade of being the first pilot to become an ace by scoring all his victories entirely as a member of the AAF in the ETO.

August

In the Middle East the Tidal Wave strike on Ploesti went ahead on 1 August, with mixed results. The refineries were badly bombed, although confusion on the target run-in was a contributory factor in the loss of 41 B-24s. No escort was provided. Administratively August also saw the creation of the 65th Fighter Wing within

VIII FC, this resulting in greater freedom to plan operations when bomber escort was not required, which remained the top priority.

On the 12th the loss rate for the Eighth's heavies rose when the primary targets were at Bochum, Gelsenkirchen and Recklinghausen. For the first time over 100 B-17s were damaged — and 23 were shot down by fighters and flak. Taking a little heat off the bombers during the penetration and withdrawal stages of the mission, the 4th, 56th, 78th and 353rd Groups (the last on its second ETO mission) flew P-47s fitted with steel drop tanks for the first time. These tanks were still of the 'figure hugging' type fitted flush to the belly of the aircraft similar to the earlier 200-gallon type, but they were pressurised which enabled them to be retained at altitude without splitting apart. Cass Hough of Eighth ASC (Air Service Command) had laboured long and hard to design a pressure pump that could be produced in quantity for the P-47's belly

tanks and his work had finally borne fruit. Four enemy fighters were shot down with no loss to the Americans, who appeared over Bochum, Gelsenkirchen and Bonn, much to the confusion of the Jagdwaffe.

Some respite for the long-suffering heavy bomber crews was inherent in Operation 'Starkey', which began on the 15 August. A ruse to persuade the Germans that when it came, an Allied invasion would take place in the Pas de Calais, the bombing effort carried out as part of 'Starkey' attempted to enforce the deception. Already half convinced that this was the only logical landing point, the Germans were subjected to a series of medium and heavy bomber raids, mainly on French, Belgian and Dutch airfields, until 9 September. By all accounts, 'Starkey' succeeded in its purpose.

Pushing its attacks ever further into the heart of the Third Reich, VIII Bomber Command occasionally became the unwitting victim of learned analysis by its industrial advisers. A point had for example already been strongly made — and stressed by the CBO directive — for the destruction of ball-bearing plants; reducing these to ashes would soon result in the complete paralysis of all sectors of the German armed forces, the bomber chiefs were assured. As most engines required plentiful numbers of such bearings, the idea appealed and so the wheels were set in motion for one of the most notorious bombing missions in history. With the dual carrot of ball-bearings and the Messerschmitt factory at Regensburg dangling before their collective eyes, the planners arranged a double strike — both vital centres would have their production levels reduced, provided that the bombers could fight their way through to such distant targets. Fighter cover could be provided for only about 250 miles, half the distance the bombers would have to fly. The risks were enormous, but if the targets could be hit hard the first anniversary mission of the Eighth Air Force's bomber offensive in the ETO would be a milestone.

Previous dark predictions about the risks of the double strike on Regensburg and Schweinfurt came horrifyingly true for the B-17 crews on 17 August. Sixty bombers fell to the relentless onslaught of fighters and flak, the worst that most of the participants had ever experienced. The plants were, however, hit by the survivors (188 out of 230 dispatched to Schweinfurt and 127 out of 146 briefed for Regensburg) and the achievement of the force in bombing at this reduced strength should not be minimised. The 4th Bomb Wing proceeded on to land at bases in North Africa, thus inaugurating the first 'shuttle' bombing mission flown by the Eighth.

On 18 August the 353rd Fighter Group flew its ninth P-47 mission out of Raydon in Suffolk and was assigned to the 66th Fighter Wing, the second formed in VIII FC. The weather, already bad for the time of year, deteriorated further to reduce the scale of air operations for several days. It was, however, bright enough on the 24th when the fighters covered the return of the bombers that had flown the double-strike mission of 17 August. *En route* back from North Africa, the B-17s arrived over Bordeaux/Merignac aerodrome around noon, while in the afternoon, Villacoublay aerodrome was bombed by 1st Wing Forts from England. It was the latter force that mainly occupied the AAF escort and of six German fighters claimed in the resulting combats, one fell to the P-47s of the 353rd Group. One other kill was the first by

Francis S. Gabreski — about whom much more would be heard — and Eugene P. Roberts, commanding the 84th Squadron at Duxford, brought his score to five with a Bf109 and an Fw190. Roberts thus became the 78th Group's second ace.

Noballs in France

With the confirmation that the Germans were building launching sites for pilotless flying bombs in the Pas de Calais and on the Cherbourg Peninsula, the Allied high command initiated Operation 'Crossbow', an all-encompassing codename to cover counter-measures aimed at neutralising new-type German weapons. VIII Bomber Command flew the first of many short range 'Noball' operations to obliterate all the known sites for the V1 flying bomb. The Eighth was joined by RAF Bomber Command and the heavy bombers' efforts were supplemented by tactical AAF B-26s.

Missions by the American heavies during this period encompassed numerous other targets of a tactical rather than strategic nature as the Allied air forces went out to devastate many of the forward German airfields on the Continent. The invasion of Europe was months in the future, but every mission that helped to reduce Luftwaffe fighter strength was worthwhile. Escort by the American fighter groups often resulted in less reaction by enemy fighters to these shorter

Above: Almost as important as guns to a single-seat fighter pilot were his maps. Marking these with emergency airfields, route waypoints, turning areas, enemy flak belts and 1,001 other details, were just some of the keys to survival. Assuming that the P-47D's partly visible code is 'HV', 'Okley and Tobe II' belonged to the 61st FS, 56th Group. *Imperial War Museum*

Above: One of the characters who made the 4th such a cosmopolitan and successful fighter outfit was Howard 'Deacon' Hively. *Imperial War Museum*

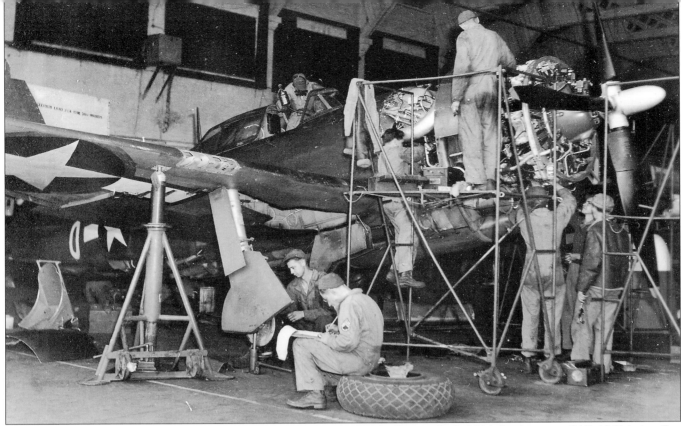

Above: Major overhaul for a P-47 (with red surround to the national insignia) of the 78th Fighter Group at Duxford. Units based on prewar RAF airfields had excellent facilities compared with those 'in the field' when the tactical groups moved to France. *Imperial War Museum*

Above: This P-47D, one of George Preddy's early mounts in the 352nd Group, was, like all his aircraft, named 'Cripes a'Mighty' after an English colloquialism. *Sam Sox*

penetration raids and as crews of the medium bombers could happily confirm, the enemy placed an increasing emphasis on defending targets in the Reich rather than the rest of Europe.

Further build-up of the AAF fighter force in England saw the 352nd Group at Bodney, Norfolk, flying its first P-47 mission on 9 September. Shorter range missions continued throughout that month and generally brought a very low rate of loss, few fighter victories — and numerous aborted sorties as bombers tried in vain to circumvent the worsening autumn weather. On 27 September the P-47s were again able to extend their reach to appear over Emden, 375 miles from their bases in England — for the bomber crews the escort gap was slowly closing.

October

Missions were again mounted against industrial targets at Emden and Bremen by early October and on the 4th of the month, a mission to Frankfurt went badly awry as the B-17s and B-24s were led 100 miles off course. This did not result in a disaster and although 16 bombers were lost, this was less than the many reported attacks by enemy fighters might have indicated. Bomber gunners were usually able to give as good as they got, but the Germans' losses were difficult to quantify. As had rapidly become commonplace, the bomber gunners claimed to have destroyed considerably more German fighters than were actually lost. Claims made in good faith were duplicated many times when every man who fired at a Bf109 or Fw190 and saw it dive away trailing smoke became convinced that he had shot it down.[1]

Wolfpack success

Fighter activity in support of the bombers on the 4th was a massive 223 P-47s. The day included victory claims of 18 enemy fighters, all but three being credited to the 56th in the group's most successful day to date. Captain Walker M. Mahurin became an ace with three Bf110s destroyed near Düren to give him a total of six.

Attacks on Germany picked up in October, as did the fighter opposition. A very long-range mission to Poland on the 9th was followed the next day by a crack at Münster. The Luftwaffe defence was intense and 30 B-17s were shot down, including 12 of the 14 from the 100th Bomb Group. Gunners defended their ships bravely and wildly over-claimed, while the US fighter escort numbered 216 P-47s from the five groups in England. If the high figures for enemy fighters destroyed had borne much relation to true losses, the Luftwaffe would have all but ceased to exist inside a month. Fighter scores were much nearer the mark and the Münster raid brought victories of 19 enemy aircraft, Major Dave Schilling, then 56th Group operations officer, becoming an ace with his single Fw190 kill. Two other Wolfpack pilots, Captain Gerald W. Johnson and

Above: Jack Jenkins of the 55th Group (in cockpit) going over some last-minute mission details with Lt Russell F. Gustke before take-off on 23 October 1943. *USAF*

Above: One of the leading aces of the Wolfpack, Dave Schilling ended the war with 22.5 victories. *Paul Conger*

Lieutenant Robert S. Johnson, became aces with respective scores of a Bf109 and Bf110 and a Bf110 and an Fw190. Captain Walter C. Beckham of the 353rd shot down an Me 210[2] and two Bf110s to also reach ace status.

New Ninth

Under a major Army Air Forces restructuring programme geared primarily to basing enough tactical aircraft in the UK to support the invasion of Europe, a new Ninth Air Force was established on 16 October. The effect on the Eighth was positive in that more than a dozen new fighter groups promised additional escort capability. That and the fact that some of these Ninth Air Force groups were to be equipped with the P-51 Mustang, a new

fighter known to have substantial range, was encouraging. The saga of how the P-51 was turned into a long-range escort par excellence by substituting a Rolls-Royce (Packard) Merlin engine in place of the original Allison is well enough known not to need repeating at length here; suffice to say that the reports on the converted P-51B's performance were soon substantiated.

Risky as it was for bombers to return to targets within a short time of the original raid, VIII Bomber Command nevertheless decided that a second crack at Schweinfurt was necessary. Accordingly, the proponents of unescorted daylight bombing were allowed one more indulgence. When on 14 October another 60 B-17s failed to return in an almost carbon copy (in terms of losses) of the first strike, the terrible day

marked the end of what might be termed the first phase of the Eighth Air Force's bold experiment. The command would attempt no further deep penetration missions without fighter escort. And as the autumnal mists closed over the many empty bomber hardstands on the East Anglian aerodromes, the answer to this problem was quite close in terms of time if not physically.

Lightnings return

In line with the starkly revealed need for 'all the way' escort to the heavy bombers, the P-38 returned to operational status in the ETO on 15 October. The 55th Fighter Group, led by Lieutenant Colonel Frank B. James and based at Nuthampstead, Hertfordshire, flew several theatre indoctrination sweeps along the Dutch coast without incident and two days later was scheduled for a bomber escort mission. When the heavies were recalled, the would-be escort, comprising the 55th's P-38s and the 356th's P-47s, carried out an uneventful sweep over northern France; real action for the Lightning pilots would not materialise until November.

The 55th Group got into the escort business on the 3rd and the day's mission turned out to be a memorable event. P-47s of the 56th were also part of the bomber escort and when the USAAF formation was attacked by JG 1 over The Netherlands the Lightning group defended the bombers magnificently. Put at some disadvantage from the start, in that they took off in driving rain, the Germans lost badly. Several fighters crashed as a direct result of the bad weather, and when the air battle finally ended 13 of their number had gone down. The 55th took credit for four, the 56th seven.

An ominous peripheral event for the bombers at this time was Hermann Goering's rage at seeing the Americans storm across Germany 'as though on parade'. The Reichsmarschall ordered each individual Jagdflieger to ram the bomber he was attacking if his ammunition was exhausted before it went down. Such a ridiculous order was ignored by all but a few hotheads, but JG 1 was among those Jagdgeschwader that initiated their own head-on bomber attacks in late 1943. These had been tried before as they were potentially more lethal to the bombers than attack runs from other quarters and marginally less dangerous to the attacking fighter — although that margin was always terribly slim.

Above: Virgil K. Meroney back from another successful mission. The five kills chalked up made him the first ace of the 352nd Group at Bodney. The aircraft is his personal P-47D-5, 42-8473. *Sam Sox*

Right: The port side of Virgil Meroney's Thunderbolt was reserved for his wife, 'Sweet Louise'. The scoreboard includes nine victories and numerous sweeps denoted by tiny brooms. *Sam Sox*

Below: Starboard side of Virgil Meroney's P-47D with the names 'Miss Josephine' and 'Hedy', who were the wives of his ground crew. *Sam Sox*

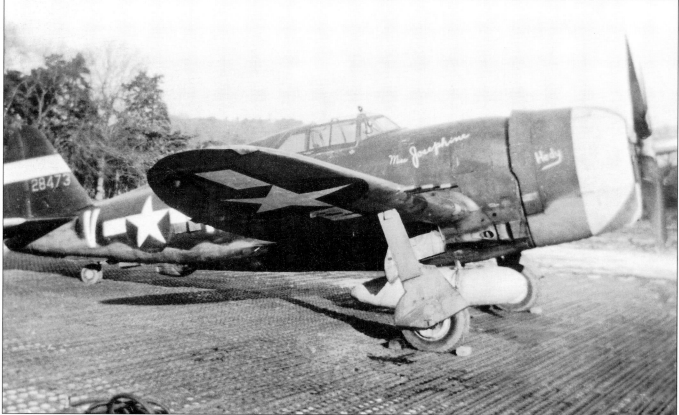

Above: World War 1 style German pattée crosses were the choice of John C. Meyer of the 352nd Group to display victories on his P-47D-5 (42-8529/HO-M). *Sam Sox*

Above: Denied any escort missions with early P-38s due to the needs of Operation 'Torch', the Eighth got more units flying them in late 1943. On 12 December the 55th Group took its aircraft to Bassingbourn, Cambridgeshire, to escort the 91st Bomb Group. *USAF*

Lieutenant-Colonel James of the 55th and Colonel Jack Jenkins, one of the outstanding proponents of the P-38 in the ETO, soon realised that the European theatre was less than ideal as regards operating conditions for the Lockheed twin. To begin with there were too few Lightnings to make up numbers when weather-related technical malfunction kept them off the mission rosters. Eighth Bomber Command began to demand an ever higher ratio of fighters to bombers and, although shorter range withdrawal support was available in abundance because the AAF could always call on the RAF to provide this if enough P-47s were not available, the immediate future did not appear to hold any positive answers to closing the 'escort gap' completely.

However, with Mustangs about to join the Ninth Air Force and more P-38s and P-47s (the 361st and 362nd assigned to the Eighth and Ninth Air Forces respectively had gone operational on 30 November), the picture ahead looked much brighter. As the end of 1943 approached, the Eighth could count on a virtual one-to-one ratio if the composition of the bomber force was around 550. Adding another 200 or so bombers to a given mission size widened the ratio, although this still remained low enough for the fighters to cope. Much depended on the size and aggressiveness of the

Luftwaffe riposte, the line of approach, the position of the bombers in relation to the escort at the time of the intercept and the disposition of the bombers themselves. If tight formations were maintained while under attack, a single element often proved capable of defending itself until the escort appeared. Numerous German fighters were to fall solely as a result of flying into the range of the bombers' guns, which had always been capable of inflicting fatal damage.

Among the drawbacks facing the German pilots was that they could form up in substantial numbers for a potentially devastating opening attack but once their run had been completed, it was natural for flights to break off and get clear of defensive fire as rapidly as possible. Re-forming in any strength for repeat attacks was difficult, particularly so if they were challenged by the escort. The introduction of heavier armament and greater protection for the Fw190 resulted in the conundrum of potentially greater bomber killing power being compromised by higher weight and lower performance. This brought about a gradual erosion of any technical edge the Germans had enjoyed over US fighters, which was in any event small: the early

model P-51s had already begun to open that gap to the advantage of the Americans to the point that the Germans could not easily close it. From their viewpoint it was about to expand again.

New Mustang

Few military aircraft of the war period did not benefit from a development programme that upped their power rating, armament, equipment and so forth and the P-51 had been progressively developed through most of its existence. The ultra-significant change to the Packard Merlin powerplant was a giant step, but other changes were soon necessary. The armament of the B model left much to be desired, for example, as did visibility from the original 'greenhouse' cockpit canopy. North American's updating of the Merlin Mustang began with the installation of a bubble canopy on the 10th P-51B-1 (43-12102). With a cut down rear fuselage the P-51D looked good and flew well and the modified wing was adapted to take six rather than four 0.50in machine guns. The first 'full' change to the new configuration was made on two P-51B-10s (42-106539 and 42-106540) and test pilot Bob Chilton made the maiden flight on 17 November 1943.

Above:
Carrying the big,
165-gal steel drop tanks
that would get their
charges right into
Germany, ground crews
go about their business
at a P-38 base. The
aircraft was from the
55th Fighter Group.
Imperial War Museum

Left:
The numerous servicing
tasks around a fighter
base were ably assisted
by bicycles as this view
of a grass dispersal
shows. Unfortunately
for the pilots, the
ground crews soon had
a huge workload at
P-38 bases trying to
'keep 'em flying'.
Imperial War Museum

Chilton was positive about the new model's capability, and the improvements NAA proposed for production P-51s were endorsed by Eglin Field.

As early as July 1943 a contract for 2,500 NA-109s had been approved and the new model was built in quantity as the P-51D-5. Delivery of the first 800 examples began in March 1944 to be followed by 200 more, the initial examples from Dallas, in June. The P-51D was therefore in England in small quantities by D-Day.

December 43
With fewer operating days available due mainly to bad weather, the Eighth's bomber crews kicked their heels awaiting some improvement as 1943 drew to a close. Bombing was still carried out visually and although the enforced stand-downs were interpreted as the Eighth licking its wounds after the losses on the second Schweinfurt mission, the weather was actually a greater deterrent to bomber operations than any number of fighters or flak defences. Not that the Fortresses and Liberators were actually sitting idly on their hardstands, for the Eighth Bomber Command mission schedule had to be met as far as the conditions allowed.

Above: Col Jack Jenkins in his famous 38th Squadron P-38H (42-67074/CG-J) named 'Texas Ranger'. The man who first saw Berlin from a fighter cockpit, Jenkins led the 55th Group from February to April 1944. *Imperial War Museum*

On 1 December the weather all but ruined an effort by 15 groups of Fortresses and Liberators to bomb industrial targets in Solingen and Leverkusen. Seven groups of P-47s and one of P-38s covered the force. The 3rd Division was forced to abandon the mission while the 1st and 2nd Division groups bombed the secondary target. The fighters saw plenty of action and came home with 20 destroyed for the loss of seven of their own — these actions actually proving to be the most intensive for the entire month.

When their bombers could not fly, the American fighters were still able to make life miserable for the enemy, albeit on a modest scale. Having more or less perfected dive-bombing with the P-47 — without any special sighting aids — the 353rd went to Gilze-Rijen on 4 December escorted by the 56th. The 352nd Group acted in a diversionary capacity by carrying out its own sweep, the result of the operation being three enemy aircraft destroyed for no losses.

Mustangs at last
A mission on the 5th was again almost completely disrupted by the weather — just two B-24s and one B-17 from the total of

548 aircraft dispatched being able to bomb St Nazaire. Less than five tons of bombs were dropped at a cost of nine bombers lost to various causes, including one Liberator blasted apart by a direct flak hit. Although they were probably unaware of the fact, the most important event of 5 December for the bomber crews was the dispatch of the first P-51Bs as part of the escort. There were 36 Mustangs of the 354th Group, plus 266 P-47s and 34 P-38s on a less than auspicious mission in terms of results during which the 56th lost one Thunderbolt — but the die had been cast.

The most effective escort for the month so far took place on the 11th when the 354th fielded 44 P-51Bs as part of an eight group escort for a strike on Emden. The B-17s and B-24s poured over 1,000 tons into the port area shortly after midday and one Mustang went down in the dogfights to keep the Luftwaffe off the bombers. The Wolfpack came home to claim a spectacular 17 downed for the loss of two P-47s in a collision. As they had done previously, pilots from the new 20th Fighter Group flew as part of the 55th Group's element of 31 Lightnings.

Above: Lt William H. Allen of the 343rd FS, 55th Group, flew 'Pretty Patty', an example of the much improved P-38J model (42-67966). *J. V. Crow*

The German ports were pounded on 13 December, bombs falling on Bremen, Kiel and Hamburg. Fighter support was hardly needed, although the P-47s of the 359th Group based at East Wretham in Norfolk flew their debut mission, a sweep to the Pas de Calais area.

Little fighter action accompanied the escort missions on 16 and 20 December, the latter date recording the first P-47 mission for the 358th Fighter Group based at Leiston, Suffolk, which although it had been assigned to the Eighth, was subsequently to transfer to the Ninth and win fame in the tactical role as the 'Orange Tails'. Overcast created less than ideal bombing conditions on the 22nd when the fighters nevertheless clashed with the Luftwaffe and claimed 15 for the loss of four, the Eagles putting their stamp on three of the enemy.

Another dive-bombing mission to Gilze-Rijen was carried out by the 353rd on 23 December, sections of the 56th acting as escort to the bomb-laden Thunderbolts flown by their colleagues.

A massive Christmas Eve attack on V-weapon sites in the Pas de Calais by 722 B-17s and B-24s brought no reaction from the Luftwaffe, the bombers consequently enjoying a relatively trouble-free, short-range run. It was the strongest force the Eighth had yet sent out and 541 fighters ensured a safe passage, without any bomber or fighter losses. However, flak damaged no fewer than 85 of the heavies taking part. From the 670 effective sorties the sites received 1,745 tons of bombs.

There followed a week of low-key activity as the weather clamped down, but 1,394 tons were dropped on targets at Ludwigshafen on the penultimate day of December. The escort, which included the P-38s of the 20th Fighter Group on their first full mission, found itself very busy. The US fighters took heavy losses: 11 P-47s, two P-51s and 12 pilots were missing after the mission. Claims were filed for seven German fighters destroyed.

Large scale air engagements also took place during the last day of the month when the fighters again covered a short-range bomber mission to enemy airfields in France. A heavy, 548-strong fighter force of P-47s and P-38s plus the P-51s of the 354th warded off Luftwaffe attacks, the Lightnings doing well to claim three out of a total of nine for the day, which recorded four US fighters posted as missing. One of these, flown by a pilot from the 55th Group, ditched and was rescued by ASR. That fuel soon became critical for the P-47s when missions included combat was shown by the fact that six pilots from the 358th made forced landings in Kent with their tanks all but dry.

Notes

1 This phenomenon fooled many a gunner. The German fighters characteristically gave off a plume of smoke when they added boost to increase speed.
2 Numerous Allied combat claims were filed for Messerschmitt 210s, although this type's limited production and service mainly in North Africa made frequent encounters highly unlikely over Europe. The finer points of the virtually identical Me410 were not always appreciated when viewed through a gunsight at 350mph.

Above: When it could beat the European weather the P-38 could dish it out well enough. The only US fighter with a 20mm cannon based in Europe, it had very effective firepower and was highly thought of by the AAF top brass. A Lightning's ammunition load was impressive, as this view shows. *Imperial War Museum*

Above: With its distinctive twin boom layout the Lightning was one of the most recognisable of wartime fighters. This P-38H coded CL-Y from the 338th Squadron, 55th Group, was the subject of many press photos in late 1943. *Imperial War Museum*

Above: Incorporating a simple ammunition feed system without too many awkward twists and turns, the P-38's generous nose gun bay gave armourers room to work. *Imperial War Museum*

3 Horse Trading

When American interest in the re-engined P-51B finally picked up, the AAF procurement organisation still failed to feed every example off the assembly line straight to the Eighth in England. Instead the first Merlin Mustangs in Europe were sent to the Ninth Air Force to be flown on tactical ground support duties. The fact that a P-51B could fly from England to Berlin and beyond apparently went unnoticed by the very officers who were tearing their hair out about Thunderbolts and Lightnings being unable to do just that. They did take notice by the end of 1943, but it took precious time – time that VIII Bomber Command did not have.

The 354th Fighter Group had come to England not knowing exactly what to

expect from its assignment to the ETO; it was assumed that it would soon be used in anger on ground-attack sorties when the Ninth Air Force was further into its stride. Higher command had other ideas. Soon after it arrived on 4 November the 354th was based at Greenham Common in Berkshire awaiting delivery of aircraft. It moved to Boxted, Essex, nine days later, assigned to the Eighth Air Force for escort missions. Reversing the policy that had decreed that the P-51 was to be a tactical, ground-attack aircraft, the AAF ensured that the next Mustang group dispatched to join the Ninth was exchanged for a P-47 group. The P-51 unit in question was the 357th based at Leiston, which traded places with the 358th, then flying P-47 escort missions. This was the start of a

rationalisation which would group the P-47s into the ground-attack formations (to which the Thunderbolt was very well suited) of the Ninth, while the Eighth got most of the Mustang groups.

The Eighth held onto the 354th for months, a decision which few of the pilots disagreed with. The chance to hone their skills against the best that the enemy had was an unexpected bonus and hardly an issue with Colonel Ken Martin's determined young men. When the next Mustang group allocated to the Ninth, the 363rd, arrived in England, the tactical force was allowed to keep it, though it required some weeks of nurture by the 354th before it could be deemed combat-effective. It was in the event very fortunate that the 363rd was retained as it later

Above: A whole new ball game: this was the combination that stopped the martyrdom of the Eighth Air Force bombers — the P-51 Mustang and the Rolls-Royce (Packard) Merlin engine. S/Sgt George W. Leonard (left) and Sgt Robert L. Seager were pictured at work on a 354th Group P-51B on 13 January 1944.
Imperial War Museum

Above: Not quite so hot was the design of the P-51B's gun bay and ammunition feeds. Prone to jamming, the angled guns could leave pilots almost defenceless in combat. Armourer Sgt Marvin Lippoff eases a belt of 0.50in ammunition into position on 13 January 1944. *Imperial War Museum*

became a very useful tactical reconnaissance outfit in the Ninth.

For the time being, the Eighth made no decision on the future of the P-38; fighters were needed in substantial numbers in all war theatres and the Lockheed twin, while suffering more than its fair share of mechanical problems in Europe's hostile climate, was highly thought of elsewhere and had development potential. Remedies of its major ills were being addressed by the manufacturer and Lightnings continued to serve in the ETO.

January 1944
With the issue from the chiefs of staff of the Pointblank bombing directive and the formation of USSAFE under Carl Spaatz on 1 January, the USAAF formalised its commitment to the CBO. Spaatz now had the strategic Fifteenth Air Force in Italy as well as the Eighth in England under his control, the former having the potential to hit targets in Eastern Europe and the Balkans, thus saving the Eighth from flying all of the most dangerous, maximum range missions.

On the 4th the heavy bombers returned to Kiel in strength, their mission being the destruction of port facilities. Seventy P-38s

and 42 P-51s provided the escort and there were several inconclusive engagements as the Luftwaffe fighters attempted to counter. A 354th pilot shot down a Ju88 over Kiel, but a P-51 and P-38 were lost. The second mission of the day saw the bombers heading for Münster under the watchful eyes of 430 fighter pilots. The enemy made an appearance and lost seven fighters for his trouble, while the American side came home with another ace. Peter Pompetti of the 84th FS, 78th FG, had shot down a Bf109 near Coesfeld for his fifth kill.

The 56th was well pleased with improved models of the P-47 which had that day flown their first operation fitted with a performance-boosting 'paddle bladed' propeller and engine water injection.

There was a partial return to airfield targets for the heavies on 5 January, the bombers also going to shipyards at Kiel, and ball-bearing production at Elberfeld. Fighters covered all three bomber elements at a cost of 12 of their own against 27 German machines.

Phased-escort
By 7 January the Eighth was able to send off 463 P-47s, 71 P-38s and 37 P-51s to escort and support the bombers heading for the IG Farben plant at Ludwigshafen. This impressive fighter total included the P-47 flown by James A. Goodson of the 4th Group, who shot down two Fw190s to become an ace. Seven enemy fighters were claimed.

This was also the first occasion when the fighters employed a phased-escort tactic, under which specific groups relieved each other at precise times and places along the bombers' route. Fighters also began taking the most direct route from the UK to conserve fuel; with an adequate number of fighters on hand, this system enabled each group to stay with the big friends longer than it had previously. This proved so effective that it remained in force until the end of hostilities.

New groups of bombers joined the Eighth during the month, the force approaching the point where it could make good even heavy losses much more quickly than before. The build-up similarly ensured that important targets could have a substantial number of bombers, around 5–600, dispatched against them. Pointblank, the Allied strategic air offensive against Germany, officially began on 11 January with a selection of targets for the 663 heavies dispatched by the Eighth.

Also receiving high level sanction on the 11th was the first 'freelance' fighter sweep in front of and on the flanks of the bomber stream. This important change in deployment enabled the fighter pilots to make surprise attacks on enemy air units as they assembled to attack the heavies. As mentioned previously, if this could be achieved quickly, the Germans would lose valuable time – re-forming the attack formations would mean that the bombers would pass through many intercept sectors before a substantial force could react. The P-38, P-47 and P-51 pilots would also do their best to ensure that fewer enemy interceptors were able to assemble. The 56th Group made the first freelance sweep

deploying 'A' and 'B' groups of 36 and 48 Thunderbolts respectively; things went entirely according to plan when the 56th A Group claimed 11 victories between 11.05 and 11.15 hours.

Medal of Honor

When the German fighters did almost inevitably break through to the bombers, a small group of them regretted their boldness. Over Halberstadt, crews of the Bf110s of ZG 76 met the P-51Bs of the 356th Squadron, 354th Group. 'Riding shotgun' on a small group of B-17s being harried by both twin- and single-engined fighters, Major James H. Howard waded into the opposition. An ex-American Volunteer Group pilot, Howard had already achieved two aerial victories in combat with the Japanese, and that January day over Germany he did far more than merely add to his score. Suddenly finding himself alone as he opened the combat at 11.50 hours, Howard kept his gun triggers down until he had blasted two Bf110s and an Fw190 and probably

destroyed a second Focke-Wulf. At the time the score seemed higher, certainly to the bomber crews, who initially reported that as many as 11 Bf110s had gone down. The Germans finally sheared off at 12.15 hours, much to Howard's relief because he then had very little to fight with. Being set at an angle due to the thin inner wing section of the P-51B, the ammunition feed to the outboard guns was not very direct and the design caused no end of stoppages. This happened to Howard, and as the Germans retreated his Mustang was down to just one operable gun. When he returned to Boxted, the full story of one fighter pilot's bravery against heavy odds was recounted. The upshot was that Jim Howard was awarded the Medal of Honor, the only fighter pilot recipient of America's highest award for gallantry in the ETO.

Weather disrupted much of the bombers' effectiveness on the 11th and numerous crews dropped on targets of opportunity observed literally through holes in the cloud. Steps were being taken to overcome

Above: One more element made the Mustang the success it was — drop tanks. Sway braces held them firmly in place until release time and members of the 354th ground crew are shown here tightening them down. *Imperial War Museum*

Above: Easy does it! Those lugs had to be tight, for no pilot wanted tanks that dropped prematurely. This is one of many scenes shot at the 354th's first operational base at Boxted to publicise the new Ninth Air Force fighter. Note the P-51B's generous area of flap, which drooped as hydraulic pressure bled off. *Imperial War Museum*

the overcast weather as a B-24 equipped with H2X radar was flying its first combat mission that day. A period of bad weather then further highlighted the need for a target locating radar, H2X being an American design based on the successful British H2S set.

'Socked in' targets in Germany invariably released the heavies for a further pounding of the Noball sites along the French coast. The full weight of a 522-strong force of Liberators and Fortresses was thrown against 21 V-weapon locations on 14 January. All but one site was deluged with high explosive — 1,500 tons in all. No fewer than 645 US fighters rode with the bombers, which attracted the attention of the Jagdwaffe. In the resulting combats, 13 German fighters were claimed in an aerial mêlée that sprawled across France and Belgium for almost an hour. Don Gentile of the 336th FS became an ace when he shot down two Fw190s over the Bois de Compiègne in 20 minutes' combat. Another ex-Eagle Squadron pilot who was now adding to his score, Gentile had knocked down two while with No 133 Squadron.

A week's inactivity in deference to the weather was ended with a bang on 21 January when 795 bombers went to the French coast again. Heavy cloud brought mixed results, 400 aircraft returning home with their bomb bays still full. That left

395 to drop on 26 sites and several aerodromes. A record escort force of 628 fighters included the 361st Group flying its first mission in P-47s.

The 56th claimed another first for the day when it filed claims for enemy fighters destroyed on the ground. One of the few air forces officially to give credit to claims for ground victories, the Eighth thereby recognised the extremely hazardous nature of strafing which was none the less an effective operational tactic available to General William 'Bill' Kepner, VIII FC C-in-C. Always ready to try anything that would whittle down the odds in favour of his boys, Kepner knew that such bold tactics could deny the Germans more fighters, burn fuel stocks, wreck facilities and generally unnerve ground crews. Pilots frequently indulged in strafing *en route* back to England from escort duties from this point on.

A few more fighters were added to the mission schedule on 24 January when 678 were dispatched, but the main point of the exercise was abandoned when the bombers experienced a huge mix-up during assembly and the mission was finally cancelled. The fighters meanwhile had also

to abandon a new area patrol tactic which was an expansion of the earlier group relay system in that specific groups were briefed to operate in particular areas along the bombers' route. All was not wasted, however, for combat claims were made for 21 enemy fighters in return for nine P-38s, P-47s and P-51s, all the pilots of which were killed.

Gee and G-H navigational aids were now coming into service to be fitted to Eighth Air Force bombers configured as pathfinders and on 28 January the fighters — 122 of them — escorted a B-24 PFF mission which led two 2nd Division groups to V-weapon sites near Bonnières, but the gremlins struck to render the bombing largely ineffectual owing to errors in target identification. On 29 January the Eighth launched its largest strategic mission to date when 863 B-17s and B-24s were briefed for industrial targets in the Hamburg area. More than 1,800 tons of bombs were dropped in 806 effective sorties. The escort of 632 fighters claimed 44 enemy fighters shot down, although they were powerless to prevent the loss of 11 B-17s that bombed targets of opportunity at Ludwigshafen; otherwise

Above: Wing drop tanks needed to be braced a bit more on Thunderbolts, as indicated by the 'plumbing' on the 108-gal steel (grey coloured) tanks carried by P-47D-15 (42-75587/B8-V) of the 379th FS, 362nd Group. *Imperial War Museum*

fighters and flak brought down 29 Forts and Libs.

An indifferent month in regard to weather rounded out with two more days of aerial activity: on the 30th, 703 bombers attacked industrial targets in Brunswick and Hanover with 635 fighters in an escort and support role. The fighter box score rose to 47 claimed and 1st Lieutenant Michael J. Quirk became another 56th ace. Lieutenant Virgil K. Meroney of the 487th Squadron, 352nd Group, thought he had also brought his score to five, but his fifth was subsequently downgraded to a damaged claim. Not until 3 February could Meroney make sure of kill number five.

There was an 'all fighter' show on the 31st, the P-47s of the 4th, 78th and 355th Groups making a series of dive-bomber attacks on Gilze-Rijen aerodrome, escorted by P-38s and additional P-47s. Each of the dive-bombers carried a single 500lb bomb. Covering their charges well, pilots of the 4th shot down five Bf109s near the target, while the P-38s of the 55th Group wrought further havoc on the Jagdwaffe to the tune of six 109s and two 190s during a separate sweep of the Eindhoven–Venlo–Arnhem area.

February 44

Rationalisation of the tactical air support element of the Ninth Air Force took place in February, Major-General Elwood 'Pete'

Quesada taking over as CO of Air Support Command, which henceforth controlled all fighter groups and effectively rendered the former IX Fighter Command a 'paper' organisation. Colonel Clarence B. Crumrine then briefly headed XIX ASC which would be one of the major tactical fighter organisations for post D-Day operations. There was some immediate indication that the changes in the Ninth were too radical as by the 4th, Major-General Otto P. Weyland had replaced Crumrine and IX ASC had been given the 84th Fighter Wing HQ but was still without any assigned groups.

In the meantime the build-up of Ninth fighter groups in the UK continued and all of them began flying missions as soon as possible, as European theatre combat experience would soon be vitally important.

On 3 February VIII FC literally flew headlong into another natural hazard in the form of strong winds. With 632 fighters up to escort the heavies, some of the pilots encountered these severe conditions on the way out. This in turn led to fuel starvation unexpectedly early and eight pilots were lost to this primary cause. Combat was, however, joined and the force claimed six German fighters downed. Further combats took place on the 5th and 6th, the latter day being memorable for

Captain Robert A. Lamb of the 56th who became another 61st Squadron ace after shooting down a Bf109 near Beauvais.

Fourteen enemy fighters were downed on the 8th, the fighter escort amounting to 533 aircraft, including the P-38s of the 20th Group and the P-51s of the 354th. Both these units went down to hunt trains during their return to England and seven locomotives were claimed. That the Germans could defend their trains just as well as other targets was shown by the disproportionate loss of three pilots from the Pioneers. As the only AAF fighter to pack a 20mm cannon, the P-38 found a new usefulness on ground-attack missions, where its closely grouped nose guns could puncture the boilers of locomotives; if the fighters could remove all motive power from the prime mover, the flatbed cars and wagons it was hauling could usually be destroyed piecemeal provided that the train was not bristling with mobile flak, as many were.

Attacks on pre-invasion targets were now stepped up and the V-weapon offensive continued to absorb many sorties by medium and heavy bombers; the amphibious operation to land armies in France was mere months away and the air forces had the vital task of making the move inland as safe as was humanly possible. Worried that the chosen landing points in Normandy might be guessed by the Germans, the Allied opted for a 'broad front' interdiction of all forms of transport and the necessary road, waterway and rail connections, plus radar stations and airfields, to avoid this happening. There was indeed some risk — but the enemy had already convinced himself that nobody would cross the Channel anywhere but from Dover to the Pas de Calais, the shortest possible sea route.

On 10 February further strength was added to VIII Fighter Command's strength when the 364th began P-38 operations from Honington in Suffolk.

Joining the 67th Fighter Wing, the group was led initially by Colonel Roy W. 'Ozzie' Osborn, who had been called away from the 352nd Group when the new unit's designate CO was killed on a mission with the 20th Group. The 364th took its Lightnings over Europe for the first time on 2 March.

The bombers meanwhile went to Brunswick and charged headlong into one of the most intense air battles to date. There were 446 fighters to cover the 1st Wing B-17s, 141 of which had been dispatched. Five P-38s and four P-47s were reported lost when the fighters returned to England — but Eighth Air

Force intelligence officers were amazed to find themselves logging total claims for 60 enemy aircraft, the highest number to date. 1st Lieutenant Vermont L. Garrison of the 366th Squadron became another 4th Group ace during the course of the day's actions, his personal (fifth) Bf109 falling near Dummer Lake, a prominent landmark and fighter rendezvous point.

Day of aces

Another fighter group debut, that of the 357th Group, took place on 11 February. As only the third P-51 unit in the ETO, the 357th took to escort work without qualms and its subsequent combat record

Above: One of the many: Steeple Morden from the air gives a fair idea of a typical Eighth Air Force fighter airfield with the distinctive 'frying pan' hardstands for aircraft plainly visible. *Author's collection*

Far Left:
'King of Strafers'
James A. Goodson,
14-victory ace of the
4th Group. *Author's
collection*

Left:
John T. Godfrey,
long-time member of
the 336th Squadron,
who finished the war
with 16.333 victories.
Author's collection

Above: Eugene Roberts became the first ace of the 78th Group. *Imperial War Museum*

Above: Capt Jack Price of the 78th Group named all his P-47s and P-51s 'Feather Merchant' and scored five victories. *Imperial War Museum*

showed that the change was nothing but positive; this particular group of Mustang pilots eventually turned in one of the best records in the Eighth. On the 11th the 357th carried out a sweep to Rouen which was unchallenged by the Luftwaffe. Otherwise the Eighth sent out 482 P-47s, 82 P-38s and 38 P-51s and in combat with the Jagdwaffe the Germans lost 30 in return for 14 AAF fighters shot down with their pilots. These modest figures belied the experience of the American flyers, five of whom returned to base as new aces: 1st Lieutenants Stanley B. Morrill (62nd FS, 56th FG); Frederick J. Christensen, Jr, (62nd FS) and James M. Morris (77th FS, 20th FG); Captain Richard E. Turner (356th FS, 354th FG) and Colonel Kenneth Martin, CO of the 354th Group. Of these, only Martin failed to return when he collided with another P-51 after destroying an Me410. He became a prisoner and the 354th was taken over by Colonel Jim Howard the following day. Otherwise these pilots all shot down Bf109s to achieve their ace status.

Another new arrival in England on 12 February was the P-38-equipped 370th Group, assigned to the Ninth. While the newcomers were settling in at Aldermaston,

Berkshire, 2nd Division B-24s led by pathfinders using G-H attacked V-weapon sites at St Pol/ Siracourt under close escort by the P-47s and P-51s which also conducted an uneventful sweep.

A further directive aimed primarily at destroying Axis airpower was issued on the 13th, the target list stressing the need for concentrated attacks to demolish the objectives rather than to spread the offensive over too many locations. Particular emphasis was laid on targets associated with the German aircraft industry. More Noball targets were bombed with heavy fighter escort, part of which dealt with six Fw190s attempting to intervene, the combats spreading between the Channel and Paris.

During a period of limited air operations in deference to the weather, the Ninth Air Force had established an advanced headquarters at Uxbridge by 17 February, this being intended to direct tactical air operations in France immediately following the invasion. The period was something of a 'calm before the storm' as the Eighth launched the first of its 'Big Week' attacks

on 20 February. Otherwise known as 'Argument' this campaign had the dual purpose of ensuring that at least one large scale bomber strike was made every day for a full week to draw German interceptors into combat. The targets themselves would be mainly those associated with aircraft production, the first being to Leipzig, Brunswick and Tutow aerodrome — and for the first time the Eighth would attempt to put 1,000 bombers over a German target. In the event, the inevitable technical problems with a proportion of the participating aircraft reduced this to 823 effective sorties. Some crews were obliged to seek targets of opportunity but in the main the primaries were bombed. A record 835 fighters were airborne and if nothing else the sheer number of returns on German radar showed the enormous task now facing the Jagdwaffe. Destroying even 10% of the bombers had always been difficult, but the presence of so many escorts made numerous interceptions seem like an easy way to commit suicide. Nevertheless the German fighter pilots tried, as always, to do their duty and at the

Above: Lt James M. Morris chats to his crew chief, T/Sgt Joseph H. McCarland, on 10 February 1944. Morris, who hailed from Detroit, flew with the 20th Group, became an ace the next day and finished his war on 7 July when he was shot down with a total score of 7.333. The P-38J behind him was assigned to group CO, Col B. M. Russell. *Imperial War Museum*

Above: Not a fighter pilot although he was qualified to fly all types, Lt-Col Cass Hough was an indispensable technical troubleshooter to the Eighth Air Force in England. *Author's collection*

end of the day the occupants of 59 US aircraft had suffered death, injury or at best a crash-landing or bail-out. In addition, the prowling American fighters found two Ju88s which they quickly dispatched. Another nail in the Luftwaffe's coffin was that the white-starred fighters were now right over Germany — for the day was marked by the first use of 150-US gallon (125 Imp gal) belly tanks. In addition, the fighters were in a position to disturb the Germans twice that day when the 55th, 356th, 361st and 362nd Groups were able to fly their first double missions.

The steadily rising number of aces in the ranks of the American fighter groups increased by six on the 20th when Captains Don M. Beerbower and Jack T. Bradley of the 353rd Squadron of the 354th Group each shot down Bf109s. Beerbower also nailed a Bf110, as did Captain Lindol F. Graham, a P-38 pilot with the 79th Squadron, 20th Group, who accounted for two of the twin-engined *Zerstörers*. The victories credited to Captain Leroy A. Schreiber of the Wolfpack's 62nd Squadron took him past the baseline five, his three Bf109s bringing his score to 7.5. At the controls of another P-47, 2nd Lieutenant Grant M. Turley's victory over a Bf109 added to the laurels of the 78th Group. And the 355th Group's Captain Norman E. Olson (357th FS) also made ace with a Bf109 kill near Siegen.

'Pete' Quesada's appointment as head of the IX Fighter Command became effective on 21 February, the command's role now being defined as 'operations and training for all Ninth Air Force fighter units'. Weather again disrupted bomber operations to some extent, but the fighters, 679 strong, again found combat with the enemy to down 27. Two more aces were thus created, 1st Lieutenant Charles F. Gumm, Jr, continuing to add to the stars of the 354th when he shot down a Bf110 over Brunswick, a feat duplicated by Captain Robert W. Stephens, also from the 355th Squadron. These aces were the first for the Ninth Air Force in terms of pilots who had scored kills only in the ETO.

The recent use of the Bf110 to intercept bombers reflected the desperate measures the Jagdwaffe was being driven to by the Allied air assault. Ill-equipped in terms of speed and manoeuvrability to survive against enemy fighters, the Messerschmitt twin was used only sporadically. Heavy losses were doubly wasteful in that a number of the individuals who went down were night-fighter crews whose expertise — and indeed aircraft — were much better suited to nocturnal interceptions of RAF bombers. Wasting them against the USAAF daylight juggernaut was folly in the extreme, but there was a tendency to throw everything at the bombers as they entered various sectors of the Reich defence area.

Big Week continued the inexorable toll of the German defenders when the Eighth and Fifteenth Air Force joined forces on 22 February to strike aircraft factory targets simultaneously from two directions. This was an ideal goal of the AAF high command, although the Italian-based bomber force was as yet small. However the bad weather over its airfields had already been detrimental to operations, something few had predicted. It was already well known how the weather over England could throw the Eighth's heavy bomber operations out of kilter and during this ambitious operation 544 out of 799 B-17s and B-24s were forced to abort or heed a recall order. This left just 81 1st Division B-17s to make attacks on Aschersleben and Bernburg while 100 more went after targets of opportunity. Adding embarrassment to navigational error, the B-24s of the 2nd Division unloaded over four Dutch towns when they believed they were in German airspace. Heavy bomber losses made this a day the Eighth had to put down to experience, although 118 B-24s from Italy made a mess of the Obertraubling Messerschmitt assembly plant at Regensburg. B-17s also hit another Messerschmitt facility at

Above: A galaxy of 4th Group aces shows (from left to right) Duane Beeson, Nick Megura, Don Gentile, John Godfrey and Jim Goodson. *Author's collection*

Prufening, among other locations.

The fighters from England again emerged from the chaos of the day with battle honours and additions to the Eighth's list of aces. The 365th Group concurrently made its IX FC debut on loan to the Eighth to swell further the number of P-47s available for bomber escort duty.

There was also a downside for the fighter groups when Major Walter C. Beckham, 18-victory ace with the 353rd Group's 351st Squadron, was brought down whilst strafing dispersed Fw190s at Ostheim. Beckham was then the leading Eighth Air Force ace, and his capture and incarceration were to be shared by many of the top-scoring pilots in future months. In this the American experience was in marked contrast to that of the Jagdflieger, so many of whom were killed outright or fatally wounded in aerial combat.

New aces on 22 February were: Donovan F. Smith of the 56th's 61st FS, George Hall and Captain John W. Vogt, Jr, both of the 63rd FS; Captain James N. Poindexter, 352nd FS, 353rd Group and Major Jack J. Oberhansley of the 82nd Squadron, 78th Group. These pilots accounted for 6.5 enemy aircraft (the half share was Oberhansley's) from the day's total of 57 fighters, a Ju88 and what was described in combat reports somewhat mysteriously as an Italian flying boat.

It was not always easy to have a kill officially verified, as 1st Lieutenant John B. Carder of the 364th FS, 357th Group, found on 23 February. His was a very unusual victory in that the gun camera film clearly showed German markings on a P-47, but despite being backed by Carder's eye-witness account, the claim was denied. A number of P-47s had by then been captured by the Germans and in common with a similar practice followed by the Allies with German aircraft, these were maintained as far as possible in flying trim for the purposes of demonstrating their salient points to fighter and bomber pilots.

Another mission co-ordinated with the Fifteenth Air Force was laid on by the Eighth on 24 February, this bringing savage reaction by the German fighter force, which relentlessly attacked the bombers using aerial rockets as well as cannon and machine guns to bring them down. Ten of the Fifteenth's 2nd Group B-17s were lost, even before their target was reached, but battling through the fighters and flak the 87 remaining Fortresses all but wiped an aircraft components facility at Steyr off the map and for good measure destroyed a stock of ball-bearings at another location. Subject to further flak assault once clear of the flak belt, four more bombers were shot down before the cavalry arrived in the

shape of the 87 P-38s and 59 P-47s that constituted the withdrawal support.

The 82nd (P-38) and 325th (P-47) Groups from Italy did well with a score of 12 German fighters, while the Eighth, briefed to attack five plants associated with the German aviation industry, sought instead alternate targets due both to mishap and bad weather. Some bombed the primary at Schweinfurt and Gotha, escort cover at both locations being 767 fighters of all three types. The Eighth's 359th and 365th Groups flew double missions. For their trouble all participants claimed a total of 37 fighters and a Ju88, mostly over Germany but also within Austrian airspace. Ten AAF fighters were lost. Among the most successful pilots that day was 1st Lieutenant John H. Trulock, Jr, who enhanced the reputation of the Wolfpack and his own 63rd Squadron by shooting down an Fw190 to become an ace. He was joined in that elevated position by Major James C. Stewart of the 61st Squadron, whose Fw190 kill brought his score to five. On the fringes of the action, the Ninth's 363rd Group flew its debut mission, its Mustangs being on loan to the Eighth for the time being.

Schweinfurt's air raid sirens had hardly cooled down when they began again — the RAF was over the town on the night of 24/25 February. It was a demonstration of how local the war could become to one

Above: Don Gentile's distinctively marked P-51B 'Shangri-La' being waved away on another mission. *Imperial War Museum*

Above: Close to, the details of the streamer of kills on Gentile's P-51B can be seen to advantage as Duane Beeson shakes his colleague's hand. Both pilots helped make the 4th one of the top scoring groups in the Eighth. *Imperial War Museum*

area when the British were able to combine their efforts with those of the Americans under the CBO plan.

Big Week concluded on the 25th, the Eighth dispatching 685 bombers, the Fifteenth 139, to more aviation industry plants at Augsburg, Fürth, Regensburg and Stuttgart. Bombers of the latter air force had no escort during the target penetration phase of the mission, due once more to the fighters' lack of range. Coming under heavy German fighter attack, the B-17s briefed for Regensburg lost 11 machines. Down to just 25 Forts, the formation hit the target squarely, just before the fighter attacks began again. Harried for 30 minutes, the bomber gunners blazed away to claim 31 enemy fighters down, a proportion of which were undoubtedly real enough casualties.

A massive 899-strong force of Eighth and Ninth air force fighters covered the bombers, the 361st, 363rd and 365th P-47 groups flying two missions each to do so. Two P-51s and a single P-47 was the modest cost in return for 25 victory claims over fighters and two Ju88s. 1st Lieutenant Frank Q. O'Connor flying a P-51B as part of the 365th Squadron, became a Pioneer Mustang Group ace when he shot down a Bf109 near Mannheim.

The daily mission strategy of 25 February included a double blow against the Prufening Messerschmitt factory at Regensburg — the Eighth following up an early attack by the Fifteenth — which had sustained a high, 24% loss. The crews from England found the air relatively clear as they struck just as the German fighters were replenishing and refuelling after their earlier exertions, allowing the 267 bombers to unload without much interference. Even though the 50 fighters that did attack them shot down 12 B-17s, the attack all but destroyed the Prufening factory and severely damaged the Regensburg plant.

The Eighth thereafter flew short range, anti-V1 Noball sorties until the 29th when the heavies returned to Germany to carry on the offensive against German aircraft industry plants in and around Brunswick. The bomb tonnage was recorded as 425 tons and, although the 554-strong escort lost four pilots, none fell to enemy fighters. A victory over a single Ju52 spoke volumes — the pilots estimated that the Luftwaffe fighter force had all but been exhausted by its efforts during Big Week which, overall, was counted as an AAF success.

Left:
A good ground crew was almost as important as a good wingman and Don Gentile had S/Sgt Harry F. East, here expertly probing the innards of Gentile's P-51B to ensure that it would not let the ace down. *Imperial War Museum*

Above: P-47D flown by 1st Lt Dick H. Mudge, Jr, which suffered superficial battle damage on 29 January 1944. Mudge was later shot down and made a PoW. *Bill Crimmins*

Left:
Lt Robert H. Knapp of the 83rd FS, 78th Group, who flew a total of 119 missions between 16 February 1943 and 23 February 1944, was said to have reached terminal velocity while diving his P-47 named 'Percy'. There were several reports of dives at sound barrier speeds by piston-engined fighters in England during the war. *Imperial War Museum*

Below:
In common with other aces of the 4th, Duane Beeson gave his P-51B a distinctive personal insignia, in this case 'Boise Bee', which recalled his home in Idaho. *Author's collection*

Above: Detail view of the P-47D's internal bullet-proof windscreen, rear-view mirror and gunsight bracing in front of Lt William S. Swanson of the 82nd FS, 78th Group, who was killed in action on 11 February 1944. His personal aircraft was P-47D-6 (42-74733/MX-P). *Imperial War Museum*

4 Build-up to 'Overlord'

March 1944

Both tactical and strategic targets were drawn by the heavies on a fairly regular basis in the months leading up to D-Day, that on 2 March being typical. Aerodromes and marshalling yards, the latter the large and important junction at Frankfurt-am-Main, were on the mission schedule, although thick cloud prevented the full force of 327 aircraft from bombing. In such a situation, rather than bring their bombs home, the Fort and Lib crews unloaded on targets of opportunity of which there were many inside the Reich borders. As was becoming more or less routine, VIII FC did not come home empty handed, but claimed 16 enemy fighters.

The 2 March mission was the third for the 4th Group in the P-51B. Teething troubles had led to some disappointment among the pilots, as they had expected so much from the long-awaited P-47 replacement. Don Blakeslee gritted his teeth and persevered — he was not alone in seeing the great potential of the North American fighter. Two enemy fighters were downed on the mission.

Weather disrupted the 3 March bomber missions to Berlin, Oranienburg and Erkner, although the day included an historic footnote when Colonel Jack Jenkins, CO of the 55th Group, peered through the gloom from his P-38 cockpit to see the suburbs of Berlin slide away underneath. He was the first USAAF fighter pilot to get a sight of the German capital from a single-seat fighter, the Lightning being part of a 730-strong force which included the P-38s of the 364th Group which was flying its debut mission. The victory tally reflected the poor flying weather — eight German fighters for eight American. The latter, six P-51s, a P-38 and a crash-landed P-47, translated into six pilots listed as MIA. The modest victory tally nevertheless brought ace status to Lieutenant Vermont Garrison of the 336th Squadron, a Bf109 shot down near Berlin raising his personal score to an unwieldy 7.333 (a carry over from the RAF scoring system). Garrison himself did not get home to Debden to celebrate, as he was shot down by flak near Boulogne to become a PoW.

Below: A typically heavy ground-attack load for a P-47 was two 500lb bombs and triple-tube M-10 rocket launchers, plus a belly tank. The big fighter lifted it all with ease as this 353rd Group ship shows. *J. V. Crow*

'Personal' air cover

In its forward planning for the invasion, the Ninth Air Force was in the process of subdividing its fighter assets to offer direct support to specific US armies, once these were in action on the Continent. In this way the fighter-bombers would, it was hoped, be able to spread their efforts evenly and not duplicate each other in certain sectors. This practice was more clearly defined in terms of fighter deployment due to the very 'localised' strafing and bombing the single-seaters would be asked to carry out. Ninth Air Force bombers were not so tied to ground formations, their attacks of necessity ranging from the front lines to the rear areas to disrupt the flow of supplies into the German frontline battle areas. As a result of this policy, the 84th Fighter Wing began early in March to plan the operations for several of its subordinate groups.

The weather continued to be responsible for indirect losses of fighters and bombers, and on 4 March there was a minor disaster when 24 of the latter failed to return. It was a small percentage of the 770 sorties

dispatched, but losses into double figures were viewed as serious, such was the upper hand that the USAAF was beginning to get used to, however large the opposition. One day's loss figures were made worse if a disproportionately high number of aircraft and/or pilots were from a single unit and in this case it was the 363rd Fighter Group which counted 11 fewer P-51s by the end of the day. The incident was made worse by the fact that enemy action was not a factor. The unit had sent off 33 Mustangs and these were recalled as most of the bombers had similarly aborted in bad weather. Three pilots who did not hear it completed an escort to Münster and returned via the Dutch coast. The rest had presumably set course for England but had become lost and disorientated in the overcast, run out of fuel and, one by one, had gone into the Channel. Blame was mostly laid at the door of poor instrument-flying training but the loss of 11 pilots was a disaster whatever the cause. On 5 March the P-47s of the Ninth's 405th Group came into Christchurch in Hampshire to boost further the tactical order of battle which was by that

time approaching its full complement, as was VIII Fighter Command.

Combat always carried the risk of losing pilots whose expertise extended beyond the cockpit into the important realm of tactical planning, training and the generally smooth running of a group. Losing a commanding officer was always a setback and the 357th Group experienced this on the 5th when Colonel Henry R. Spicer was shot down and taken prisoner. Fortunately the AAF had planned that such an eventuality would not create a leadership void to the detriment of group performance and had initiated a system whereby there was usually a deputy on hand quickly to fill the shoes of a missing CO. There had to be such a system when fighter group leaders regularly flew missions, which many of them continued to do, despite the occasional persuasive offers for them to remain on the ground and use their experience in an important if less stimulating arena behind a desk. It was also not unknown for fighter pilots to play down the number of missions they had flown in order to extend their tours of duty

Above: As the Ninth blasted targets across northwest Europe before and after the invasion it relied on tried and tested weapons. Parafrags were deadly and bunches of them were hung in multiples on fighter wing racks for maximum target impact. A P-51B has a typical load here. *Imperial War Museum*

Above: Johnny Godfrey (left) and Don Gentile by the latter's P-51B which had a red and white checkerboard below the exhaust stacks on both sides.
Imperial War Museum

Above: The deadly effects of German light flak were seen on all fighter bases, but some P-47s never got home to tell the tale. Attacking Châteaudun aerodrome in France on 26 March 1944, P-47D-5 (42-8443) of the 355th Group flown by Lt Kenneth R. Williams was shot down. A member of the 353rd Group, Williams was on TDY with the 'Steeple Morden Strafers' to gain experience. He evaded capture and got back home. *J. V. Crow*

Above: Williams' P-47 suffered a landing heavy enough to rip the engine out of its mountings and looked a little truncated when the Germans came on the scene. *J. V. Crow*

Above: The fetching nose art of 42-8443 was 'Miss Clean Sweep'. Marked as a 354th Squadron aircraft when it was lost, it had previously been part of the 358th Squadron and had probably been named by its original pilot, Lt James Upchurch. *J. V. Crow*

beyond the date when the AAF system would normally have rotated them home. Entered as local training flights and other non-combat hops, there were log book entries that were not all they seemed at first glance. Numerous individuals flew one tour and called it a day while others volunteered for second or third tours, which were usually allowed, depending on the war situation at the time.

'Big B'

The probing attacks on Berlin culminated in the first USAAF bombing raid on the 'big city' on 6 March. A maximum effort comprising 504 B-17s and 226 B-24s was launched, the objectives including several of the many industrial plants in and around the sprawling German capital. But the distance Berlin lay from England had previously helped protect it from the full weight of air attack, and this was no exception. Cloud cover prevented a great concentration of bombs falling on the primary targets, 474 bombers seeking secondaries. As was anticipated, the Jagdwaffe was prepared to defend the Reich capital vigorously, having had ample indicators that the Americans would sooner or later appear in force. The Focke-Wulf and Messerschmitt reception committee enforced the apprehension the bomber crews undoubtedly felt about the

distant location and importance of their targets; aggressive attacks chopped down 53 Fortresses and 16 Liberators and damaged a total of 347 more. Fifteen of the B-17s were from the 100th Bomb Group which thus sustained the highest one-day toll taken of a single group to date. Escort was a record 801 fighters, comprising 615 P-47s, 100 P-51s and 86 P-38s which frequently engaged the enemy, to come home with record air combat claims of 81 downed.

The individual dogfights stretched for many miles along the bomber routes and the AAF fighter losses were remarkably light at 11 aircraft. Among those missing was the 334th Squadron's CO, Major Henry L. Mills who had brought his personal score to six shortly before he was forced down during an engagement with an Fw190. As he was taken into captivity, Mills could not have known that he was more fortunate than 2nd Lieutenant Grant M. Turley of the 82nd Squadron, another six-victory pilot who was killed in combat over Barenburg. Such a high score of enemy aircraft included a number of kills credited to pilots who became first-time aces on the Berlin show, including Joseph W. Icard of the 56th, Glenn T. Eagleston of the 354th and Pierce W. McKennon of the 4th.

Another 300-plus B-17s and 150 B-24s were launched against the

Berlin/Eckner aircraft industry complex on 8 March, the force dropping nearly 1,000 tons of HE in the process. Pushing the fighter to bomber ratio even higher, VIII FC dispatched 891 Lightnings, Mustangs and Thunderbolts, 18 of which failed to return — as did 77 of the enemy. The fighter element included both P-47s and P-51s of the 352nd and 355th Groups, their transition from one type to another not being allowed to interrupt the mission schedule. New aces from the day's combats were Captain Joseph H. Bennett of the 56th and three from the 4th: Major James A. Clark, 1st Lieutenant John T. Godfrey and 1st Lieutenant Nicholas Megura.

The briefed return to Berlin on 9 March was turned from a precision attack on specific factories to an RAF-type area bombing attack as the B-17s were again frustrated by the weather over the city. The B-24 force went elsewhere for the same reason and 808 escort fighters saw no action.

After a break, the 11 March part of the main area of bomber operations was the French coast and Noball targets; the 352nd Fighter Group toted 500lb bombs to St Nazaire's submarine pens in a somewhat ambitious attempt to cause substantial damage to the mighty concrete structures. Coming in from the seaward side at very low level, the P-47s skip bombed the pens, taking the Germans completely by surprise. The fighters strafed their way out of Brittany *en route* to England. Münster was the target for 124 B-17s, covered by 90 P-47s and 50 P-51s which made no combat claims.

Over the next few days a trio of fighter groups joined the Ninth Air Force — the 474th (that air force's first P-38 outfit) the 366th and 368th, both flying P-47s. The 366th was soon in action: on the 15th the group carried out its first dive-bombing mission, each of seven Thunderbolts carrying a single 250lb bomb on the belly rack for delivery to St Valery-en-Caux aerodrome.

A larger weight of ordnance for the single-seaters was tested over Holland by two 353rd Group P-47s which hauled two 1,000lb bombs apiece on the wing racks to drop on a barge in the Zuider Zee. The 353rd became a leading Eighth Air Force proponent of dive-bombing with the P-47, although the group had to absorb a steady rate of pilot loss, including several former instructors.

Escort missions on 15 March included a run to Nienburg for 1st Lieutenant Joseph L. Egan, Jr, who shot down an Fw190 to become another of the 63rd Squadron's aces, a feat he shared with Frank W. Klibbe of the 61st Squadron, who also destroyed an Fw190. The Wolfpack was definitely outstripping the Eagles in terms of kills, a fact noted by Don Blakeslee with no little irritation. The 4th had the desired P-51s, but despite this, victories were still hard to come by.

March operations continued with an 868-fighter escort to bombers attacking Augsburg, Ulm and Gessertshausen on the 16th, the fighter element being made up by 237 fighters from Ninth Air Force groups. Aircraft from the Eighth's groups shot down 75 enemy fighters along the bomber routes; among the victors was Glendon V. Davis of the 364th Squadron of the 357th Group, who claimed a Bf109 for his fifth kill as well as a part share in a Bf110. Captain Jack D. Warren, another P-51 pilot from the same squadron and group, also became an ace when he downed an Fw190 and two Bf110s near Augsburg. Warren's success was to be short lived, as he was shot down and killed two days later. The 4th fell on packs of Bf110s harassing the bombers like hungry wolves and shot down 13 of them. Wrestling with various P-51 malfunctions the Debden pilots nevertheless made

March 1944 an outstanding month for victories on the ground as well as in the air.

The gradual development of fighter sweeps from innocuous glimpses over the parapet for groups new to the ETO to full-blown strafing missions both after escort and independent of the bombers began to take shape in the spring of 1944. VIII and IX Fighter Commands had enough aircraft to provide ample escort to the heavy bombers while conducting their own ground attacks. These were primarily designed to whittle down Luftwaffe fighter strength and were mainly against airfields, with the goal of completely ejecting the Luftwaffe from the Normandy area before D-Day.

On 17 March the 78th, 353rd, 359th and 361st Groups sped through the overcast to rip up German airfields — they were not the planned ones but the results of rapid changes made as the weather clamped down. The fighters had plenty of French airfields to choose from and any and all attacks were viewed as worthwhile. Strafing had the drawback of possibly removing experienced fighter pilots from the scene in a few seconds of accurate ground fire and the 78th Group lost Peter E. Pompetti to this cause while he was strafing an aerodrome near Paris.

The 78th flew the first triple mission for VIII FC on 18 March, its 96 P-47s being divided into 'A', 'B' and 'C' groups, while 284 1st Division B-17s bombed German

airfields and aircraft plants at Oberpfaffenhofen, Landsberg, Lechfeld and Memmingen; 198 2nd Air Division Liberators went to similar targets at Friedrichshafen and 196 B-17s from the 3rd Division attacked various targets around Munich.

Working hard to keep their charges safe, the fighters destroyed 38 enemy fighters, the victors including Ralph K. 'Kid' Hofer, the baby-faced boxing enthusiast of the 334th Fighter Squadron who thus became an ace. Back in the saddle after a first tour in which he got four kills was Lieutenant Colonel Mark E. Hubbard of the 20th Group. At the controls of a P-38, he nailed a brace of Bf109s to take him past the basic score to be counted as an ace. Hubbard was another pilot whose success was seemingly a passport to disaster, as he was himself assailed by a German fighter soon after his victories. He went down to become a prisoner. A worse fate awaited Captain Lindol F. Graham who was already an ace with the 20th. He was killed when his P-38 hit the ground during a strafing run.

Sixteen Ninth Air Force P-47s flew a short range mission to Boulogne on 19 March, the pilots honing their dive-bombing skills against the coastal aerodrome. P-47s also escorted bombers to V-weapon sites further along the coast while yet another group of Thunderbolts from the 78th Group dive-bombed Gilze-Rijen.

Above: Priding itself on its close escort work rather than high individual pilot scores, the 356th Group was initially equipped with the P-47. The group's 360th Squadron is rolling in this view. *J. Lambert*

Above: Lt Lawton E. Clark in the cockpit of a P-47D with one of the better artistic renderings on aircraft in the 78th Group. Clark was killed while strafing a train on 10 September 1944. *J. Lambert*

While there was no official ETO 'ace race' apart from that run by the pilots in each group who watched their chosen rivals with more than a little professional interest, it was inevitable that some of the faster scoring fighter pilots would emerge as the leading 'hot shots' of the theatre. On 20 March Major James C. Stewart of the Wolfpack's 61st Squadron shot down two Bf109s to bring his tally to 11.5 confirmed. The 56th was patrolling Charleville during the morning, but otherwise the heavy cloud cover prevented much further action despite there being 353 fighters over the Continent as would-be escorts to an aborted mission by the heavies.

On 21 March the 4th's Captain Kenneth G. Smith of the 334th Squadron become another 'brief ace' when he shot down a Fi156 Storch, the ultra-slow German observation aircraft, near Bordeaux. For his trouble Smith was himself shot down and made a prisoner. The pilots of VIII Fighter Command claimed 10 enemy aircraft during the day, which involved a sweep of the Bordeaux area by 48 of the Eagles' Mustangs. Inclement weather obliged the heavies to switch to targets of opportunity rather than the briefed factories at Oranienburg and Basdorf on 22 March. Their gain was

Berlin's loss as 1,471 tons of bombs fell in the city, the US heavies being covered by 817 fighters. It was secondary targets again the following day, although the score for the fighters rose to 20, 18 more than that for the 22nd. A Bf109 that fell to the guns of 1st Lieutenant William J. Simmons of the 355th Squadron gave the 354th Group another ace.

While B-24s bombed tactical targets, the B-17s went to Schweinfurt on 24 March, a mission that was way down on the number of effective sorties, with only 60 Fortresses attacking the primary. The largest force of the day was 162 Fortresses dispatched to Frankfurt, there being hardly any German reaction to the American bombers, giving the escort little to do but keep watch.

A directive issued on 25 March confirmed that the two Ninth Air Force P-51 groups were to continue to make Pointblank targets their priority, which meant that bomber escort took precedence over other types of mission. Otherwise the P-47 and P-38 groups were to shift increasingly to tactical targets to pave the way for Operation 'Overlord' — rail

centres, V1 sites, airfields and industrial locations were to be attacked, as specified. This overall plan was verified by Dwight D. Eisenhower, Supreme Allied Commander designate, the following day.

In accordance with the urgent need to eliminate all known V1 launching sites before D-Day, 500 heavies struck at 16 sites in the Pas de Calais and Cherbourg areas where most of them were concentrated. IX ASC sent its fighters to attack marshalling yards, V-weapon sites and German Army installations across France.

Then on 27 March it was the turn of Luftwaffe personnel to experience the fear and discomfort of falling bombs as B-17s and B-24s hit 11 aerodromes, under the watchful eye of 960 US fighter pilots who made up the escort. Despite the size of this armada, the Luftwaffe challenged and lost a dozen more fighters in combat. Major Walker M. Mahurin of the 63rd Squadron raised his total to 19.75 when he and three other pilots took a share in the destruction of a Do217 near Chartres. Mahurin's luck almost ran out as flak brought down his P-47, but rather than be captured Mahurin evaded, to return to England on 7 May. But he would not fly again in the European theatre.

It was a general policy to have evaders who had had local assistance transferred away from the theatre to avoid any risk of them being captured on a subsequent mission. The Luftwaffe maintained remarkably complete dossiers on many USAAF pilots and under skilful interrogation they were quite likely, however inadvertently, to give away details of the people who had helped them avoid capture on a previous occasion. The 'lifeline' organisations which helped Allied pilots out of occupied territory were vitally important and there was no desire to put these brave civilians in danger from German reprisals. Later, as the occupied countries were liberated, this rule was relaxed. Mahurin went to the Pacific where he was soon at the controls of a P-51. But the enemy 'bag' of American aces was still swelled that day as Major Gerald W. Johnson, the leading Wolfpack ace with 16.5 victories, was shot down by flak as he made a pass over a train.

Following a relatively uneventful heavy bomber mission to tactical targets on 28 March, a fighter escort to Brunswick brought action on the 29th and the mantle of ace for Lieutenant-Colonel Everett W. Stewart, executive officer of the 355th

Group at Steeple Morden. Ten AAF pilots were lost — but 46 enemy fighters were destroyed in return. Another 4th Group pilot became an ace that afternoon when good shooting by 1st Lieutenant Charles F. Anderson, Jr, brought him credits for two Fw190s last seen going down near Gifhorn.

On the penultimate night of March the CBO received a setback when 90 RAF bombers were lost in a raid on Nuremberg, an event that temporarily curtailed the British part in the offensive. The month ended with a tactical fighter mission by the Eighth, 12 P-47s each from the 359th and 361st Groups dive-bombing Soesterberg and Eindhoven aerodromes respectively on the 31st. The 78th concurrently dispatched 22 Thunderbolts on a Rhine River tour, the fighters strafing shipping, an adjacent marshalling yard and a flak tower, plus three Dutch aerodromes.

April 44

Chemical plants were the primary target for the heavies on 1 April, but all B-17s participating in the mission were forced to abort while the B-24s sought targets of opportunity — it was unfortunate that crews of 36 Liberators believed Schaffhausen to be a legitimate target. The Swiss authorities took a different view and accepted $1 million from the US government in compensation.

As part of the escort the 352nd Group took off with both P-47s and P-51s, the latter being concentrated in the 480th Squadron, whose pilots then had about five hours' experience on the new type. A total of 475 fighters managed to get off, although four groups were grounded by bad weather. Five enemy aircraft were claimed. This weather front was persistent and it was 5 April before the fighters could go into action once more. The day beforehand saw the personnel of the 339th Group arrive at Fowlmere, Cambridgeshire, to await delivery of P-51B Mustangs which would be under the command of Colonel John B. Henry. Other new arrivals in England were the 404th and part of the 373rd, two new Thunderbolt outfits destined for service with the Ninth Air Force.

Surprise

On 5 April the fighter pilots braved the elements — which included thick cloud and falling snow — to escort the few bombers that were flying and, in the case of the 4th and 355th Groups, to make surprise ground attacks on 11 airfields around Munich. By so doing, the pilots claimed 96 German aircraft destroyed. The 355th's flyers made a name for themselves on low-level attack as the 'Steeple Morden Strafers', their handiwork proving very destructive to the enemy.

Above: Building its ground-attack force around the mighty P-47 and trading its Mustangs to the Eighth, the Ninth Air Force helped create a war-winning combination. A NMF P-47D of the 36th Group's 23rd FS taxies out in this view. *Author's collection*

Above: Combat author Marvin Bledsoe 'told it like it was' in a postwar autobiography. He flew a P-47D in the 353rd Group named 'Little Princess' for his baby daughter. *Imperial War Museum*

Above: As the P-38 force in Britain expanded, so attempts were made to make the aircraft more effective in the ground-attack role. Thus was born the 'droop snoot' lead ship which carried a bombardier to guide conventional Lightnings onto the target. This P-38J shows the extent of the glazing in the modified nose. *Lockheed*

Captain Duane W. Beeson, 17.333-victory ace of the 4th Group teamed up with two other pilots to destroy a Ju88 when his P-51B was hit by flak. Forced down near Brandenburg, Beeson was made a prisoner, one of four pilots from the 4th who went into German captivity that day.

More days that brought fog as well as snow held the bombers back until 8 April when once again the conditions allowed only opportunity targets to be attacked. Escorting AAF fighters pushed the enemy loss table to a record 88 in the air and 49 on the ground in strafing runs. Such figures brought more individual pilots the accolade of ace, among them James B. Dalglish of the 354th who was that day flying as part of the 363rd Group, the Ninth's second tactical Mustang unit. His Bf109 kill gave him five. Don Gentile, the colourful ace of the 4th, had one of his best days with claims of three Fw190s, bringing his score to 21.833. Due to rotate home, this was Gentile's final tally. Other 4th Group pilots who further depleted the Luftwaffe that day were Captain

Raymond C. Care and 1st Lieutenant Willard W. Millikan.

Two 356th Squadron pilots became aces in the 354th Group on 9 April when the Eighth Air Force bomber effort was again down on numbers. As part of the 791-strong escort, 1st Lieutenant Robert E. Goodnight shot down an Fw190, as did 2nd Lieutenant Thomas F. Miller. The enemy aircraft went down near Kiel and 19 more were claimed by the AAF fighters.

B-24s hit Noball targets in France on the 10th as well as aerodromes and aircraft factories, similar targets being briefed for the B-17 crews.

An innovation introduced by the 20th Fighter Group on 10 April was the so-called 'droop-snoot' version of the P-38J, fitted with a clear-vision nose containing a seat and equipment for a bombardier. In an attempt to concentrate bombing by P-38s (the designation 'B-38' was used for a time) a formation of standard aircraft

would be led in to the target to release their ordnance on the bombardier's signal. The 20th Group dispatched 29 standard P-38s loaded with bombs to carry out such a precision attack on Florennes aerodrome, but in the event all the HE ended up in the Channel when the target was found to be obscured by cloud. A second droop-snoot mission went off later that day, 16 P-38s of the 55th Group managing to drop 17 tons of bombs on Coulommiers aerodrome, the secondary target. Two P-38s went down to defending flak as this airfield, along with numerous others, was well used to air attack and was defended accordingly. Piloting one of the missing P-38s was Colonel Jack S. Jenkins, the 55th Group commander, who became a prisoner. The 20th also ran a mission into Germany to test the droop-snoot technique further, 27 P-38s escorted by 46 P-47s from the 359th Group attacking Gütersloh aerodrome. Only 13 tons of bombs were dropped, however, for the cost of one P-38 and its pilot.

While escorting the P-38s, the P-51s of the 355th Group strafed Villaroche aerodrome, while the 4th's Mustangs ranged over three countries as part of the bomber escort. 1st Lieutenant Paul S. Riley of the 335th Squadron found a hapless Bu131 trainer over Romorantin/ Prunières aerodrome which he shot down for his fifth kill.

More than 90 P-47s were dispatched by the Ninth Air Force on 11 April, the fighters attacking the aerodrome at Gael and nearby military installations. The heavy bombers meanwhile ranged across Germany with 819 fighters making up the escort. Among the groups that saw action against enemy fighters was the 357th's 364th Squadron whose John B. Carder came home an ace after shooting down a Bf109. Don McDowell, flying a 353rd Squadron P-51, added his name to the spiralling list of 354th Group aces when he also destroyed a Bf109. The 4th Group's Lieutenant Hipolitus T. Biel nailed an Me410 and 110 to give the

Eagles another ace and Robert L. Shoup of the 356th Group also made ace when he shot down a Bf109 near Munich.

The 371st Fighter Group, another P-47 outfit assigned to the Ninth Air Force, made its combat debut on 12 April, a day when the conditions over Germany resulted in a total recall for all 455 bombers dispatched. Left with nothing to escort, 748 fighters went hunting and shot down four Ju87s and 13 German fighters. Captain John J. Hockery of the 78th Group made ace by claiming one of the downed Stukas. Charles F. Anderson of the 4th became a double ace with his score of two more Bf109s.

The B-17s returned to Schweinfurt on the 13th while the B-24s attacked various targets including Lauffern, Lechfeld and Oberpfaffenhofen. Stirring up a hornet's nest of interceptors, the bombers were subjected to what many participants described as the heaviest enemy attack on a long-range AAF mission since November 1943. It resulted in 38 bombers going down. Nine US fighters were also lost from the 871 dispatched, although the

Germans again lost heavily, with the toll rising to 42 fighters and a trainer. Lieutenant Alwin M. Juchheim, Jr, of the 78th Group became an ace when he shot down an Fw190, as did Louis H. 'Red Dog' Norley of the 4th. Carl M. Frantz of the 354th nailed a Bf109 for his fifth kill.

Strafing toll

A mass strafing attack on aerodromes in Germany took place on 15 April, the fighters also shooting down 17 aircraft in aerial combat. Bad weather was a contributory factor in the loss of 33 of the AAF fighters, with 30 pilots listed as MIA, among them Raymond C. Care of the 4th, who then had six victories. He fell to flak and became a PoW. Leroy Schreiber, 12-victory ace and CO of the 62nd Fighter Squadron, was killed when his P-47 was also hit by flak over Flensburg aerodrome.

The Ninth Air Force made some changes to its structure on 18 April, IX and XIX Air Support Commands becoming Tactical Air Commands (TACs).

Above: Posing in the cockpit of 'Silver Lady', the P-47D (42-2604/HV-Q) that several 56th Group pilots flew and scored kills with, is Capt Jim Carter. The P-47D was actually assigned to Maj Leslie Smith. *Paul Conger*

Above: Capt William R. O'Brien of the 363rd FS, 357th Group, at Leiston in May 1944. The P-51B has the coveted RAF-derived Malcolm hood, which greatly improved visibility over the original 'greenhouse' canopy. *J. V. Crow*

The 18th was not the most memorable day the 4th Fighter Group had ever had, as during an escort the 335th Squadron lost its CO, Major George Carpenter. Having shot down an Fw190 and a Bf109 which were later confirmed, Carpenter brought his final score to 13.833 before his P-51B was brought down in combat with enemy aircraft near Navuen. He became a PoW, one of five pilots listed as MIA that day.

Improving spring weather usually enabled large scale bomber missions to be mounted, but during April 1944 it was singularly unreliable in this respect. Eighth Bomber Command grabbed its chance on the 19th and sent 741 aircraft from all three divisions to a wide range of targets, including aerodromes in Germany. The escort was mounted by 697 fighters with about 500 others flying sweeps throughout northwest Europe.

The enemy reacted and about 100 interceptors were seen in the air, of which 16 were claimed as destroyed by US pilots. Bomber losses amounted to five and the fighter groups lost two, although one of the

P-51s was flown by Lt Charles F. Anderson, Jr, an ace of the 4th credited with 10, who was killed in action (the exact cause remaining unknown) in the vicinity of Brussels. The reverse side of the coin was the new aces made that day: John Thornell (352nd Group), Bernard J. McGratten (4th) and Thomas L. Hayes, Jr (357th).

Further action over the next few days saw the fighters carrying out dive-bombing attacks as well as escorts, although operations continued to be hampered by bad weather. What VIII Fighter Command counted as the first true fighter-bomber mission by P-51s was flown on 20 April when 33 Mustangs of the 357th Group attacked Cambrai/Epinoy aerodrome covered by 31 P-47s of the 78th Group. Each Mustang carried a pair of 500lb bombs. One pilot, either mistakenly or in an act of sheer bravado, bombed Vitry-en-Artois aerodrome on his own. The 48th Fighter Group, which had

recently joined the Ninth Air Force, also made its combat debut on the 20th.

On 22 April Captain Albert L. Schlegel of the 4th's 335th Squadron became an ace by shooting down two Bf109s, Lieutenant Kendall E. Carlson of the 336th getting the one more he needed for his baseline five in the form of a Bf109. 'Swede' Carlson of the 336th Squadron additionally damaged two more '109s and was credited with a half claim in another.

While the P-38 was generally a little disappointing in the ETO due to its high rate of engine malfunctions, the squadrons of the Eighth and Ninth did their level best to make the aircraft effective. Among those who became aces on Lightnings while operating from England was Captain Robert L. Buttke, a 343rd Squadron pilot; when elements of the 55th Group ran into Messerschmitts near Hamm, Buttke's single victory gave him a score of five.

There was another P-38 droop-snoot mission on 23 April, the 55th and 20th Groups flying bombing sorties to Laon and Tours, and Châteaudun aerodromes respectively. P-47s of the 78th and P-51s of the 352nd Group provided escort to the Lightnings, while the 361st went to Denain/Prouvy aerodrome to carry out a dive-bombing attack.

While the 353th Group ranged over Germany attacking T/Os on the 23rd, the 356th's P-47s made a glide-bombing attack on Haguenau aerodrome before strafing it. Glide-bombing was a target approach technique used by P-47s as an alternative to dive-bombing whereby pilots approached the objective at a shallow, much flatter angle than they used in dive-bombing. Either tactic was valid and widely used, and although diving from altitude ostensibly put the fighter in the sights of ground gunners that much longer, the approach speed was greater, which tended to even things up.

P-51s carried out both dive and glide bombing, notwithstanding the fact that the Mustang was rather more vulnerable than the P-47 if it ran into ground fire while doing so. A single bullet in the coolant tank or radiator was enough to bring a P-51 down, as several pilots found to their cost.

Airfields and industrial targets occupied the bombers on 24 April, the 867 fighters that comprised the escort accounting for 66 enemy aircraft over western Germany. Among the 17 American fighters lost was the P-51 flown by Lieutenant Hipolitus Biel, who had so recently become an ace in the 4th Group. He was killed in air combat near Worms. A second 4th Group ace, Lieutenant Paul Riley of the 335th Squadron, was also shot down in the same locality to become a prisoner.

The run of high-scoring pilots in the 354th Group continued with another pilot, Edward E. Hunt, becoming an ace when he shot down a Bf109 near Ingolstadt;

Captain Robert E. Woody had an outstanding day when he got the better of four Bf109s to return home a seven-victory ace and Henry W. Brown shot down a further two Messerschmitts to become another of the 355th Group's aces. Fletcher E. Adams and John B. England of the 357th Group's 362nd Squadron achieved ace status with three Bf109s apiece.

Lower-key activity on 25 April saw more P-38 droop-snoot, escort and dive-bombing sorties against aerodromes, the 474th Fighter Group making its ETO debut flying the P-38. A similar pattern of operations was repeated on the 26th and 27th. This time the weather remained poor over Germany and the heavies attacked V-weapon sites without interference from the Jagdwaffe, which stayed on the ground, apparently due to the poor flying conditions.

Cloud continued to hamper the bombers on the 28th and again smaller formations were dispatched. On 29 April VIII FC

Above: 'Tear down' maintenance gave ground crews a thorough insight into what could go wrong with fighters damaged in combat. In a yard obviously shared by the RAF, a P-38J is being stripped to the bone, possibly in the interests of cannibalisation to obtain parts for others. *Imperial War Museum*

was able to put 814 fighters over Berlin and, although a large number of enemy fighters appeared, only 11 of them were claimed shot down as against 13 American aircraft. A Bf109 destroyed by Lieutenant Lowell K. Brueland brought his score to five and made another ace for the 354th Group.

The ratio of escort fighters to bombers was now better than two to one, a situation highly appreciated by the Fort and Lib crews; on 30 April the 284 bombers dispatched were covered by 644 fighters. Droop-snoot missions continued with an attack on Tours aerodrome, the 20th Group trying out bombing from a higher altitude than before, each Lightning carrying four 500lb bombs. Escort for this force of 44 aircraft was by P-38s of the 55th Group and, with bombing completed, the fighters swept areas ahead of the bombers. In the afternoon the 20th sent out 22 P-38s escorted by the similarly equipped 364th Group. The droop-snoot lead swept over Orléans/Bricy aerodrome followed by the fighter-bombers which distributed some seven tons of fragmentation bombs across the runway and dispersals.

The Mustang-equipped 339th Group made its combat debut by joining in the sweep ahead of the bombers and the 353rd's P-47s dive-bombed Romorantin/Prunières. All the peripheral fighter attacks were designed to switch attention from the heavies as well as to cause material damage to enemy installations and aircraft. When the Germans did clash with the bomber formations they lost 18 fighters, the dogfights making aces out of Lieutenant Richard A. Peterson, Captain Joseph E. Broadhead and Lieutenant Joseph F. Pierce, all members of the 357th Group.

May 44

On 1 May three more tactical groups, the 50th at Lymington, Hampshire, the 370th at Aldermaston, Berkshire, and the 404th at Winkton, Dorset, were declared operational and, although the 4th Group accounted for five Bf109s, the bombers did not range much further than the coast of France to pour more tons of high explosive onto V1 launching areas. More Noball targets were struck on the 2nd and the 3rd, and it was 4 April before the Eighth scheduled another long-range mission, to

Berlin. This was all but aborted due to cloud cover and 40 B-17s bombed tactical targets in The Netherlands. With fewer heavies than usual to look after, the pilots of 516 escort fighters found enough aerial action to keep them busy and 11 of the enemy were downed. Captain Frank Q. O'Connor of the 356th Squadron, 354th Group, ran his personal score up to a final 10.75 by destroying a Bf109 near Hanover. There was some doubt about the aircraft type claimed by O'Connor, there being some indication that it was a new version of the Fw190.

By the late spring of 1944 the quality of the P-51 as an escort fighter had been proven to the point that Eighth Fighter Command decided to re-equip all its P-47 groups without delay. This process went ahead for each group as soon as enough Mustangs could be delivered to the UK, although the process was steady rather than rapid. The 359th Group had all but converted by late April and undertook its first mission after making the change to Mustangs on 6 May. The group was part of a 185-strong force that escorted the bombers to Noball targets on the French coast but which made no contact with the enemy.

Above: The pilot of this 385th Squadron, 364th Group P-38J (coded 5E-H) appears to need a new spinner on the port engine. *Author's collection*

Bridge attacks

On 7 May the Ninth Air Force launched a far-reaching tactical campaign to destroy all the bridges carrying rail lines serving the Normandy area in advance of the invasion. Attacks by medium bombers and fighters were concentrated on bridges up to 150 miles from the beaches, particularly those spanning the Seine and Meuse rivers. The P-47 pilots became extremely adept at knocking down bridges — which eight of them proceeded to demonstrate on the 7th; each aircraft made its run-in at low level and dropped the maximum load for a P-47 of two 1,000-pounders squarely on a rail span at Vernon.

Berlin was again hit by the heavies on the 7th, the bombers also attacking targets in Münster and Osnabrück. Shepherding their B-17 and B-24 charges were 754 fighters, a force that lost three pilots, probably to flak, in a day of low-key German fighter reaction.

P-47 strength in the Ninth Air Force was about to reach its pre-D-Day peak with the operational debut of the 36th and 373rd Groups, on 8 May. While Berlin again felt the thunder of American four-engined bombers (386 of them), the fighter pilots did their best to ward off the enemy fighters which aggressively pressed home their attacks. Numerous combats developed along the bombers' route between 09.30 and 12.35 hours. As capable of 'dishing it out' as they had always been, irrespective of the size of the opposition, the USAAF pilots wreaked havoc among the Jagdwaffe, shooting down 56 enemy aircraft at a cost of 13 of their own.

The number of Eighth Air Force aces increased by a further five for the 352nd: Captain Clayton E. Davis, Lieutenant Carl J. Luksic, Lieutenant-Colonel John C. Meyer (CO of the 487th FS), Major Stephen W. Andrew and Captain Frank A. Cutler. Captain Robert S. Johnson of the 56th brought his personal tally to his ultimate figure of 27 and Lieutenant Robert J. Booth of the 359th got three.

Ninth's full quota

On 9 May the 367th (P-38s) and 406th (P-47) Fighter Groups went operational to complete IX Fighter Command's full complement of 18 groups. Concurrently the Allied Expeditionary Air Force, Eighth Air Force and RAF Bomber Command launched a full scale offensive against Luftwaffe airfields in France and Belgium designed to eject enemy air forces from the invasion area completely, Operation

'Overlord' having been set for 4 June. USAAF fighters escorted bombers from all three Eighth Air Force divisions and also joined in the assault on aerodromes, as did the AAF medium bombers; 668 fighters from the Eighth and 202 from the Ninth flew support and escort missions. Seven AAF fighters and five German aircraft were destroyed in combat.

Deciding not to try penetrating a bad weather front on 10 May, VIII Bomber Command abandoned missions into Germany and, apart from some tactical sorties by P-47s and P-51s, the UK-based air forces stayed on the ground. The planned effort was again slightly reduced in terms of numbers on 11 May, but fighter escort was required for afternoon missions by B-17s, 471 fighters from both air forces taking part. Airfields in France, Belgium, Germany and Luxembourg received another rain of bombs, as did several marshalling yards and other tactical targets. Taking on the German fighters that rose to intercept the bombers, the 354th Group again did well and claimed 10 downed over a wide area of Germany and Luxembourg. A marshalling yard in Luxembourg city was included on the target list for 53 of the Fortresses. Two more 354th Group pilots became aces during the various combats — Lieutenant Robert D. Welden and Captain Charles W. Lasko.

Target – oil

Violent enemy reaction was encountered by bomber crews on 12 May, the day that marked the first Eighth Air Force mission to a German oil target. Nearly 1,700 tons of bombs fell on various refineries as far afield as Brux in Czechoslovakia as 814 B-17s and B-24s ploughed their way through the fighters and flak. A leading 3rd Division formation of B-17s was slaughtered by the enemy fighters, 41 out of 43 Forts being lost as well as three B-24s. Nearly 1,000 fighters — 735 from the Eighth and 245 from the Ninth — battled the Luftwaffe for control of the airspace. The combat, which saw 67 German and 10 American aircraft shot down, was a series of no-quarter duels which claimed both the novice and the experienced; Lieutenant John B. Carder, an ace of the 357th, was shot down and captured. In terms of aerial victories the Americans had as usual gained the upper hand and there was cause to celebrate at several airfields when the boys returned.

New aces for the day were: Captain James W. Wilkinson (78th Group) and Captain Clarence E. 'Bud' Anderson and Lieutenant William C. Reese of the 357th. Captain Joe H. Powers of the 56th brought his score to 14.5 and Lieutenant Robert Rankin, who was also flying with the Wolfpack, had an outstanding tally of five Bf109 victories to bring his score to nine and make him one of a select band of US pilots who achieved the feat of becoming an 'ace in a day'.

Conversion from the P-47 to the P-51 continued for Eighth Air Force units and the 361st Group marked 12 May as its first all-Mustang mission. Apart from the 56th, which was allowed to retain its P-47s until the end, this official goal of standardisation was not appreciated or liked by all. Numerous individual pilots baulked at the changeover imposed by an unfeeling, unrealistic and downright blind high command which, they believed, was completely out of touch with reality. This bitterness was particularly felt by some of those who were getting well used to the Lightning which, despite its earlier technical troubles, was an excellent aeroplane. The developed P-38J and L models fitted well into the tactical war, as their Allison engines functioned far better when they were not subjected to the freezing cold air the earlier models had found on high-altitude bomber escort missions.

However valid a reason the pilots had for resisting change, such decisions were rarely reversed and in most cases, protesters soon found that the P-47 or P-51 was equal if not superior to the P-38 on the type of operational sorties they were called upon to fly. The protests tended to die away rapidly after a few sorties in the replacements — but it was undeniable that trading the safety of two engines for one gave numerous P-38 proponents more than a few anxious moments.

Sorties into Poland

Extending its reach into western Poland on 13 May, part of the UK-based B-17 force was thwarted by bad weather in an attempt to bomb primary oil industry targets. The Forts were instead diverted to Stettin and Stralsund on the Baltic coast, while Liberators also hit an aircraft factory at Tutow and other B-17s attacked Osnabrück. This day saw the combined Eighth and Ninth escort force swell to over 1,000 fighters for the first time, at 737 and 370 respectively. This huge phalanx of warplanes proved all but impregnable, although the German fighters tried, as ever, to make some impression on it. Their efforts contributed to the destruction of a dozen US bombers and nine fighters at a cost of 54 of their own.

Two names would stand out from the newly created aces that day: Major George E. Preddy and Colonel Joe L. Mason. At that time Mason was CO of the 352nd Group, while Preddy commanded one of the component squadrons, the 487th. Both pilots shot down two Bf109s to achieve ace status, while Lieutenant Francis H. Horne upheld the honour of another 352nd Group squadron, the 328th. Captain Wallace N. Emmer also claimed a pair of Bf109s to place his name on that ever-lengthening list of aces accruing to the Pioneer Mustang Group. All was not completely rosy for the Bodney group, however, as Frank Cutler was among the nine American pilot casualties on 13 May. Having become an ace just five days previously, Cutler was shot down and killed just after he nailed a Bf109 over the town of Neubrandenburg.

Longest trip

On arrival back at its Hertfordshire base the 355th Fighter Group found it had completed its longest target penetration mission to date, the P-51s having covered 1,470 miles on the round trip to Poland.

Apart from Noball sorties and preparations by the 10th Photographic Reconnaissance Group to obtain coverage of all German airfields within range of the Normandy beaches, the next few days of May were relatively quiet in terms of fighter and bomber operations.

The PR side was of course ultra-important for the success of the invasion; with continually updated visual and written data on the air and ground situation, the Allied high command could plan its combat missions to achieve the greatest effect. An important pre-invasion task for the 10th PRG was to assemble photographic mosaics to show all the planned paratroop drop zones, all main roads in the invasion area, the traffic over the Seine bridges between Paris and the sea and those over the Loire between Orléans and Nantes, and every flak emplacement, particularly those defending Liège in Belgium.

The mid-month weather remained decidedly unreliable and a number of fighter-bomber missions were called off when the targets became completely obscured. An opaque haze hanging over the Continent caused a number of sorties over France to be aborted on 19 May, but pushing further afield, 495 B-17s and 272 B-24s reached several objectives around Berlin. Cloud was very much in evidence over the German capital, however, and dozens of bombers were forced to drop on secondary and alternative targets. German interceptors were up against 964 Eighth and Ninth Air Force fighters and lost 71 of their number against an American loss figure of 19 aircraft and 17 pilots.

Combat ranged over Germany and out across the Baltic between 12.20 and 16.15 hours and once again a number of individual US pilots reached ace status. Major Leslie C. Smith, CO of the Wolfpack's 61st Squadron, shot down two Fw190s, while Lieutenant Ray S. Wetmore of the 359th brought his score to five with a pair of Bf109s. There were two more 4th Group aces, both flying with the 334th Squadron: Captain Howard D. 'Deacon' Hively and Lieutenant David W. Howe.

Lower-key activity in terms of AAF pilot victories followed this hectic day, but on 21 May the ETO fighter force opened Operation 'Chattanooga Choo-Choo'. As the name, taken from a popular song, implies, this was an all-out war on the rail systems of France, Belgium and western Germany designed to paralyse all enemy movement into Normandy. An estimated 500 P-47s and P-51s accordingly went out to bomb and strafe any locomotives and rolling stock they could find. That the attacks were successful is shown by the figure of 46 locomotives claimed as destroyed plus 11 others probably wrecked beyond repair and quantities of wagons and rail facilities badly damaged. Nine fighters failed to return.

'Chattanooga' sorties by VIII Fighter Command extended into Germany and these added 91 locomotives destroyed out of a total of 225 attacked. Most targets of opportunity were also associated with rail transport and vital though these were, fighter losses were inevitably higher proportionately than the figures for air combat. Attacks on virtually any defended ground target could be lethal and trains were no exception, a fact reflected in the highest loss the command had yet suffered — 27 aircraft shot down, with 26 pilots listed as MIA. Among them were two from the 357th Group, seven-victory ace

Lieutenant Joseph F. Pierce and Lieutenant William C. Reese, whose score was five. Both were killed.

By ranging ever further into Germany the American flyers came across numerous enemy aircraft including trainers, bombers and transports which had not previously figured highly in kill claims. Now, flying right into 'the enemy's own back yard' the pilots included eight trainers in the 21 aircraft claimed on the 21st.

On 22 May the loss rate of the German fighter arm continued to climb as the American fighters escorted their bombers to Kiel. Combat with enemy fighters resulted in claims of 23. Of the 568 USAAF fighters aloft, seven aircraft and six pilots were lost. F/O Evan D. McMinn of the 56th shot down two Fw190s to become an ace, and double ace Captain Nicholas Megura of the 4th, raised his score to 11.833 by sharing a Bf109 with a P-38 near Kiel. But fire from the Lightning accidentally damaged Megura's Mustang and he limped out of the battle area to make a landing in neutral Sweden where he was interned.

First thousand

On 23 May the Eighth Air Force dispatched a record 1,045 B-17s and B-24s on a single mission; their targets were aerodromes and rail transport throughout France and Germany, but, as was all but inevitable, the number of aircraft actually able to bomb fell, to 814 in this case. A record number of fighters matched the size of the bomber force, there being 1,206 sent off from England, 562 from the Eighth and 644 from the Ninth. Four were lost and no air combat claims were made.

It was back to V-weapon sites for the B-24s on the afternoon of 24 May, the tactical fighters concurrently attacking airfields and escorting 517 B-17s to Berlin. From the German fighter intercepts the US pilots destroyed 32 for 16 lost, the latter figure including several aircraft that went down in strafing attacks on rail targets en route to base.

On the 25th the Eighth introduced a variation in sorties against tactical targets made by heavy bombers, in that small formations, independent of each other, went after specific targets including German coastal gun batteries and rail links. Fighters escorted the 325 bomber sorties by sending out 604 (from the Eighth) and 207 (Ninth). Twelve enemy aircraft were claimed for the loss of 12

Above: Among the most striking P-51 markings was the 'half and half' olive drab and NMF design adopted by the 55th Group for a time in 1944. This 343rd P-51D, 'Miss Marilyn II' has the full treatment. *Author's collection*

AAF fighters, the latter figure including Captain Joseph H. Bennett of the 4th who then had 8.5 victories. His P-51B went down and he was taken prisoner.

The last Eighth Air Force fighter group to go operational, the 479th based at Wattisham in Suffolk, made its debut in P-38s on 26 May when it mounted two uncontested familiarisation sweeps along the Dutch coast. VIII FC then had 15 operational groups.

Along with the Ninth's medium bombers which had been pounding away at tactical targets for months, the fighter-bombers flew across the Channel on the 26th to attack aerodromes and bridges. All three types of US fighter in the ETO participated on a day when there were no heavy bomber escorts.

Targets in France and Germany occupied the heavies on 27 May, the fighter escort totalling 1,155 from both commands. The bomber force was again divided into division attacks, this being practical in that it tended to avoid mixing B-17 and B-24 formations. Each aircraft had its own characteristics — speed, preferred bombing altitude, equipment and so forth. Some sorties were also more specialised than others. For example, the

B-24 element sent out on the 27th bombed gun emplacements under H2X radar control. Standardisation was also on the cards for the Eighth's bombers, the B-17 being preferred over the B-24, which was concentrated in the 2nd Air Division. Steps were taken to change completely to the Fortress, although in the event this was never fully achieved.

During their morning escort duty on 27 May, the American fighters accounted for 34 enemy aircraft, most of them going down as a result of a concentrated air engagement that developed at 12.30 hours. Among the victors were Major George L. Merritt, Jr, CO of the 361st Group's 375th Squadron based at Little Walden, Essex. A single Fw190 kill brought his score to five. In a later engagement which was part of the afternoon cover for bombers hitting a plethora of targets inside Germany, Captain Thomas L. Harris of the 357th Group became the second new ace of the day when he chopped down two Bf109s over Colmar.

Another 1,341 heavy bomber sorties were dispatched against German targets on 28 May, although heavy cloud cover at many of the targets caused some 500 aircraft to abort the mission. Others unloaded on secondaries and T/Os, of which there were literally hundreds within the borders of the Reich. From the record 1,224 escort sorties, 14 fighters were lost, including that flown by Captain Alwin M. Juchheim, Jr, nine-victory ace of the 78th Group, who survived a mid-air collision with another P-47 and was taken prisoner. Nobody saw what happened to the P-51 flown by Lieutenant Don McDowell of the 354th; an 8.5-victory ace with the Pioneers, he was never heard from again.

The missions for 29 May saw 888 effective attacks by heavies on targets in eastern Germany and Poland; 1,265 fighters provided the escort, the pilots of which shot down 41 German fighters. Four of these were Me410s destroyed by Lieutenant Dale F. Spencer. Lieutenant George Doersch of the 359th Group became an ace with part shares in two

Above: A more subdued scheme with green and yellow group trim was most common in the 55th, typified by this P-51D which has the green stallion painted on the fin rather than the rudder. *Author's collection*

Fw190 kills. Lieutenant Glennon T. Moran of the 352nd also became an ace when he destroyed an Fw190 and a Bf109.

D-Day preparations began on 30 May with loading of shipping that would bear the first wave of the assault forces across the Channel. In the air, US fighter-bombers attacked rail bridges while a substantial force of heavy bombers sought out targets in Germany escorted by 1,309 fighters, a new one-day record. Among the US losses was Captain Fletcher E. Adams, nine-victory ace of the 357th Group, who was killed in action. Into captivity went the 4th's Captain Willard W. Millikan after he collided with another P-51. As a long-time member of the

Eagles, 'Millie' was sorely missed at Debden, which changed in character from the quasi-RAF days the more the older members of the 4th were lost or rotated home. The 58 German aircraft the American escort destroyed on 30 May brought the 357th Group three more aces: Captain Robert H. Becker, Lieutenant Gilbert M. O'Brien and Captain William R. O'Brien.

Decidedly un-spring-like weather disrupted some of the scheduled bomber targets on 31 May, but aerodrome and marshalling yard attacks were carried out

in France. Over Germany the bombers also struck rail targets in lower numbers than normal due to the prevailing overcast; the fighter escort set a new record with 1,329 sorties, yet reported no contact with the Luftwaffe. Thunderbolts of the 353rd and 56th Groups dive-bombed Gütersloh aerodrome while the 20th sent 35 P-38s to stir up Rheine/Hopsten — they were supposed to hit Lingen but failed to find it. The Wolfpack hunted down five Fw190s while blasting Gütersloh, and the P-38s claimed five enemy aircraft destroyed on the ground at Hopsten.

5 Invasion Front

As part of the pre-planning for the ground support for the invasion the Ninth Air Force established a network of ground-air controllers who would work with the 21st Army Group. Riding in vehicles of the forward echelons as the army advanced, these men were to maintain radio contact with the fighter-bomber pilots so that objectives immediately in front of the troops could be attacked. Also planned was a more sophisticated coverage of Europe by mobile microwave radar teams. As the pre D-Day planning entered its last phase the USAAF finally flew the first shuttle mission to Russia on 2 June. This was codenamed Operation 'Frantic Joe' and was undertaken by the Fifteenth Air Force.

During the first few days of June American fighter-bombers, mediums and heavies maintained their pressure on the various types of target, many of which were becoming very familiar indeed to the pilots. The fighters found little air action before the 4th when Eisenhower ordered that, due to the bad weather, the invasion would not be launched until the 6th. Tension was high as the meteorologists sought some positive sign that the low cloud and rain would ease just long enough for the great endeavour to proceed. Meanwhile more bridges were attacked and enough rail cuts made to ensure that, even if the Normandy area was not completely sealed off, any German reinforcements heading for the coast would have an exceedingly difficult task in reaching the area.

While the Allied high command agonised over the weather, the huge logistical preparations continued — then in the early hours of the 6th the first troop carriers took off and set course for France. With a great sense of anticipation AAF ground crews completed routine maintenance and repair work and topped up the fuel tanks of hundreds of aircraft. Fighters, medium bombers and transports, now all with black and white Allied Expeditionary Air Force stripes around their wings and fuselages, prepared to take off at set times. Each group in the Ninth Air Force was allocated a specific objective; pilot and crew briefings began at 03.00 hours, an abnormally early time that

convinced everyone that the big day had arrived. There had already been considerable air activity by the time the first five Ninth Air Force fighter groups taxied out for take-off. Their task was to intercept and destroy any Luftwaffe aircraft that attempted to attack the amphibious landing forces.

Despite Ike's assurance to Allied naval forces that '... planes overhead will be ours', he was taking no chances with the notorious penchant of warship gunners to blaze away at aircraft — any aircraft — that came within range. It was therefore decided that the first fighters they would see would be ultra-recognisable Lockheed P-38s. Consequently all four Eighth and the two Ninth Air Force Lightning groups also took off early to carry out their convoy escort duty.

As the invasion began, the Ninth's single-engined fighter-bombers went in over Utah Beach to blast any signs of life from the enemy side. But there was, to the dismay of numerous troops wading ashore, plenty. It had not been possible to neutralise all the heavily fortified positions by air bombardment and these retaliated as the first rounds of naval shells crashed onto French soil. Survival for the ground troops depended very much on which of the five assault beaches the troops had been assigned; those drawing the short straw faced the formidable and largely intact defences of Omaha which proceeded to inflict crippling casualties.

As the air effort was stepped up, the reports from Normandy generally praised the accuracy with which the air forces pounded gun positions. Beyond sight of the first troops to land, the Ninth, assigned cover of the Utah and Omaha Beach areas, attacked six bridges and a rail embankment. Heavy bombers meanwhile put in a massive effort to prevent the German troops they knew were down there from moving on the beaches in strength. But the Germans were in no hurry to do so as Hitler and some of his key generals still believed that Normandy was merely a diversionary thrust to mask the true invasion in the Pas de Calais. This fiction, fuelled by excellent Allied intelligence, subterfuge and aerial 'spoofing' flights

designed to divert attention away from Normandy, was maintained long enough for a bridgehead to be established.

In total, US fighters and fighter-bombers flew 2,185 sorties on D-Day, this amounting to at least one mission by every unit in the Eighth and Ninth Air Forces, to maintain a continuous air umbrella over the amphibious operation. Of this total, 1,719 sorties were classed as escort or patrol, with an additional 466 fighter-bomber sorties completing the total. By any yardstick it was an enormous effort in a single day.

Faced with such overwhelming force, the Luftwaffe wisely played a waiting game and not until the afternoon of the 6th was any intervention attempted. It has passed into folklore that two Fw190s made a firing (or non-firing depending on the source) pass along the beaches and fled. There are many contenders for the feat, but JG 26 appears to have the most substantive claim for making the first appearance of the Luftwaffe on D-Day. Other enemy aircraft that ventured anywhere near the beaches were quickly intercepted, attacked and driven off, if they were not destroyed. The first US air victory was reported at 12.25 hours: an Fw190 falling to an F-6 reconnaissance pilot of the 19th TRG who claimed it over Dreaux aerodrome.

The Germans were powerless to inflict any significant damage on the Allied armada despite having elements of most operational fighter Gruppen in France at that time. Those units that did attempt to disrupt operations suffered grievous losses in the period after 'Overlord' began. The Germans even deployed outmoded Ju87s with predictable results, losing 12 of them on the 6th. In addition, 12 Fw190s — which increasingly became the only Luftwaffe ground-attack aircraft able to survive in such a hostile operational area — were shot down on that first day.

Ground fire was the most lethal deterrent to Allied ground-support sorties and 25 aircraft and 24 pilots were lost. Ten of these were from the 4th Group, among them Captain Bernard J. McGratten, an 8.5-victory ace. He was KIA in combat with enemy fighters near

Above: For D-Day all AAF fighters in the ETO received AEAF recognition stripes. A fully marked example was this P-51B of the 358th FS, 355th Group, awaiting attachment of its drop tanks. *Author's collection*

Rouen. The 56th Group also lost an ace when F/O Evan D. McMinn who had five, went down near Bernay, apparently as a result of flak.

While ships and troop carriers poured in reinforcements and materiel to feed the bridgehead, the fighter-bombers continued to attack objectives along the Normandy coast. On the 7th P-47s from the 365th, 366th and 368th Groups began taking off at 06.00 hours to strike chokepoints caused by interdiction further afield. On-call to US Army ground forces throughout the day, the Thunderbolt units responded, attacking most objectives in squadron strength. During the day 35 such missions were completed by 467 aircraft from the three tactical groups. Using guns, 1,000lb bombs and clusters of fragmentation bombs, the pilots were able to deal with a variety of targets.

The Ninth's P-47s were not, of course, the only American fighters in the air. Other elements of the Ninth flew convoy cover and a host of other sorties, while the Eighth provided 820 patrol and escort sorties as well as 653 strafing sorties at a cost of 14 fighters and 12 pilots. The Ninth's fighters did not end their day until 22.30 hours.

The attempt to seal off Normandy from German reinforcements involved a continuing air effort throughout the rest of June, which was not surprising considering the importance of the invasion. On 8 June all Eighth Air Force fighter groups participated in 1,353 sorties beginning at

05.30 hours and comprising escorts, sweeps, patrols and ground attacks throughout the day. The cost was 22 aircraft and 21 pilots in return for 38 enemy aircraft claimed. Another ace lost on the AAF side was Lieutenant Robert J. Booth from the 359th Group. With eight victories to his credit, Booth, another victim of the deadly German flak, was taken prisoner. Of the German aircraft claimed, seven fell to the guns of Ninth Fighter Command and Major Rockford V. Gray of the 371st Group clobbered a trio of Fw190s near Cabourg to become an ace.

The expected worsening of the weather that had so nearly forced a disastrous postponement of 'Overlord' finally struck with a vengeance on 9 June, causing the entire US air forces in England to remain on the ground. There was a little improvement on the 10th, but the weather still disrupted bomber operations. The fighters were able to fly 1,491 sorties, engage the enemy in the air and shoot down 29 fighters and a single Ju52. Lieutenant Christopher J. Hanseman of the 339th Group came home with a single Bf109 claim to make him an ace. On the debit side 24 Eighth Air Force pilots were lost.

Losing no time in establishing its own foothold on the Continent, IX TAC headquarters shipped out to France to better support the US First Army. Mission cancellations were still in force on 11 June, although there were 914 effective fighter sorties over the beaches. These were completed without too much reaction from

the Germans, who lost 10 of their own in skirmishes with the 55th and 356th Groups. Allied fighter pilot casualties rose to their worst of the war during this period and on 12 June the list of missing extended by another 16 aircraft and 15 pilots. However, the American groups usually managed to claim more than double their own losses from the ranks of the enemy.

From the German viewpoint this was due to several factors, the most important being that the American pilots were better trained and flew better aircraft than they did. The cream of the Luftwaffe's experienced pilots had been lost in three years of large scale combats in Europe, Russia and the Mediterranean, and the Allies enjoyed a numerical superiority that sometimes rose to three to one over the fighters the Germans could put into the air. And to add to their woes, the Germans had also to contend with the escort fighters of the Twelfth and Fifteenth Air Forces from Italy, both of which exacted a steady toll of skilled pilots during missions to targets in the Reich.

In such a position of superiority in the air the Americans could regularly announce a fresh crop of fighter aces, 12 June seeing Flying Officer Steve Gerick of the 56th join that illustrious band with a victory over a Bf109 near Evreux.[1]

As Germany still enjoyed the protection of the overcast on 13 June the heavies instead attacked tactical targets in France while the fighters escorted the long- and short-range bombers. Combat claims were again down, there being but 10 victories for the American side in return for half that number of fighters and their pilots lost to VIII Fighter Command. Among the victors reaching ace status was Lieutenant Colonel Joseph J. Kruzel of the 361st Group, who shot down a Bf109 for his second enemy aircraft kill in Europe. The first three victories had been Japanese aircraft when Kruzel was stationed in Java in 1942.

Still the weather contrived to reduce the Allied air effort on 14 June, although, as on most such occasions, some elements of the tactical air forces tried to find their briefed targets. It was vital to prevent any Panzer reinforcements reaching the bridgehead and when 168 Eighth Air Force fighters found German armoured columns near Chantilly, south of Allied positions, they did not hesitate to bomb and strafe them. Also hit was a Luftwaffe headquarters in the same area. German air reaction to the day's sorties resulted in more casualties on both sides. P-51 pilot Lieutenant Robert M. Shaw of the 357th Group scored over an Fw190 to become an ace, as did Lieutenant Clayton K. Gross of the 354th Group when he accounted for a Bf109.

During the night of 15/16 June, after a small beginning three days before, the Germans managed to open their V1 offensive in earnest and about 150 flying bombs fell on England — but the tactical air forces had been instrumental in postponing that fearful event until after the invasion. AAF tactical fighters would take little part in combatting the V1 offensive, which was handled in the main by RAF Fighter Command under its unwieldy new title Air Defence of Great Britain. Several US fighters accounted for V1s, however.

On the 16th the first American fighters began operating from strip A-2 in Normandy near Criqueville. A landing ground bulldozed flat by men of the IX Engineer Command, it was used by the P-51s of the 354th Group to fly ground-attack missions against the German Army. Although primitive, the beach-head airstrip saved valuable time in that the fighters did not have to fly back across the Channel

until nightfall. It was the first of many 'frontline airfields' built by the redoubtable engineers. Otherwise 16 June was notable for the first use of drop tank 'bombs' by Eighth Fighter Command. It had been found that if a number of fighters could release their long-range tanks accurately enough to fall within the confines of a sizeable target and then strafe them, an impressive blaze would result. Not having napalm bombs available in Europe at that time, the AAF made use of these makeshift petrol bombs on several occasions. When 500 fighters dropped their tanks on rail targets on the 16th, they succeeded in destroying nearly 400 railway wagons.

Escort sorties to heavy bombers flying morning missions on the 17th rose to 427, plus 99 by P-38s attacking rail and other ground targets. In the afternoon B-24s bombed aerodromes in France and 270 more fighter sorties took place, both to escort the Liberators and to attack ground targets. In total, the day saw the loss of seven aircraft and their pilots for AAF fighter claims of 17.

The control of all tactical missions in France was assumed by IX TAC headquarters which had established its

advance headquarters on the Continent by the 16th. The operational deployment of the V1 had given a new urgency to Noball targets and these were hit on the 18th, the fighter-bombers ranging out to the Cherbourg area to bomb and strafe these and other targets located on the peninsula.

More fighters headed for new bases in France, including the P-47s of the 48th Group, which quickly began operating out of A-4 Deaux Jumeaux in Normandy. And despite laying on the first major strategic strike on Germany since D-Day, Eighth Fighter Command received no reports of contact with the Germans from the 537 escort fighters. The heavies, bombing oil refineries around Hamburg, Hanover and Bremen, lost 11 B-17s and B-24s to random fighter attacks and flak, cloud cover causing many bombers to turn back.

Cloud cover dispersed the Eighth's bombing of French aerodromes on 19 June and the heavy escort lost six P-51s and four P-38s. A second mission to V-weapon sites bombed under G-H control, the similarly heavy escort meeting no opposition in the air. The Ninth announced that the 368th Group was the first to be assigned a 'permanent' base in France, this being A-3

Above: Poised for another sortie, a P-51D of the 339th Group's 503rd Squadron retains the black recognition bands first applied to the P-51B/C in white over camouflage paint to avoid confusion with the Bf109. *Author's collection*

Cardonville, another ALG built by engineers. Action on 20 June was centred on Noball sites and airfields in the Paris area, the Eighth's fighters shooting down 16 enemy aircraft, while the Ninth continued to move its tactical units to France as soon as airstrips were ready; the 366th Group's occupancy of A-1 St Pierre-du-Mont began on the 20th.

Second shuttle

The Schweinfurt-Regensburg mission of 17 August 1943 was an ambitious bombing plan not least because it marked a new phase in operations, that of 'shuttle bombing'. Having reached North Africa the bombers had returned to the UK in due course — but Frantic missions were intended to become much more ambitious by having bombers based in Britain regularly using airfields in Russia. There they would be refuelled and bombed up to enable strikes to be made on German targets in Eastern Europe on the way back home. The Fifteenth had successfully carried out the first Frantic mission on 2 June and when the Eighth's heavies went back to Berlin oil targets on 21 June, 114 of the B-17s did not attempt the return leg but carried on across Eastern Europe. Of the 958 fighter pilots manning the escort, only a relatively small percentage saw action, while 70 Mustangs from the 4th and 352nd Groups accompanied the bombers eastwards. To conserve precious fuel the shuttle escort pilots were advised to avoid combat unless absolutely necessary. Over Germany the action was intense; 17 German aircraft were accounted for and seven more were claimed in Polish airspace.

As always there would be action for only some of the participating fighters, depending on where the Germans struck. Some pilots on the fringes of the developing air battles could only imagine what went on and many did not see enemy aircraft at all. Among those who did were Lieutenant John F. Thornell of the 352nd who dispatched an Me410 with the help of another Mustang pilot, to bring his personal score to 17.25. Two more Me410s were shot down by Captain George M. Lamb of the 356th Group to make him an ace. Lieutenant Joseph L. Lang and Captain Frank C. Jones of the 4th Group both scored victories over Bf109s to make two more aces for the group. Both American pilots scored over Poland, Lang's victim falling near Warsaw, Jones getting his near Kobrin.

With creditable navigation the fighters of the 4th and 352nd Groups found their base at Piryatin in the Ukraine while the bombers put down at nearby Poltava. Warmly greeted by most of the frontline Russian troops they came into contact with, the Americans were soon at home. But the feeling of joining forces against the common enemy did not reach as far as the Kremlin. For months before the first Frantic to Russia, US diplomats had worked hard to convince Stalin that using his bases would be another blow to the Germans. The Soviet leader agreed only reluctantly to foreign aircraft being based in Russia.

During 21 June the Luftwaffe had tracked the flightpath of the B-17s and during the early hours Ju88 pathfinders led He111s of KG 53 in to attack Poltava with devastating effect. When dawn broke, the wrecks of 73 B-17Gs were a sorry sight to the crews of the groups which had been the hardest hit.

Despite this setback, the flyable B-17s were moved to bases further to the east of Poltava to await their return to England with their escort, the fighter force having been virtually untouched by the attack. The Germans raided Mirgorod and Piryatin again on the night of the 22nd/23rd but the birds had literally flown and there were no Allied casualties. The German bombers did however further deplete stocks of US fuel and bombs, which they had also hit in the first raid. Frantic missions continued, but the lack of any great enthusiasm for them on the part of the Soviet authorities, plus events on the ground, made the need for them less acute than at the time they were first mooted.

Marshalling yards, V-weapon sites and aerodromes were the familiar bill of fare to the Eighth's fighters and bombers alike on 22 June, while US troops battled a tenacious enemy defence of the port of Cherbourg. Ninth Air Force fighters were called upon to make more than 1,200 sorties against this important target, for capture of the port would greatly ease the Allied supply situation. The cost was 24 aircraft. Medium bombers also carried out their largest such attack of the war when they laid a rolling barrage of bombs in front of friendly troops over a period of 55 minutes.

By regularly flying multiple daily escort missions, the Eighth's fighters invariably made contact with the Luftwaffe — which could no longer challenge every air raid in strength — and during afternoon and evening sorties, 20 enemy aircraft were claimed by the USAAF pilots. Lieutenant Clarence O. Johnson of the 479th Group scored an unusual kill in the shape of an Fi156 which he dispatched to become an ace. This was also Johnson's first victory in the ETO as four had been achieved while he was flying a P-38 with the 82nd Group in the Mediterranean. P-47 pilot Major Randell O. Hendricks, CO of the 368th Group's 397th Squadron, also reached ace status with a single Bf109 kill.

Weather gremlins struck the Eighth Air Force heavy bombers on 23 June, although 12 V-weapon sites were attacked using G-H. Fighters strafed ground transport and bridges while the Ninth's fighter-bomber pilots claimed another Storch and five German fighters. Two more groups moved to France, the 354th's P-51s occupying A-2 Criqueville on a permanent basis and the P-47s of the 371st Group taking station at A-6 Beauzeville.

Missions to France for the Eighth during this period could be relatively trouble-free in terms of aerial attack; on the morning of 24 June a series of small scale raids by B-24s and B-17s resulted in the loss of four aircraft including one from the 307-strong escort. Similar light casualties occurred during the afternoon — further proof that the German fighters were generally being held back to fight over the Reich itself. A later mission to oil targets at Bremen could only be partially completed due to bad weather diversions to alternative targets.

On 25 June the Ninth's strength on the Continent was boosted by the P-47s of the 50th Fighter Group which flew into A-10 Carentan. US ground forces concurrently captured Cherbourg/Maupertus aerodrome, thus removing another of the many airfields from the AAF target list. Others would follow as the ground forces advanced and some of those same airfields would similarly house American squadrons. Cherbourg fell to the US First Army on the 26th, a day that saw the Eighth and Ninth Air Forces all but totally grounded by inclement weather.

The most action for some elements of the ETO groups was provided by the force returning from Russia, but not flying direct to England. Accompanied by 103 P-51s, 72 B-17s bombed an oil plant at Drohobycz in Poland, after which the Fortresses set course for Italy, their escort swelled by Fifteenth Air Force fighters by the time they reached the specified bases.

Above: Invariably called the 'Hun Hunter FROM Texas', any close-up will show how Henry Brown's Mustang was really marked in the 355th Group. Brown (*right*) is standing with Brady Williams. *T. R. Bennett*

Bad weather continued over Europe on the 27th to keep sorties down once again. Some bombing of French targets was alarmingly random as bombers became separated, a not unusual phenomenon in poor visibility. The under-employed escort also attacked T/Os. Aerodromes were attacked by fighters in the afternoon, but the largest air effort of the day was reserved for the 700 Ninth Air Force fighters which patrolled the Normandy area and attacked targets as they were identified.

Low-key, weather-restricted activity followed on the 28th but picked up on the 29th, when the 365th Fighter Group moved to A-7 Azeville. Otherwise the Eighth bombed German targets in some strength, although 400 out of 1,150 aircraft dispatched to Leipzig had to abort

when heavy cloud over England disrupted assembly. The fighters found some limited action, while the 48th Group made A-4 Deaux its home, having begun limited operations from that ALG from 18 June.

Escorting the Leipzig bomber force the fighters clashed with the Jagdwaffe's interceptors and exacted a toll of 35. The 357th Group became the first for some time to record new aces following combat kills, Captains Don H. Bochkay, James W. Browning and Robert W. Foy achieving that coveted status. All pilots were members of the 363rd Squadron.

Among the air engagements on 30 June was an unusual kill for a P-47 pilot of the Eighth's 5th Emergency Rescue

Squadron, who shot down a V1 over England. While fighters dashed across the Channel to strafe various targets including bridges and transportation links, many bomber crews kicked their heels after returning early. Those who could bomb did so only by using G-H. Thus a day of untypically low-key air activity finished the most momentous month in the history of the USAAF in the European Theatre.

Notes

1   Gerick was an RCAF officer who initially retained the rank of flying officer in USAAF service; he became a lieutenant in late June 1944.

6 Breakout

July 1944 opened with the activation of IX Air Defense Command to oversee, as the title implied, all defensive operations behind friendly lines in France. The HQ moved to the Continent by the end of the month, a relocation followed by IX TAC's 100th Fighter Wing which occupied Criqueville. This formation's task was to direct the operations of the groups under its control in close support of the US Army. The 405th Fighter Group also moved from England to operate henceforth from A-8 Picauville.

Weather again grounded the Ninth's bombers on 2 July, although tactical fighters got off to cover the Normandy beach-head and attack a German Army headquarters plus fuel dumps, rail lines and strongpoints along the Loire river. In the course of carrying out afternoon sorties, the fighters engaged the Luftwaffe. Two enemy fighters downed made Lieutenant Colonel Robert L. Coffey, Jr, an ace. As the CO of the 365th Group, Coffey was one of a number of Ninth Air Force fighter pilots who found themselves in a position to shoot down five or more enemy aircraft. This was something their Stateside ground-attack training had hardly stressed, but, needless to say, they were elated that the opportunity came their way. Having their aerial claims verified could, however, be far more difficult for pilots wearing a Ninth rather than an Eighth Air Force uniform patch. The tactical air forces appeared almost actively to discourage the destruction of enemy aircraft by issuing edicts to the effect that pilots should wait to be attacked before retaliating. The Ninth was unusual not only in denying fighter pilots claims for ground kills but by adopting the ambiguous 'unconfirmed destroyed' classification. In numerous cases pilots were convinced that they would officially have become aces had the Ninth's system been more flexible.

More group movements to forward landing grounds in France were made on 2 July, the P-47s of the 362nd Group occupying A-12 Lignerolles and the aircraft of the 67th TRG moving into A-9 Le Molay.

On a day when escort fighters scored well against German interceptors the 4th was making its way back from Italy having escorted part of the third shuttle mission, by bombers of the Fifteenth, to Russia. Most of the day's victories fell to the Fifteenth's fighters, although Don Blakeslee increased his wartime score to 14.5 when he shot down a Bf109 near Budapest. It was apparently Bf109s of JG 52 that clashed with the 4th, and the German formation included — according to subsequent reports — the redoubtable Eric Hartmann. When Kid Hofer failed to return to Debden and his body was subsequently found near Mostar, Yugoslavia, it was assumed that he had become a victim of the leading German *Experten*. In any event, another of Debden's most colourful characters had gone.

After a day's break in operations, the Eighth's heavies attacked more tactical targets on 4 July, but the bad weather hampered many crews. Better luck attended the B-24 force that also bombed targets on what had become the 'invasion front'. Aerial combat developed for some of the 569 escort fighters, the 56th finding great form on its escort to Conches aerodrome and returning home with claims for 19 — which took the Wolfpack's wartime total to more than 500 enemy aircraft destroyed. Captains James R. Carter and Mark L. Moseley, respectively of the 61st and 62nd Squadrons, were new group aces. In addition, tactical fighters shot down a further four enemy fighters in a day of 900 ground-support sorties which saw much of the medium bomber force grounded by the weather.

Eighth Fighter Command emerged victorious from another series of combats on 5 July, 31 German aircraft being claimed. Lieutenant Dale F. Spencer achieved ace status with a Bf109 kill, as did Lieutenant Robert J. Keen of the 56th, although the latter pilot got three Messerschmitts. Lieutenant-Colonel Francis S. Gabreski, then operations officer of the 56th, also shot down a Bf109 to bring his personal total to 28 confirmed. Although 'Gabby' could hardly be sure what the future held, he had destroyed his last enemy aircraft in World War 2. He

was then due to rotate home. The 363rd Group's P-51s moved to A-15 Cherbourg/Maupertus and on the 6th the 404th Group occupied A-5 Chippelle.

Action on 6 July included over one thousand VIII Fighter Command escort sorties and quite sizeable heavy bomber formations over France to attack Noball sites and transportation targets. At lower altitudes, the Ninth gave its able support to the ground forces and covered medium bomber strikes, losing five fighters and four pilots in the process. Victories for the day went to the fighter pilots of the strategic covering force, the Eighth's groups shooting down 21 enemy aircraft. Lieutenant George Bostwick of the 56th became an ace with a single Bf109 kill and Major Kenneth W. Gallup, CO of the 350th FS, did likewise to become another ace in the 353rd Group.

On 7 July Captain Felix M. Rogers of the 354th added his name to the roll of aces when he shot down two Fw190s over Perdreauville. The Pioneer Mustang Group, so vital to the safety of the strategic bomber force for some six months, was by then flying missions as part of the Ninth's tactical battle order.

German targets occupied the heavy bombers at a cost of 37 lost and 390 suffering varying degrees of battle damage. The escort fighters also made strafing attacks on airfields and the European rail network and, although six US fighters and their pilots were lost, Captain James M. Morris of the 20th Group brought his victory tally to 7.333 when he shot down an Me410 at 09.35 hours. Just afterwards Morris himself was jumped by another *Hornisse* and had his P-38 shot from under him. He was taken prisoner. Another experienced fighter leader failed to return when flak nailed the aircraft flown by Colonel Glenn E. Duncan, CO of the 353rd Group. Getting safely down, Duncan managed to evade capture but had to remain in hiding; it was not until 22 April 1945 that he finally returned to England. Duncan's loss was another blow to the 'Slybird Group' at Raydon as he was the third group commander in a row to be shot down. In retribution for their own losses the American pilots made the

Above: This well-known view of fighters gathered for a group commanders' conference at Bottisham on 31 August 1944 shows a variety of P-51, P-47 and P-38 markings post D-Day, the only sheep in the wolf's lair being a T-6 at the far end of the nearest line. The P-51D in the foreground has the early markings of the 20th Group. *USAF*

Above: Low over the sea, a P-47D of the 361st Squadron, 356th Group has its wing leading edges cleaned back to NMF to improve performance. In common with hundreds of others, these P-47s were delivered unpainted and had topside paint applied 'in the field' at unit discretion. *J. Lambert*

Germans pay the price of another 77 aircraft destroyed.

These enemy machines were not all fighters: Captain Fred J. Christensen, already an ace in the 62nd Squadron of the 56th, could not believe his luck when he came upon a formation of lumbering Ju52 transports approaching an aerodrome at Gardelegen. Taking his time, Christensen shot down six of the transports to bring his score to a final 21.5 confirmed. Lieutenant Billy G. Edens, also of the 62nd Squadron, was part of the same Wolfpack formation and his destruction of three of the transports brought him ace status.

An 8 July series of heavy bomber missions to tactical targets was disrupted by bad weather, with over half the dispatched crews aborting. The huge fighter escort carried out a spot of train-busting and came home to report 15 locomotives destroyed. One fighter and its pilot was lost and in terms of aerial combat the Ninth did well to claim three enemy fighters shot down.

The weather continued to impose restrictions on bomber targets on 9 July, although by now Eighth Air Force planners were adept at switching attacks from cloud-covered primaries to secondaries that the bombardiers could

see. Despite the availability of G-H the planners preferred to rely most heavily on visual bombing, particularly in the occupied nations. The target list remained long and ever-changing as the ground forces made progress. The 353rd Group added the name of Captain William J. Maguire to its list of aces but Billy Edens of the 56th, who had enjoyed ace status for 48 hours, was shot down by flak near Trier in Germany and captured.

Although the Ninth's fighter-bombers attacked T/Os on 10 July, the weather generally forced a stand-down of much of the US airpower in England.

On 11 July pilots of the 366th Group came upon a German Panzer column threatening a First Army position near St Lô. Intense flak greeted the Thunderbolts as they dived through driving rain to destroy pillboxes which had been their briefed target, before turning their attention to the Panzers. Keeping very low, the P-47s bombed and strafed the armoured column, severely damaging enough tanks to prevent any attack on American troops. Flying back to base the 366th rearmed and returned to shoot up

more tanks and in a memorable day flew a third mission to attack yet another enemy Panzer column. The results of the group's effort were called 'decisive' by US Army ground forces in the area.

Bad weather continued to disrupt bomber operations on 12 July but the fighter-bombers were able to carry out most of their support missions and to shoot down six enemy fighters. Radar aiming was the only option for many of the bombers sent over Germany, and the escort fighters reported no contact with the Luftwaffe.

Much the same conditions prevailed on the 13th but operations were carried out as far as was possible. Operation 'Cadillac' on 14 July was a supply drop by the heavies to Maquis forces around St Lô, Limoges and Vercors. The 499 accompanying P-51s helped ensure the drops went ahead as scheduled. Ground controllers called in fighter-bomber attacks on various points and enemy fighters attempted to intercept some AAF sorties. IX TAC pilots shot down 11 over France, losing five of their own in the ensuing dogfights.

Widespread, almost total, cancellation of operations marked 15 July but a more normal flight schedule was possible on the 16th, VIII and IX Fighter Commands sending out escort and ground-attack sorties; the 358th Group moved to A-14 Cretteville.

With the two sides continuing to fight a bitter ground war for control of northwest France, the AAF directed its heavy bombers to isolate the German Army further by bombing bridges over the Seine and Vire rivers. After escorting the heavies, the fighters strafed transport T/Os to claim the destruction of 23 locomotives and 55 wagons as well as 18 motor vehicles. V-weapon sites were also pounded in separate missions.

Rocket Thunderbolts

For the first time on 16 July IX TAC fighters were able to add weight to their attacks with aerial rockets. Twelve P-47s armed with four rockets apiece made a terrible mess of the marshalling yard at Nevers, the rockets granting the fighters a degree of immunity from the flak, as they could be fired from much further out than was possible with guns. Napalm was another new weapon that made its appearance that day when 14 P-38s of the 370th Group used it against targets around Coutances. The 36th Fighter Group moved into A-16 Brucheville, while American fighter pilots accounted for another 11 of the enemy over France.

Radar bombing was necessary on 18 July, the bombers attacking oil targets as well as the Luftwaffe experimental stations at Peenemünde and Zinnowitz. The escort found a gaggle of Ju88s and shot down 10 of them plus seven fighters over various areas of Germany.

Transportation targets located in western Belgium were 'on the board' for the TAC fighters on 19 July, this area representing the furthest they had flown since D-Day. The weather remained poor but numerous tactical sorties were completed successfully. German flak, rarely prevented from firing, claimed the P-47 flown by Captain Joseph L. Egan, Jr, of the 56th, who was killed when his aircraft fell near Nancy. The Ninth Air Force's 373rd Group moved to A-13 Tour-en-Bessin and in England the 55th Group completed its transition from the P-38 to the P-51. In the air combats that embroiled the escort to bombers attacking various targets in Germany and Austria, saw Captain William J. Hovde of the 355th become an ace when he destroyed a Bf109.

'Gabby' downed

A force totalling 1,077 B-17s and B-24s attacked oil, industrial and transportation targets in Germany on 20 July, the force being protected by 476 fighters which included the 20th Group making its debut in Mustangs. In keeping the enemy fighters away from the heavies, the Eighth Air Force claimed 10 and a Do217, Captain Norman J. 'Bud' Fortier of the 355th Group becoming an ace when he shot down a Bf109. Eight US aircraft and seven pilots were lost, one of the latter being 'Gabby' Gabreski who only went along on the mission while awaiting final orders to go home. Flying the first P-47M received by the 56th Group, he made a pass over an aerodrome at Bassenbeim. Keeping low to avoid the flak, the red-nosed Thunderbolt suddenly touched the ground, giving Gabby no choice but to make a crash-landing. This he survived to become a prisoner, and the Germans thus had, along with the other experienced AAF fighter pilots, the top-scoring American ace in the ETO.

As the penultimate development of the P-47D model line the P-47M was the culmination of all the experience gained in the tough combat arena of the ETO. Delighted to be the first (and, as it transpired, only) unit in Europe to be equipped with it, the 56th's initial enthusiasm waned when the technical problems that had plagued the early model Thunderbolts in 1943 began to reappear.

Above: Don Blakeslee was one of the driving forces behind the success of the Eighth's fighter offensive. A highly respected pilot and leader, he ended the war with 14.5 victories. *Author's collection*

Above: Maintenance on P-38Js and all other aircraft was aided greatly by useful work stands, which were seen everywhere and adapted to various heights. *Imperial War Museum*

In almost a carbon copy of what had occurred in those days the P-47M began to develop a long list of faults — particularly engine malfunctions — that resulted in individual aircraft being grounded for lengthy periods. As soon as one set of malfunctions appeared to have been cured, others would arise, to the point where the 56th had to return to the 'tried and tested' but marginally less capable P-47D in order to meet its mission schedules.

When it was finally found that the P-47M actually had few inherent faults and that the problems experienced by the 56th were traced to insufficient care having been taken to 'pickle' the engine for its long sea voyage across the Atlantic, the remedy was a straightforward engine change. Months had passed while other areas were probed for the cause of the trouble, but the P-47M did return to service and the Wolfpack pilots' collective nightmare of having to re-equip with the dreaded 'Spam cans' (Mustangs) did not come about.

The air activity possible over Normandy on 21/22 July was, at least in tactical terms, way below what had become normal for the Ninth Air Force, but once again the weather was to blame for keeping many

aircraft on the ground. The Eighth was able to mount only small scale missions on the 23rd, but on the 24th Operation 'Cobra' was scheduled to begin. This was a big air effort designed to assist the US First Army to break out of the Normandy beach-head by carpet bombing German Army positions hampering the advance. The weather forced a one-day postponement. On the 24th, the fighters attacked targets in the Normandy area and destroyed 10 enemy fighters in the process. The 370th Group moved into A-3 Cardonville during the day.

'Cobra' began on the 25th, with eight of the Ninth's fighter groups attacking their set objectives in squadron-strength columns spaced at three-minute intervals starting at 09.38 hours. Each aircraft bombed and strafed an area 250 yards deep by 7,000 yards wide to the south of the St Lô–Périers road. When the fighters had left 1,503 B-17s and B-24s poured high explosive into a similar small area one mile deep by 5 miles wide. To complete the job, seven Ninth Air Force fighter groups swept

in at 11.00 hours, bombing and strafing to the east and west of the main target areas. Concurrently the first US troops moved forward. By 12.23 hours, as the last fighter-bombers departed, IX Bomber Command's mediums were overhead to spread fragmentation and HE bombs.

With such a concentration of fire it was hardly surprising that the main objective of 'Cobra' was realised: the German troops who survived the onslaught were totally immobilised, allowing the Americans to advance quickly. No fighter-bombers were lost in the operation, making the bombing error which killed friendly troops during the latter part of the air operation even more of a tragedy. The heavy bombers involved in 'Cobra' were escorted by 483 fighters of which two were lost; 77 P-47s led by a droop-snoot P-38 attacked a fuel dump at Fournival/Bois-de-Mont while the TAC fighters patrolled out to Amiens, Ghent and Laval, on-call for targets. These operations were challenged by the Luftwaffe to some extent, but the Germans lost 17 aircraft in combat, among them a

Bf109 dispatched by Captain John F. Pugh to make him another of the 357th Group's aces.

Fighter-bombers continued to support the breakout of the First Army on 26 July, responding to calls by ground forces to hit a variety of targets impeding the advance. Eighth Fighter Command sent 40 P-47s to attack one fuel dump and 93 Thunderbolts to another. Unable to find the latter target in the overcast, the pilots dropped their bombs on a marshalling yard. A variation on an established doctrine was that IX Fighter Command introduced armed reconnaissance missions under which pilots were free to attack any authorised target within the mission area. Such sorties soon became the normal practice for groups under the tactical commands.

In another innovation 70 four-plane flights of TAC fighter-bombers were attached to the various American armoured units to provide 'column cover'. This involved fighter-bombers being controlled by experienced tactical pilots riding in forward vehicles especially adapted to maintain the air-ground link via aircraft radio sets. The 'ground pilots' and their army counterparts were trained to direct gun, rocket and bomb attacks and were able to appreciate what could be accomplished by different types of ordnance. The driving force behind this idea was Major-General Quesada who adapted and updated an established tactical technique to speed up and greatly increase the destruction of enemy objectives. In time, surprisingly small targets such as single pillboxes, buildings or vehicles could be knocked out using this system.

In successive days of operations the busy TAC fighters also found more aerial combat and destroyed 32 enemy aircraft over the 26–28 July period. American fighter-bomber pilots had become wise to the Luftwaffe's penchant for sending up sections of fighters to close and appear aggressive, whereupon the American pilots would release their ordnance in anticipation of combat — at which point the Germans often fled, having all but neutralised their ground-attack capability. For that reason the Thunderbolt pilots kept their bombs for the first few manoeuvres in the hope of driving off a feint attack. The fighter-bombers were also doing their bit to deny the Germans their long-enjoyed respite during the hours of darkness; on the night of 27/28 July IX TAC briefed a mission to drop delayed-action (DA)

Above: Jacks were also much used for raising belly-landed aircraft onto their wheels. In this view a crew watches a demonstration from the horizontal tailplane of a P-38J-20 (44-23574) which makes an ideal bench. *Imperial War Museum*

bombs on selected road junctions in areas held by enemy forces.

In common with the Ninth's tactical effort the Eighth Air Force fighters made a huge contribution to the safer passage of the ground forces with numerous strikes at ground objectives, while maintaining the primary mission of heavy bomber escort.

As the Allied armies pushed on into the French countryside it was clear that the incessant pounding from the air was having a significant effect on their adversaries. Having suffered appalling personnel and matériel losses ever since 'Overlord', the German Seventh Army had been contained and limited to achieving, at best, mere holding actions. It was perceptibly retreating by late July, a predicament not eased by the heavily interdicted roads, which had the effect of pushing AFVs (armoured fighting vehicles) and trucks into traffic jam 'chokepoints' where further air attacks on exit routes created chaos. On 28 July P-47 pilots of the 405th Group noted an immense vehicle jam which they proceeded to attack. In six hours of carnage the Thunderbolts destroyed an estimated 12 tanks, 400 trucks and various other vehicles. In addition, air combat resulted in the destruction of seven enemy aircraft by the TAC fighters of the Ninth, and during the night of 28/29 July they repeated the DA bombing of road junctions.

Over Germany itself 652 B-17s bombed the Leuna synthetic oil plant at Merseburg and 36 the Taucha oil plant in Leipzig. Escort was by 386 fighters including the 364th Group flying its first Mustang mission after converting from the P-38. Bomber crews reported their first sighting of the Me163 rocket-propelled interceptor, but otherwise losses of US bombers and fighters totalled nine for three German fighters and a Ju52.

While Liberators visited airfields and other tactical targets in France, the B-17s made a second attack on the Leuna plant and 442 2nd Division B-24s were sent to an oil refinery at Bremen. While fighting off conventional German interceptors, the escort made the first Eighth Air Force claims against the Me163 and Captain Leonard K. 'Kit' Carson made ace when he shot down a Bf109 near Merseburg. The day's action was also the first combat experience for pilots of the 20th Group since relinquishing P-38s for Mustangs. Two groups strafed ground targets *en route* back to England and among the

seven aircraft and pilots lost was Lieutenant Christopher J. Hanseman, an ace in the 339th Group. He was killed when his P-51 hit the ground during a strafing run.

Fighter sweeps by the Eighth fighter groups on 30 July netted 18 enemy fighters, Major Richard E. Turner of the 354th Group being one of the successful American pilots. A Bf109 became Turner's 11th confirmed victory.

Another ace was made on the last day of July when Colonel Morton D. Magoffin, CO of the Ninth's 362nd Group, shot down an Fw190 to bring his score to five. The Ninth's bag from a series of armed recon and dive-bombing missions was three enemy fighters. Escorting bombers to the Munich area, Allach, Schleisshelm and Ludwigshafen cost VIII Fighter Command three aircraft and their pilots. Group moves in IX TAC saw the 406th occupying A-13 Tour-en-Bessin. Frantic IV was flown by the Fifteenth Air Force on 31 July.

August 44

In order to serve the ground forces better in their push across France and ultimately into Germany, the Ninth Air Force implemented a number of changes in mid-1944. Among the most important was the creation of separate tactical air commands to operate primarily in support of specific American armies. On 1 August XIX TAC commanded by Major General Otto P. Weyland began operations with General George Patton's Third Army which had recently been committed to combat. Then with three fighter groups, Weyland's command was soon expanded.

Kepner steps down

Changes in top echelon personnel at this time included command of the 2nd Air Division's Liberators passing into the hands of Eighth Air Force fighter leader Major-General Bill Kepner, who was temporarily replaced by Brigadier General Murray C. Woodbury. Kepner, who adopted an aggressive stance in relation to fighter operations, had helped guide the groups through their most difficult operational period. He had strongly backed the early experiments to use P-47s in the dive-bombing role and had also endorsed strafing on the return from escort missions, in line with the policy of decimating the German fighter force before D-Day.

Bombers hit the airfields surrounding Paris, dropped supplies to the Maquis and attacked V-weapon sites on 1 August, a day when the weather caused a number of aborts. Fighters destroyed four Bf109s during afternoon missions and Lieutenant William Ynge Anderson — who was born in Sweden and was nicknamed 'Willie Y' — of the 354th came home to file a claim for one of them to make him an ace with five kills.

Tactical targets were again bombed by the heavies on the morning of the 2nd, the escort losing two fighters. Afternoon missions followed a similar pattern in a day marked by near-total absence of the Luftwaffe fighter force. A single victory was claimed by AAF pilots.

On 3 August Brigadier General Francis H. Griswold replaced Murray Woodbury as head of VIII Fighter Command.

Bomber strikes were mounted against oil refineries, marshalling yards, bridges and airfields, the fighters providing their usual cover and losing six aircraft and pilots from 358 sorties. About half the fighters went down to strafe ground targets and in a separate mission 133 P-38s and P-47s sought rail traffic around Metz, Strasbourg and Saarbrücken. In the afternoon the V-weapon sites in France received another pounding and the TAC fighters scored four more kills over enemy fighters.

The rail yards at Saarbrücken were bombed by B-17s in the afternoon of the 3rd, the escort shooting down five German aircraft. The victors included Captain Leslie D. Minchew of the 355th Group whose single Bf109 kill was enough to make him an ace.

August 1944's weather was not the long sunny spell it had been in previous years and the AAF continued to battle through to its targets in conditions of low cloud. The 4th brought conditions bad enough to reduce the bombing effort against V-weapon sites, although the escort fighters made their mark on Pantlunne aerodrome as did the pilots of IX TAC, who shot down two Bf109s over Nogent.

Conditions were also satisfactory over Hamburg, Bremen and Kiel where oil targets were bombed by 221 B-17s; other formations blasted Peenemünde, various aerodromes and T/Os at a time when the Eighth was demonstrating its ability to range almost at will over the Reich, even if the weight of explosive delivered was by a relatively small number of Fortresses and Liberators. There was usually a price to be paid and in addition to the 11 B-17s and four B-24s lost, 14 of the 666 fighters went down with their pilots. Again typically the American side exacted a greater toll from the Germans and their casualties were 37 fighters. Major Donald A. Larson, CO of the 505th Squadron, 339th Group nailed two Bf109s to make him an ace. Never having the chance to confirm the fact, Larson was killed a short time later when he collided with another P-51 during a strafing run. Lieutenant James R. Starnes, a member of Don Larson's squadron, knocked down a Bf109 near Hamburg to make a personal five, while a P-47 piloted by Lieutenant David F. Thwaites of the 361st Group dispatched another, 109 in the same area to become an ace.

Bad weather on 5 August cut the number of B-17s actually able to bomb airfield and other targets in the Brunswick area by some 50% — 543 out of 1,171 dispatched. The fighter force was 573 strong and in combat the American pilots shot down 27 for six lost with their pilots. Lieutenant Glennon T. Moran, already an ace with the 352nd Group, shot down a Bf109 to bring his personal score to 13 confirmed. Lieutenant Frederick W. Glover of the 4th Group also destroyed a Bf109 to bring him a fifth kill.

V-weapon sites continued to absorb a great deal of high explosive on 6 August, the day that XIX TAC assumed primary responsibility for guarding the flank of the Third Army. This meant that Patton could concentrate on pursuing the fleeing German Army without having to worry about time-consuming 'mopping up' of enemy pockets on the flanks. Having gained this assurance of aerial protection, America's most colourful general embarked on a race that would ultimately take his tanks right through Germany and beyond. Flank protection by the fighter-bombers meant 'aggressive' armed reconnaissance and tactical sorties against all types of target.

Part of the day's operations for the Ninth was to move the 474th Group forward to A-11 St Lambert and thus complete the movement of all its component fighter groups across the Channel from England.

VIII Fighter Command meanwhile escorted 830 heavy bombers to Brandenburg to carry out a successful attack on aircraft assembly and munitions plants as well as engine plants in Berlin, six oil refineries at Hamburg, and airfields. For this effort 24 bombers were lost. With 535 AAF fighters covering the bombers, the Luftwaffe lost 30 interceptors and a Do217 over Germany. Major George E. Preddy of the 352nd Group was top among the scoring pilots with his six Bf109s. In a running battle between Lüneburg and Havelberg between 11.10 and 11.45 hours, Preddy's blue-nose P-51 systematically chopped down the enemy fighters to bring his personal score to 22.833. And six down not only made Preddy another 'ace in a day' but with his new total he was the highest scoring US pilot then active in the ETO. Other successful air combat claims were made by pilots in the 355th Group, two of whom became aces with single Bf109 kills — Captain Bert W. Marshall, Jr, and Captain Charles W. Lenfest.

Further afield the B-17s of the 3rd Bomb Division attacked an aircraft factory at Rahmel near Gdynia in Poland before proceeding east into the Soviet Union to complete the first stage of another shuttle mission, Operation 'Frantic V'. Escorting the bombers were 154 P-51s of the 55th and 339th Groups which turned at the Russian border and headed back to England. By so doing the pilots completed a round trip of 1,592 miles, their longest of the war to date. Mustangs of the 357th Group joined the big friends near Jutland in the early afternoon and shot down a Ju88 and Bf109 near Warsaw at 13.45 hours before heading with their charges into Russia.

7 Night-fighters and Shuttles

Although commanders of the US air forces in Europe soon appreciated that their tactical groups could be highly effective during the hours of daylight, night operations had not really been planned for. A number of experimental missions had proven that medium bombers and fighters could handle night sorties without difficulty, even though lack of technical aids, especially radar, led to results that were patchy at best. Items such as exhaust flame dampers had not been allowed for in any of the major bomber and fighter designs and incorporation of these, together with properly trained crews to take full advantage of night flying, awaited a specialised US design. Those night operations the AAF had undertaken in other theatres as well as Europe had been by types such as the P-38 and P-70 and the Bristol Beaufighter, but a more modern, more capable aircraft could only be a major asset to a round-the-clock air campaign. This requirement was taken up by the Northrop Corporation and in due course the P-61 Black Widow emerged. Two night fighter squadrons, the 422nd and 425th, were assigned to the Ninth Air Force, on 7 March and 23 May respectively. The 422nd was the first to move to France in late July and on 7 August 1944 two of its crews flying from A-15 Maupertus made the first recorded interception of enemy aircraft by the P-61 in the European theatre. Their claims had to be qualified as 'probable' victories, for the results obtained by opening fire on a Ju188 and Do217 could not be verified — the important point for the AAF was that it had finally committed a night-fighter to combat. It had been a lengthy wait. Later that same night at 23.30 hours, the P-61 did score its first ETO kill, however, when a 422nd crew was credited with the destruction of a Ju88 over the bay of Mont St Michel.

More conventional AAF missions on 7 August included the dispatch of 905 heavy bombers to tactical targets in northern France; 488 of these were able to release their loads, and 437 fighters were along as escort. Tactical fighter sorties by Eighth AF groups totalled 271 and in attacks on rail targets this force lost eight aircraft and their pilots. The AAF fighters destroyed 19 enemy fighters and Lt Lloyd J. Overfield of the 354th became an ace

Above: Large by any standards, the P-61 equipped two AAF night-fighter squadrons in the ETO. Note details of the rear crew entry hatch in this view. *USAF*

Above: The Ninth Air Force got into the night-fighter business with the 422nd NFS flying P-61As which were delivered both in camouflage and overall black finish. *Imperial War Museum*

when he shot down three Bf109s.

On the ground the IX and XIX TACs formed mobile headquarters which would henceforth directly support the US First and Third Armies. As of 7 August the Ninth Air Force's fighters were distributed thus:

IX Tactical Air Command
70th Fighter Wing
48th, 367th and 474th Groups
71st Fighter Wing
366th, 368th and 370th Groups
84th Fighter Wing
50th, 365th and 404th Groups

XIX Tactical Air Command
100th Fighter Wing
354th, 362nd, 363rd and 371st Groups
303rd Fighter Wing
36th, 358th, 373rd and 406th Groups

All these groupings were in no way considered permanent as they were changed in accordance with operational requirements. The TACs had permanent headquarters controlling a changing roster of subordinate groups, and they were organised on similar lines to a US Army corps.

As part of the intensive air activity of 7 August, two groups of B-17s bombed oil refineries around Trzebinia in Poland during their return from the Soviet Union under Operation 'Frantic V'. These Forts were escorted back by the 357th which had accompanied them on the outward leg. In combat with German fighters, Major John A. Storch, CO of the group's 364th Squadron, made ace with a single claim over a Bf109.

The Ninth had a new commanding general from 8 August when Lieutenant-General Hoyt S. Vandenburg replaced Lewis Brereton.

In two separate missions the heavy bombers attacked the main concentration of V-weapon sites in the Pas de Calais and other coastal areas, while others attacked T/Os. Escorting fighters were divided into two groups, to carry out strafing of various ground targets. Falaise was now a focal point in the Allied drive out of the invasion area and 497 Eighth Air Force B-17s gave direct support to Canadian troops operating there. The bombers' targets were Wehrmacht troop concentrations and strongpoints; including an assault by RAF Bomber Command the previous night, the American contribution brought the total tonnage aimed at the German positions to 5,200 tons — the second largest since D-Day. Again the danger inherent in using heavy bombers against relatively small tactical targets was highlighted when 25 Canadian troops were killed when some of the bombs fell short. Escort for the B-17s was provided by 91 P-51s, another 175 fighters of all three VIII FC types concurrently attacking rail centres. Seven US fighters and their pilots were lost from both operations that day, but victory claims from combat were 12 German fighters credited to pilots of both air forces.

A slight change of scene for the 4th Group on 8 August was to send 41 Mustangs as escort to RAF Coastal Command Beaufighters flying an anti-shipping strike off Norway. Three US fighters and their pilots were lost. In a phased operation to complete 'Frantic V', part of the B-17 force escorted by elements of the 357th Fighter Group attacked Bizau and Zilistea aerodromes in Romania before peeling off to land at bases in Italy. That flak could be deadly, even when the fighters were not at zero feet, was shown by the death of ace Captain Frank C. Jones, whose Mustang was hit *en route* to Italy. As if to pay back for that loss, a 357th pilot nailed a Bf109 over Crocil.

Night-fighter success

On 9 August the 422nd NFS (Night Fighter Squadron) continued to find trade after dark and a P-61 crew intercepted and shot down a Ju88 near Caen at 02.35 hours. This was some hours before 149 Eighth Air Force P-47s escorted by 40 Mustangs appeared over several French communications targets. The Ninth also sent fighters out to strafe tactical targets, among them Reims/Épernay aerodrome where Don Beerbower, newly promoted CO of the 354th Group's 353rd Squadron, was shot down by flak and killed. In a coincidence that the pilots found hard to believe, Beerbower's replacement was also shot down that very afternoon. Major Wallace N. Emmer who had 14 victories, 1.5 less than the late CO, was hit by flak while on a patrol near Rouen. More fortunate in that he survived to be captured, Emmer later contracted myocarditis and died in a German PoW camp.

During the day's operations the Ninth's fighters shot down 14 enemy fighters in three actions that began at 09.35 hours, continued at 13.30 hours and ended after another contact at 18.00 hours. Overcast conditions prevented all but 25 B-24s (out of 824 Fortresses and Liberators dispatched) from finding their briefed targets in Germany. Secondaries were bombed by the majority of aircraft which were escorted by 570 fighters. In combat, these pilots claimed 29 enemy interceptors and a trainer, Lieutenant-Colonel John B. Murphy, 370th FS CO becoming another 359th Group ace with a single Fw190 kill.

Sending out a 238-strong force on 10 August VIII Fighter Command also directed its groups to strafe rail and other transportation targets. This order proved unlucky for 11 pilots, including Lt-Col Kyle L. Riddle, CO of the 479th Group, who was shot down over France. He evaded capture and was back at the head of his command by 1 November. Fifteen German fighters were shot down by the Americans during the course of the day, which saw the movement of Ninth Air Force groups further into France when the 362nd relocated to A-27 Rennes. Similar moves by the 354th Fighter Group and the 10th PRG were undertaken the following day, the Mustangs going to A-31 Gael and the photo ships moving into Rennes. Otherwise 11 August was a fairly typical day for the fighter and bomber groups, there being five bombers and one fighter lost. IX TAC P-47s dropped supplies to the US 30th Infantry Division which was cut off at Mortain — the kind of service long since denied the Germans in France.

On 12 August the last of the Frantic V B-17s returned to England from Italy, bombing Toulouse/Francazal aerodrome *en route*. Their escort was 58 of the 357th Group's P-51s that had accompanied the Forts to Russia, plus 42 more fighters out from England to rendezvous with them. On other escort duties and strafing attacks that day, the Eighth's fighter force was depleted by 10, one of the missing P-51s being that flown by the CO of the 361st Group, Colonel Thomas J. J. Christian, Jr, who was killed.

On the ground the Allies were about to trap a sizeable part of the German Army at Falaise. To ensure they did not escape and regroup, the Eighth sent 1,206 heavy bombers to the area on 13 August. Operating around the Seine, 844 fighter sorties hammered transport targets and claimed 776 motor vehicles during attacks on stalled German traffic, but much of this would have remained in use had the enemy had a safe exit route out of Falaise. Further pounding from the air turned a dangerous situation into a disaster for the Germans in France. Medium bombers and fighters maintained continuous armed reconnaissance patrols over the Falaise area and caused destruction on a vast scale as all possible lines of retreat were bombed and strafed. Air support was also provided for

Above: Among the modifications made to single-seat fighters was the addition of a second place for a passenger. This P-51D of the 339th Group was one of a substantial number of such hybrids that served in various second-line roles. *Imperial War Museum*

Above: A P-47D-28 (44-19909) of the 56th Group's 63rd FS over England's typical patchwork landscape. This was the fourth 'bubbletop' production version of the D model Thunderbolt and the Wolfpack was obliged to fly it longer than planned when its 'own' P-47Ms had to spend months on the ground being modified. *USAF*

Allied troops aiming to encircle enemy pockets of resistance.

Air combat on the 14th saw Major Joseph H. Griffin, CO of the 392nd FS, 367th Group, become another Ninth Air Force ace when he shot down two Fw190s to add to his three previous Japanese kills obtained over China while flying a P-40. The 358th Group meanwhile moved to A-28 Pontorson and the 36th to A-2 Criqueville.

As the Allied push across France broadened to liberate more areas, the fighter pilots were now ordered not to strafe people on the ground for fear that they were friendly. The heavies also carried on their war against German industry in a 250-strong attack on industrial facilities. A single escort fighter and its pilot were lost to give an impression (however brief) of the degree of air superiority the AAF had gained over the enemy heartland.

While Operation 'Dragoon', the invasion of Southern France, went ahead successfully, XIX TAC saw action with the Jagdwaffe over France and scored 13 victories; the 365th Group, the 'Hell Hawks', occupied A-12 Lignerolles and the 370th Group went to A-19 La Vielle. Escorting the heavies to airfield targets, VIII FC aircraft clashed with the Luftwaffe and claimed 10 enemy fighters. Over The Netherlands, the P-38s of the 434th Squadron of the 479th Group had a successful day by shooting down three Bf109s over Steenwijk aerodrome.

Sixteen Fw190s fell to IX TAC fighters on 16 August, 14 of them in a single large scale action near Maintenon involving the 354th Group's 353rd Squadron. Two pilots became aces: Lieutenants Kenneth H. Dahlberg and Charles W. Koenig claimed three and two Focke-Wulfs respectively.

Rocket fighters

While the 50th Group settled into its new home at A-17 Meutis, there was another escort to bombers for 612 aircraft of VIII Fighter Command, which had 976 B-17s and B-24s to protect. This they did well in the face of German interceptors, the air combat claims including two Me163s. Major John L. Elder of the 357th Group became an ace with claims for two Bf109s.

For the first time on 17 August the P-47s of the 56th Fighter Group hauled M-10 rockets to Braine-le-Comte, where Lieutenant-Colonel Dave Schilling, then deputy Group CO, scored a bull's-eye with a salvo to set four railway wagons ablaze. Mounted in triple tubes, the M-10 could be an effective enough weapon provided the pilot set up everything correctly; the P-47 had no special sight for weapons other than machine guns and success with external ordnance was very much the result of combat experience, good flying and combat-proven tactics.

Otherwise the 17th was a day of rest for many crews as the weather clamped down and a percentage of those that did take off

Above: Leading ace of the ETO Francis S. Gabreski has a last word with his crew chief Ralph Safford before a mission. The 27 kill marks place the date of this photo between 27 June and July 5 1944, when 'Gabby' became the top ace of the ETO. He went down to become a PoW after a strafing mission on 20 July.
Imperial War Museum

Above: The 'Polish contingent' of the 56th Fighter Group's 61st Squadron in the spring of 1944 included some of the best pilots in the unit. (*left to right*) Capt Boleslaw 'Mike' Gladych, (18 kills) Maj Tadeusz Sawicz, Lt Col Francis S. Gabreski (28), Maj Kazimierz Rutkowski (6) Flt Lt Tadeusz Andersz and Capt Witold Lanowski (4). *Jan P. Koniarek*

were advised to return. Tactical fighters participated in a 'broad front' sweep between Paris and Brussels, attacking various targets for the loss of seven pilots. Elsewhere the 406th Group moved to A-14 Cretteville.

Bridge targets in Belgium and aerodromes in France were among the targets for the heavies on 18 August, the fighters also ranging into Belgium to carry out tactical strikes. With Allied forces advancing, IX and XIX TAC's were busy flying over 1,000 sorties in the Paris–Argentan and Seine river areas. Weather disruption continued the following day and even though the bomber bases were 'socked in', the fighters usually managed to operate. The two tactical forces of the Ninth were involved in aerial combat, netting themselves another 11 German fighters. The 373rd Group moved its P-47s into A-29 St James and the P-61s of the 425th NFS landed at the unit's new base, A-33N Vannes.

Grounding orders for the heavy bombers remained in force on 20 August, but again the two TACs based in France were not so adversely affected by the weather and were able to mix it with the Luftwaffe. Seven enemy fighters were shot down.

Few sorties by any ETO units were possible on 21 August and the 22nd was only marginally better, the TAC fighters supporting ground forces also carrying on their private war with the Luftwaffe and claiming another 27 enemy fighters. With conditions on the 23rd again preventing the bulk of planned sorties from taking place, XIX TAC's German fighter score was also down, at just five. The 36th Group's P-47s moved to A-35 Le Mans and the 369th made itself at home at A-40 Chartres. With no bomber escort missions posted, the Eighth sent 80 or so fighters into Germany to attack marshalling yards at Hamm.

The weather on 24 August was bad enough to ground IX Bomber Command, but over 1,000 heavies were able to attack German targets. The day belonged to the Ninth's fighters, however, when the 474th Group's P-38s maintained a relentless pounding of German road columns driving up to the Seine river bridges, many of which had been destroyed. Bombing and strafing, the Lightning pilots persuaded the Wehrmacht to abandon much useful equipment in its haste to get out of France. With the 366th Group moving its P-47s into A-41 Dreaux/Vermouillet and the 10th PRG taking tenancy on A-39 Châteaudun, personnel of these and other units could take a close look at the handiwork of the Allied air forces. What they often found was a distinct lack of amenities and facilities if the airfield had been badly bombed.

Above: Hard landing at Manston, Kent for a P-38J-5 (42-67232) of the 384th FS, 364th Group flown by Lt David W Williams. *Author's collection*

Above: Some pilots encouraged their ground crews to keep a comprehensive log of an individual aircraft's war record as P-47D-28 (42-29262) of the 391st FS, 366th Group shows to advantage. If one Thunderbolt could inflict this much loss on the enemy, think what a whole group could do! *J. V. Crow*

Over Germany the bomber escort handled its task with the usual efficiency while four groups carried out strafing of two aerodromes and a marshalling yard. Flak nailed the P-51 flown by Captain John T. Godfrey — and another Eighth Air Force ace was taken into captivity 'for the duration'.

The events of 25 August centred quite understandably more on the liberation of Paris than a series of successful air combats fought by the tactical fighters of the Ninth Air Force. But in claiming a record bag of enemy aircraft — no less than 77 — it was the best day the pilots serving in units predominantly engaged on ground-attack work had enjoyed to date. Enemy fighter kills transcended all other targets in the eyes of most fighter pilots, particularly when the victories were scored in the air. It was somewhat ironic that the Ninth did not therefore allow aircraft ground claims by tactical pilots and it was often quite frugal with its confirmation of air combat claims.

Starting at 08.10 hours, the combats involved the P-51s of the 354th Group and Captain Maurice G. Long of the 355th Squadron became an ace with two Fw190 kills. In the afternoon the same squadron added two more names to its ace listing — Captain Warren S. Emerson and Lieutenant William B. King — with respectively two and three Fw190s.

P-38s of the 367th Group flew an intensive number of airfield attacks in the morning and in the afternoon they undertook a round trip of 800 miles to attack others at Dijon, Cognac and Bourges. Captain Laurence E. Blumer became an ace in a day when his 393rd Squadron clashed with Focke-Wulfs and he downed five of them.

For the Eighth the 20th Group's pilots shot up 20 enemy aircraft on the ground while 629 of their colleagues took 1,116 heavies to German aerodrome targets, Peenemünde and factories located over a wide swathe of the country. Seven American fighters were lost in combat, 12 enemy fighters being shared by such pilots as Captain Robin Olds of the 479th Group flying a P-38 in the 434th Squadron. He accounted for three Bf109s near Rostock.

Having achieved one aim, that of all but ejecting the Germans from France, the Allied air forces now made an attempt to eliminate as many troops and as much equipment as possible. To that end, 389 fighter sorties were mounted by VIII FC

on 26 August. Over Germany Lieutenant-Colonel Frank E. Adkins commanding the 313th Squadron, 50th Fighter Group, made ace when he destroyed two Bf109s to add to the three Japanese aircraft he had already claimed.

In an all-out effort to remove remaining targets in and around Berlin, the Eighth Air Force sent 1,203 bombers off, only to be largely thwarted when the crews experienced dense cloud at extreme altitudes. Only 188 bombers unloaded. Fighter combat during the day's escort mission claimed 10 pilots, among them Lieutenant-Colonel Cy Wilson, CO of the 20th Group, who was made a prisoner.

Hundreds of fighter sorties were flown on 28 August, despite the bombers again being held back due to bad weather. Transport was the main target for fighter guns and bombs, combat with the Jagdwaffe resulting in losses of 16 aircraft and 15 pilots, among them Captain Albert L. Schlegel, an 8.5-victory ace of the 4th Group. American victories totalled 24 by Eighth and Ninth Air Force units, the 355th Group being able to announce later that Captain Robert W. Stephens had downed a Bf109 to bring his tally to a highly respectable 13.

With the weather severely curtailing sorties on the 29th, the Ninth Air Force authorised three more base moves: the 48th Group to A-42 Villacoublay, the 404th to A-48 Brétigny and the 474th to A-43 St Marceau.

Resorting to G-H and H2X radar bombing on the 30th, the Eighth's heavies went to V-weapon sites in the morning as well as to installations at Bremen and Kiel. There was no enemy reaction, a situation that also prevailed on the last day of August when the weather prevented any Eighth Air Force sorties; only IX Bomber Command flew and the 363rd Group based its Mustangs at A-7 Azeville.

September 1944

Pursuing elements of the German Army on 1 September, the 405th Group's P-47s destroyed about 200 motor vehicles during six squadron-strength missions for the day. The 36th Group's tally also rose to some 500 vehicles when it sent out four eight-plane missions during the course of the day. Such utter devastation wrought by air attack helped break the back of the German Army in France.

Over Germany the greater percentage of heavies were recalled when heavy cloud

reduced visual bombing conditions. Near Liège, Major Quince L. Brown, commanding officer of the 78th Fighter Group's 84th Squadron, destroyed a Bf109 to bring his personal score to 12.333. Fighter bombers of the Eighth strafed and bombed rail targets in northern and northeastern France, there being 265 such sorties.

The poor weather portents held throughout the 2nd when only the 56th Fighter Group was able to operate, strafing T/Os. IX TAC headquarters moved forward to Versailles. On the 3rd 125 P-47s of the Eighth Air Force strafed transport targets in Belgium, while 55 P-51s of the 55th Group shot down seven Fw190s near Antwerp in the afternoon. The B-17s were able to attack German artillery batteries in and around the port of Brest, while IX TAC fighters set a one-day record for the entire war when they destroyed 919 motor vehicles, 757 horse-drawn vehicles and 58 AFVs. During the 2nd the 365th Fighter Group moved to A-48 Brétigny, while B-17s of the Eighth's 1st Division bombed oil targets at Ludwigshafen.

On 4 September Brussels was liberated by British troops but the Eighth and Ninth Air Forces were grounded by bad weather. The 406th Group could therefore undertake a trouble-free move into A-47 Paris/Orly, while the 406th occupied A-35 Le Mans. In a move designed to give the Ninth greater photo-reconnaissance capability — which was subsequently seen to have been only just adequate — the 363rd Fighter Group was withdrawn from frontline fighter operations to convert to PR Mustangs and undertake a tactical recon role.

Brest was pounded by 143 B-17s on 5 September and a larger force of Fortresses continued the assault on the synthetic oil facilities at Ludwigshafen, as well as an aero engine factory at Stuttgart; B-24s hit marshalling yards at Karlsruhe and VIII FC sent 217 fighters to strafe various targets. In combat, the fighter pilots claimed 25 enemy interceptors plus two German bombers over The Netherlands. In the course of these operations, Lieutenants William H. Lewis and William H. Allen of the 55th Group became aces in a day with a clutch of trainers destroyed over Göppingen aerodrome. One of the fighters claimed turned out to be a Bf109 of the Swiss Air Force, which went down near the border with Germany.

Above: Col George R. Bickell, CO of the 354th Fighter Group during its less than ecstatic period flying Thunderbolts. *Imperial War Museum*

Some of the grimmer aspects of the air war were revealed on 6 September when the 78th Group lost Major Quince Brown during an VIII FC sweep in the Aachen and Koblenz areas. Hit by flak, his P-47 went down and Brown was captured near Schleiden only to be summarily shot by an SS officer. The 474th Group moved into its new base, A-72 Péronne.

Few operations could be conducted on 7 September, although the Ninth's fighters made a sterling effort to provide support to US Army ground forces. Part of this was an attack on German road transport by the 406th Fighter Group which proceeded to bomb and strafe 300 vehicles to destruction along a 15-mile section of road. After flying back to replenish their ammunition, the pilots returned to the scene of carnage, went to work again, and claimed another 200 or so vehicles destroyed.

Even fighter activity was restricted by the weather on the 8th, the 366th Group taking the opportunity during the lull to move to A-70 Laon/Couvron, while the 367th Group headed for A-71 Clastres. Bomber support to the heavies raiding Ludwigshafen, Karlsruhe, Kassel and Gustavsburg also involved the fighters strafing targets in western Germany. No air combat was reported.

Targets of opportunity were the order of the day on 9 September, one Fw190 being shot down near Liège by patrolling fighters looking for something worth shooting at on the ground. The Eighth was the most active air force over the Continent and its bombers again attacked various categories of target. The fighters, strafing their own T/Os, also destroyed eight enemy aircraft and ranged out to the Dutch islands, where a P-47 pilot of the 353rd Group shot down a Do217.

In a further effort to deny the Germans the cover of night, the 474th Group flew intruder missions against army columns on 10/11 September. A German counter-attack on Third Army forces holding positions across the Moselle river was beaten off, ably assisted by the sorties flown by the groups of XIX TAC. The Ninth also drew up plans to interdict rail lines on both sides of the Rhine into early October, a task that would be handled by both its tactical air commands.

Over Germany a force of 1,063 bombers and 121 fighters, the latter mainly strafing targets in four major cities, were intercepted by enemy fighters which failed again to inflict much damage. Eight were

shot down. Lt Ted E. Lines of the 4th Group became an ace with three Bf109s and a Ju88 to bring his score to seven. Lt Carl G. Bickel of the 354th dispatched an He111 to bring his total to five.

The air actions of 11 September were the largest since 28 May and in terms of kills gave the Eighth's fighter pilots their best day of the war so far when 124 enemy fighters were claimed. The bait for the Jagdwaffe was 1,016 heavy bombers attacking synthetic oil plants in eight locations as their primary targets; other heavies hit depots and engineering plants at Magdeburg and Hanover, with T/Os also scheduled. The crews reported attacks by more than 500 enemy fighters which resulted in the loss of 40 bombers. Eighth Fighter Command's escort strength that day was 411 of which 17 were lost, a modest figure in comparison to the American claims. A number of pilots were able to add to their scores, among them Lt Cyril W. Jones, Jr, of the 359th Group who shot down four Bf109s; Lt-Col John L. McGinn, CO of the 55th Group's 338th Squadron got one Bf109 and Captain Benjamin H. King of the 359th Group made ace with a score of two Fw190s and a Bf109. In the 339th Group Lieutenant Francis R. Gerard came home to claim three Bf109s and an Fw190.

To divide the attention of the German defenders further, the first leg of the next Eighth Air Force shuttle mission (Frantic VI) attacked its briefed target. The mission occupied part of the fighter escort — 64 P-51s of the 20th Group — and these shepherded 75 B-17s into Russia via a synthetic oil plant at Chemnitz, which received 175 tons of bombs. One P-51 was lost.

Moving its HQ forward to Versailles, IX TAC had a quieter day, although XIX TAC supported the Third Army by warding off a German counter-attack along the Moselle. The US Seventh and Third Armies linked up to form a continuous front line across France and Belgium from the Mediterranean to the North Sea and from the Channel to the Swiss frontier. More tactical units relocated, the 368th Group going to A-69 Laon/Athies and the 36th to A-73 Roye/Amy.

On 12 September the Eighth sent 813 bombers and 579 fighters into Germany to hit various targets, and again they found the opposition heavy — 400 to 450 interceptors were reported and 35 bombers went down along with 12 fighters. Among

the victims was Cyril Jones, who had become an ace only the day before and who disappeared without trace. In return the USAAF pilots claimed 96 enemy interceptors destroyed. Lieutenants William T. Kemp of the 361st Group, Henry J. Miklajcyk of the 352nd and Robert Reynolds of the 354th all claimed victories to bring them ace status. Reynolds' personal score that day was three Fw190s, which gave him a total of seven. On separate missions, IX TAC fighters shot down six Bf109s to make this another disastrous day for the Jagdwaffe.

During the night of 12/13 September the 474th again hung bombs on its P-38s to fly intruder sorties against enemy supply columns. Pilot reports were not exactly ecstatic about the results.

A French armoured column was given support by fighters of XIX TAC on 13 September, the result being the destruction of 60 German tanks near Vittel. Other tactical fighter sorties assisted the US Army units operating around Brest, Metz and Nancy. The 404th Group moved up to A-68 Juvincourt and the 36th to A-64 St Dizier/Robinson, while XIX TAC moved its HQ to co-locate with Third Army HQ at Châlons-sur-Marne.

Although 1,026 Eighth Air Force heavies were dispatched on the 13th, only 790 were able to bomb assigned targets in southern Germany, among them five synthetic oil plants and refineries. After escorting the bombers and claiming the destruction of 33 enemy aircraft, all identified as Bf109s, the AAF fighters went down to strafe. Lieutenant-Colonel Cecil L. Wells, the 358th Group commander, was killed during these operations.

Returning from Russia, 73 bombers and 63 Mustangs of the Frantic VI force dropped 263 tons of bombs on a steel plant at Diosgyoer in Hungary en route to England via Italy. Opening its new rail interdiction campaign, XIX TAC's armed fighter reconnaissance sorties found numerous targets in and around the Aachen, Cologne, Koblenz and Wahn areas. The following day XXIX TAC was established on a provisional basis under the command of Brigadier-General Richard E. Nugent to support the new US Ninth Army.

More fighter unit base moves were made: the 358th Group occupied A-67 Vitry-le-François, the 48th Group A-74 Cambrai/Niergnies, the 50th Group A-69

Above: Lt L. W. Nelson appears mighty pleased with himself in the cockpit of his well-named 82nd Fighter Squadron, 78th Group P-51D. *Imperial War Museum*

Laon/Athies and the 365th Group moved to A-68 Juvincourt. The Ninth Air Force headquarters also moved out of England and was formally established at Chantilly, France.

In another command change on 15 September each of the three VIII Fighter Command wing headquarters and their 15 groups were placed under the operational control of the three bomb divisions. Thus the 65th Fighter Wing went to the 2nd BD, the 66th FW to the 3rd BD and the 67th FW to the 1st BD. This move was designed to ensure that escort priority was given to the bomber groups within each bomb division, and to this end, the system of coloured recognition markings and geometric symbols used by

each heavy bomber group was expanded.

The US Third Army was given able air support by XIX TAC in its efforts to repel several German counter-attacks in northeast France. A coup for the fresh US Ninth Army and XIX TAC was the surrender by a German general commanding 20,000 troops *en route* from southern to northern France. The general stated that the incessant air attacks were the primary cause of his decision to save the lives of his men; the surrender was accepted by a number of US officers including XIX TAC commanding general Otto Weyland. On a day devoted mainly

to fighter attacks rather than heavy bomber escort, the 16th rounded out with a score of 12 Fw190s by 295 IX TAC and VIII FC P-47s and P-51s operating around Aachen, Alhorn, Kaiserslautern and Mannheim in the late afternoon.

Frantic finale

As the B-17s assigned to Frantic VII took off escorted by the P-51s of the 355th Group on 17 September, 59 P-51s and 72 B-17s of the Frantic VI force returned home. With the completion of the Frantic VII operation, shuttle missions were terminated, due mainly to the fact that the allocated Soviet air bases were so far behind the front lines and because of Stalin's blatant and paranoid distrust of America's intentions in flying the missions. The shuttle missions were a qualified success and the outstanding performance of the P-51 in being able to escort the bombers all the way had undoubtedly reduced losses, but the plan really relied on two factors it lacked — much better weather in Italy and greater Russian co-operation.

The Eighth's fighters were out over Germany to knock down seven enemy interceptors, three Fw190s falling to Lt Ted Lines of the 4th to bring his personal tally to 10. The main heavy bomber effort of the day was, however, in support of Operation 'Market Garden', the attempt by Allied troops to capture a series of bridges leading up to and then across the Rhine at Arnhem; 821 B-17s and 503 fighters attacked flak batteries, airfields and other targets along the routes taken by the transports bearing the paratroops and towing gliders. Sixteen US fighters were

lost, mainly to ground fire.

During the night of 17/18 September the 474th Fighter Group continued its nocturnal intruder campaign with bomb-carrying P-38s.

The weather turned sour on the 18th, the Ninth sending out fewer than 100 fighter sorties. There were casualties, however, and Captain Michael J. Quirk, an 11-victory ace with the 56th Group, was shot down by flak and captured near Würzburg/Seligenstadt aerodrome. Eleven enemy fighters were destroyed by the AAF, four TAC P-47s also being lost in action. Further support for 'Market Garden' involved 12 groups of Eighth Air Force fighters, up to protect B-24s dropping supplies at low altitude. Two fighter groups went down to strafe rail and road traffic in the area and 50 fighters were briefed to attack flak emplacements, this latter mission causing the loss of 16 P-47s of the 56th Group. The highest single-day loss from any one group of the Eighth during the war, this disaster highlighted the danger in

directly attacking flak posts. Overall, the Eighth lost 22 aircraft in the day's Arnhem support operations. On the credit side the 357th got among the opposition to claim 25 German fighters in the Arnhem battle area. Among the victors was Lieutenant Gerald E. Tyler, who became an ace with claims filed for two Bf109s and one Fw190. Other pilots from Eighth Air Force groups destroyed three more enemy aircraft over The Netherlands.

Calls by the Polish Home Army for aerial supply support in their struggle to wrest Warsaw from the Germans were heeded by the Eighth Air Force which dispatched 107 B-24s to the city. In support of the bombers were 64 P-51s of the 355th Fighter Group and these along with the bombers did not return to England but carried on into Russia, despite the termination of the Frantic agreement. All further such operations were cancelled after Stalin refused to allow landing rights to US aircraft following the Warsaw support mission, during which the US fighters shot

Above: Over at Raydon the 353rd Group has also had a good day judging by the grins. Maj Wayne K. Blickenstaff is at far right and behind the pilots is a P-51D-10 of the 350th FS. *J. V. Crow*

down three Bf109s over Warsaw.

Over Hungary on 19 September the remaining Frantic force flew from Italian bases to bomb Szolnok marshalling yard *en route* to England, while 679 B-17s bombed various tactical targets in Germany. Escorted by 240 fighters the bombers were well protected; pilots accounted for 10 enemy fighters, and Lieutenant Thomas D. Schank of the 55th Fighter Group became an ace with a Bf109 shot down near Cologne.

Weather problems prevented the full weight of air support planned for the airborne forces of 'Market Garden', although 72 P-51s from Eighth Air Force groups flew patrols in the area. When more than 100 German fighters were encountered over Arnhem in the afternoon, the P-51s waded in to chop down 22 more of them. Lieutenant Arval J. Robertson of the 357th Group became an ace with his two Bf109s. Major Edwin W. Hiro, CO of the 357th Group, had shot down a Bf109 over Arnhem but he was himself shot down and killed near Vreden.

A day when the weather severely curtailed strategic and tactical operations across much of Europe, 20 September recorded a further effort by Eighth Fighter Command to support Market Garden. Out of 644 fighter sorties flown, the flak claimed five. Most of the succeeding days' fighter missions were to the Arnhem battle area, a magnet for the Luftwaffe fighters supporting their own ground forces which soon took the initiative and had the defenders surrounded. On the 21st, 19 German fighters were destroyed by US fighters, Major Boleslaw 'Mike' Gladych, one of the 'Polish contingent' flying with the 56th Group, getting a pair of Fw190s to bring his score to 18 confirmed. The Wolfpack put up 77 P-47s on Arnhem support on 22 September and lost one more aircraft. In various actions during the 22nd, the TACs covered the withdrawal of the US V Corps from Wallendorf and shot down 10 enemy fighters, their numerous ground-attack sorties sending them to several locations in Germany.

On the 23rd the weather again reduced the scale of operations; the 36th Group moved into A-69 Laon/Athies, while 519 aircraft from VIII and IX Fighter Commands (the latter contributing 40 P-38s) escorted glider-borne reinforcements for the Arnhem operation, now decidedly in jeopardy from aggressive German counter-attacks. One of the 14 UK-based fighters lost was the P-51 flown by Captain Clarence O. Johnson, seven-victory ace of the 352nd Group, who was shot down by a German fighter and killed over Almelo.

There were days when a single fighter unit excelled at a particular operation and 24 September belonged to the 405th Group's Thunderbolts. Called up by ground control to aid a US Third Army unit, the group's P-47s flying initially in two squadron strength found the German tank and truck columns, bombing and strafing them repeatedly despite severe weather and intense ground fire. Later the third squadron went after buildings in the same area, these attacks being designed to block roads and generally 'bottle up' the enemy. Such attacks could be highly effective in that the Germans had little choice but to spend hours clearing away rubble before their vehicles could move.

On 25 September Brest was finally in Allied hands; the port had absorbed numerous medium and heavy bomber attacks and 3,698 fighter-bomber sorties over 23 mission days. This was later judged as a wasteful and time-consuming operation that could have seen the vast airpower effort directed more profitably elsewhere. Strategic and tactical sorties during the day included dive-bombing by P-47s in support of the US First Army.

The following day the 370th Group moved to A-78 Florennes/Juzaine while TAC aircraft smashed fortifications around Metz. On escort to the heavies, VIII Fighter Command pilots shot down six of the enemy while 253 of the command's fighters also supported the forces fighting at Arnhem in company with 67 of IX TAC's P-38s.

Part of the fighter escort to the bombers hitting German targets on 27 September were Mustangs carrying the markings of the 479th Group. Newly converted from P-38s, this was the unit's first P-51 mission on a day which saw 640 escort sorties in total. Claims of 31 were made by VIII FC groups when the Germans intercepted, an additional five going to IX FC units. Captain Donald S. Bryan of the 352nd Group and Lieutenant William R. Beyer of the 361st became aces, the latter adding five Fw190s to his previous single kill to also become another AAF ace in a day.

Bad weather saw the 417 1st Division heavies dispatched from England attacking mainly T/Os rather than the primary, an oil plant at Magdeburg: only 23 B-17s reached this target but the Luftwaffe attacked with a vengeance. Interceptions were concentrated on the B-17s bombing Magdeburg and all 23 bombers shot down were from 1st Division groups. The 646-strong VIII ·Fighter Command escort waded into the Germans and shot down 30 for seven lost. Among the victorious American pilots were Lieutenants George W. Gleason of the 479th Group; Robert H. Ammon of the 339th and Ernest C. Fiebelkorn of the 20th, all of whom returned as aces, Fiebelkorn having accounted for four.

Over the 28/29 September period TAC operations were the usual fare and the 474th again attempted to achieve worthwhile results with its P-38 nocturnal intruder sorties during the night of the 29th/30th. In the event, the results of this and the three previous missions were deemed insignificant and the experiment was abandoned.

The 50th Group moved up to Y-6 Lyons/Bron aerodrome, the 'Y'-prefix denoting a second series of bases in France along with 'A'-prefix bases. On the 29th the Ninth lost one of its groups when the 371st was transferred to XII TAC headquarters and the 67th TRG relocated to A-87 Charleroi. The month ended with weather disrupting operations to a significant degree, there being no reported combats or losses from the fighter support to the heavies groping their way to various targets in Germany.

8 Into the Reich

The first day of October 1944 brought weather bad enough to keep all the Eighth and Ninth Air Force bombers on the ground; on the Continent there were more airfield relocations by the TAC fighter groups. The 474th went to A-78 Florennes/Juzaine, the 404th took its P-47s into A-92 St Trond, formerly a major Luftwaffe night fighter base, and the 36th Group went to A-68 Juvincourt. The 371st Group taking up residence at Y-7 Dole/Tavaux coincided with the 36th Heavy Bombardment Squadron (Radio Counter Measures) being reassigned to VIII Fighter Command; XXIX TAC, formerly operating under the direction of XIX TAC, was made operationally independent within the Ninth Air Force with its headquarters at Arlon. One of this latter TAC's assigned units was the reconstituted 363rd Tactical Reconnaissance Group, which was relieved from a fighter role on 29 August.

On the 2nd the base moves continued with IX TAC itself becoming established at Verviers and the 368th Group moving to A-84 Chièvres. Dispatching 272 heavies in the first major operation of October, the Eighth Air Force targeted industrial objectives in Kassel and Cologne. Other bombers went to Hamm and T/Os while 712 fighters made up the escort. Among them were the P-51s of the 353rd Group, one of the last units in the Eighth to relinquish P-47s with which it had fought a very tough but effective war to date.

Jet surprise

An entirely new phase of aerial warfare began on 2 October when two P-47s of the 365th Fighter Group encountered an enemy aircraft type neither of the pilots had previously seen. What worried them was that the bandit appeared to have a performance superior to their own fighters, as indeed it did — this was the first known clash between AAF fighters and the Messerschmitt 262. With its twin underslung turbojets, wing sweepback and well-streamlined fuselage the sleek new adversary had the potential to dominate aircraft powered by piston engines. This last fact the two P-47s pilots could certainly confirm: in a 'hairy' tailchase, the Me262 was never in a position for the Americans

to fire at it. The encounter ended when the German aircraft crashed near Münster, apparently out of fuel. Despite his guns remaining silent, Lieutenant Valmore J. Beaudreault was officially credited with the first jet kill in history.

Change continued on 3 October with the Eighth Air Force finally relinquishing the P-38 Lightning when the 479th Group, which had previously switched to the P-51, flew its final sorties in the Lockheed fighter. Otherwise it was 'business as usual' for the fighter and bomber pilots based in England. Various industrial targets were allocated to the heavies and 699 fighters made up the escort.

Flak forced down the P-51 flown by Henry W. 'Baby' Brown of the 355th Group whose score had then reached 14.25 victories. In what turned out to be a bad day for the 354th Squadron, Captain Charles Lenfest promptly landed and Brown scrambled up into the narrow cockpit. Gunning the Mustang's engine, Lenfest found to his horror that it had become mired in mud and he and his passenger had little choice but to shut down the engine and await inevitable

Above: Snow was just one of the difficulties faced by the tactical groups as they followed the front across Europe. A 366th Group P-47D-28 of the 390th Squadron displays a barred code letter denoting the second 'B' in the unit. A ground crewman wipes condensation from the canopy to ensure that it does not 'frost over' at altitude. *Robert Brulle*

Above: Refuelling a P-61 required the ground crew to have a head for heights! Believed to be at Coulommiers, the aircraft is a P-61A (42-5560), probably from the 425th NFS. *Imperial War Museum*

capture. Two aces had been lost to the group and although such bold rescue attempts by fighter pilots had been made successfully before, they were officially frowned upon for this very reason — if they failed, two pilots rather than one would be lost.

On 4 October the 365th Group moved into A-84 Chièvres on a day when even the birds were walking and the Eighth Air Force could not fly.

As if to make up for the enforced stand-down, Eighth Air Force headquarters put the entire 1st Bomb Division over German targets on the 5th, crews being able to bomb whatever they found under the protection of 675 fighters. Fighter-bombers of the Ninth offered support to the US XV Corps in the area of the so called West Wall.

In a massive operation that turned out to be the Eighth's largest to date 1,200 bombers were sent off on 6 October to attack a long list of tactical and strategic targets in Germany with 699 supporting fighters. In common with other units, the 20th Group made strafing attacks on the Baltic coast and found five German seaplane bases between Stettin and Lübeck. The pilots proceeded to shoot them up to the tune of 40 aircraft destroyed.

Fighter-bombers supporting the US Third and Seventh Armies attacked rail links around Dorsel and pilots of the 368th

Group shadowed a number of German fighters to an airfield at Breitscheld and shot down two Bf109s in the landing pattern before shooting hell out of the base and claiming 22 more 109s on the ground. In total the two US air forces claimed 22 enemy aircraft in aerial combat as well as those destroyed in ground attacks.

Records continued to be bettered as the Eighth's power over Germany targets became more or less absolute and on 7 October the number of sorties by B-17s and B-24s reached 1,401 effective. There were 521 escort fighters, of which 11 were lost along with 40 bombers. The American fighters claimed 38 German aircraft, Lieutenant Darrell S. Cramer of the 55th Group and Major Arthur F. Jeffrey, CO of the 479th Group's 434th Squadron, becoming aces with victories over conventional fighters. Lieutenant Urban L. Drew's kills were rather more exotic: the 361st Group pilot was credited with the two Me262s he surprised over Achmer aerodrome.

Following tactical missions by the fighter-bombers on the 8th, the fighters all returned safely from their escort duty on the 9th and it was 11 October before a limited number of strategic bomber strikes were mounted again. With XIX TAC moving its headquarters to Nancy on the

12th, a larger scale Eighth Air Force bomber strike was made on German industrial targets with 483 escorts. In combat while defending the bombers Eighth and Ninth Air Force pilots shot down 28 of the enemy. Lieutenant Charles E. 'Chuck' Yeager became an ace with the 357th and an ace in a day when he shot down five Bf109s near Assen in The Netherlands.

The 368th Group had its hands full in preventing the Germans from concentrating for an attack on US infantry positions near Aachen. By flying two missions with a similar purpose the P-47 pilots beat back the threat.

In another command change on 12 October the Ninth Air Force took over administrative control of the XII TAC; earlier transferred from Twelfth Air Force control, this tactical command would work closely with the European TACs as the war fronts drew ever closer.

Operating over Germany on 13 October Eighth and Ninth Air Force fighter pilots shot down 17 German interceptors, bad weather curtailing other operations in the ETO. A larger scale of operations was apparent on the 14th when the bombers were protected by 253 fighters on the day's first mission. In combat with the enemy fighter force Captain Joseph L.

Above: Maj Robert Foy's P-51D parked at Leiston during the bitter winter of 1944/5. *J. V. Crow*

Above: Among the classier names given to fighters was 'Slender, Tender & Tall', a P-51D of the 352nd Group, which in common with numerous others had the sweptback dark blue nose colour to identify the group. *Sam Sox*

Above: Awaiting its tanks if a long-range mission is scheduled is 'Duchess', alias 44-13530 flown by Capt George Arn. *Sam Sox*

Above: Utilising the sign-off line used by his wife in her letters as an aircraft name, Richard A. Peterson of the 357th Group's 364th Squadron was a 15.5-victory ace. This was his second P-51. *Author's collection*

Above: Ken Dahlberg watching the loading of the port wing guns of his 354th Group P-47D (42-29336) during the winter of 1944/5. A 14-victory ace, Dahlberg was shot down in this aircraft on 14 February 1945. *Imperial War Museum*

Lang, an ace of the 4th, was killed in aerial combat near Mannheim. Later a second mission with an escort of 732 fighters recorded little enemy reaction and no US fighter losses.

There was only one fighter engagement on 15 October, but the 78th found plenty of excitement when five Fw190s and an Me262 were shot down by the Thunderbolts. The Ninth's fighters were also busy routing a German Army counter-attack in the area held by the US XIX Corps.

October's bad weather prevented any Eighth or Ninth Air Force operations on the 16th, and on the 17th a command change saw Colonel Benjamin J. Webster succeed Francis Griswold as head of VIII Fighter Command. There were limited number of heavy bomber missions and one escort fighter was lost. Five fighters went down on the following day as the bad weather continued.

The Ninth's TAC fighters were able to operate on the 19th in attacks on tanks which were generally successful. The heavy bombers were again dispatched to report a very small percentage being able to bomb their assigned targets. Two escort fighters failed to return.

On 20 October XIX TAC was able to forestall a German plan to flood the Seille river valley and thus hamper Allied ground operations. The 362nd Group's P-47s breached a dam further up river to in effect drain off the waters of the Étang de Lindre. The TAC fighters also destroyed 20 German fighters in separate actions during the course of the day. Tenaciously braving the elements on the 21st, TAC fighters flew as many support missions as were possible.

The 373rd Group moved to A-89 Le Culot on 22 October and the 365th Group had a successful afternoon mission; clashing with German fighters, the P-47 pilots of the Hell Hawks claimed 22 shot down out of a total of 24. The XXIX TAC moved its HQ to Maastricht to join the US Ninth Army HQ and the 48th and 404th Fighter Groups came under control of XXIX TAC.

On 23 October the 36th Group moved into A-89 Le Culot with the 48th moving to A-92 St Trond but otherwise the entire Ninth Air Force remained on the ground due to the weather, a situation that also prevailed on the 24th, although 379 fighters of the Eighth were out attacking industrial targets in Germany, losing seven aircraft to ground fire.

Weather still prevented operations on the 25th, although the 1st Tactical Air Force (TAF) was formed as a 'field' organisation to fly tactical missions in the south in support of French forces and the US Seventh Army. Some improvement in the weather enabled the Eighth to renew its heavy bomber campaign against German targets of various kinds, there being little interference from the Germans and scant employment for the escort. Ninth Air Force fighters flew on the 26th and some areas of Germany were clear enough for the Eighth's bombers to strike, again without any reaction from the Luftwaffe.

On 28 October the 367th Group moved into A-68 Juvincourt and on escort missions to a bomber effort that was way below average, the fighters found no combat. The Ninth did, however, and in two separate engagements the fighters destroyed seven.

On 29 October the 363rd Group's P-51s also moved to Le Culot, while the Ninth got into air combat with the Germans and claimed 21; Capt Harry E. Fisk and Lt Bruce W. Carr of the 354th Group became aces with three and two Bf109 claims respectively. Despite launching

a massive heavy bomber strike comprising 1,300 aircraft, the Eighth had to concede to the bad weather, which allowed only 139 B-24s to get through to the primary target, two oil refineries in Hamburg.

Up to this time many of the older VIII Fighter Command hands had been continually flying, but losses in the type of higher risk strafing missions currently being flown forced higher authority to ground valuable commanders. Colonel Don Blakeslee was a victim of this policy. After landing from a 30 October mission — estimated to have been at least the 350th sortie he had flown — a transfer order to a desk job with the 65th Fighter Wing could not be ignored. Within hours the danger of continuing to fly combat 'above and beyond' the call of duty was heavily underscored. 'Hub' Zemke, Blakeslee's contemporary, outstanding leader and former boss of the famed Wolfpack, went down over Germany. Having transferred to the 479th Group to offer his experience, the 17.75-victory ace had succumbed not to the enemy but the elements. High altitude winds had ripped his P-51 apart in thunderclouds and Zemke bailed out to become a PoW.

The blanket of cloud, rain and thunderstorms over Europe did not abate as the last day of October caused another general stand-down of most of the tactical and strategic air forces in the ETO (European Theater of Operations) — and indeed the MTO (Mediterranean Theater of Operations), as the phrase 'sunny Italy' had for some time had a hollow ring. The theatre's prevailing weather had rarely lived up to expectations in terms of enabling the Fifteenth Air Force to be used to its full potential.

As November 1944 began, one of the first changes was the appointment of Colonel Kyle L. Riddle to fill Zemke's shoes as CO of the 479th Group. Riddle had plenty of experience on both sides of the lines. Having evaded capture when he was shot down on 10 August, he had returned to the group and become Zemke's executive officer.

As ever the Ninth Air Force all but ignored the weather to put up sorties vital to the well-being of the ground forces. On the 1st the fighters attacked rail lines in and around the battle area as the Allied armies pushed towards the borders of the Reich.

Above: Poor quality but interesting view of Dalhberg's P-47D coded FT-O. The skull and crossbones on a yellow cowling was applied to most of the 353rd Squadron's aircraft — probably to help raise morale while its Mustangs were absent! *Steve Blake*

As of 1 November IX Fighter Command was composed of the following units:

IX Tactical Air Command:
70th Fighter Wing
365th, 366th, 367th, 368th, 370th and 474th Fighter Groups
plus 67th TRG and 422nd NFS

XIX Tactical Air Command:
100th Fighter Wing
354th, 358th, 362nd, 405th and 406th Fighter Groups
plus 10th PRG and 425th NFS

XXIX Tactical Air Command:
84th Fighter Wing
36th and 48th Fighter Groups
303rd Fighter Wing
373rd and 404th Fighter Groups plus 363rd TRG

1st Tactical Air Force:
50th and 371st Fighter Groups
(the 371st was a Ninth AF unit which then came under XII TAC control)

Long-range escort missions were possible on 1 November, although the weather front that had curtailed operations for weeks continued to prevail. On 2 November the heavies struck oil targets in Germany and the fiercest air battles since September developed.

Some 400 German interceptors attacked the bombers and 40 were lost; of the 873 escorts there were 16 downed. But the Germans' success paled in comparison with their losses — the US escort counted 136 destroyed for a new record figure. The day's aces were Captain Donald S. Bryan of the 352nd with five and Lieutenant James J. Pascoe of the 364th Group with two downed. Lieutenant Henry Miklajcyk of the 352nd was among the pilots lost when he went down near Halle. The entire VIII Fighter Command participated in air combats on a massive scale with the enemy frantically defending Merseburg, Bielefeld, Sterkrade and Castrup/Rauxel.

In another day of little action

3 November saw the 64th Fighter Wing headquarters transferred from the Twelfth Air Force to the Ninth, with a new command post at Ludres. A heavy bomber strike on the 4th had an escort of 768 VIII FC fighters and little opposition materialised in the air. Air support to ground forces was provided by the Ninth, which carried out ground attacks on targets in the Aachen area. A similar pattern continued the following day. The heavies attacking German targets did so virtually unopposed while the TACs maintained their links with the ground forces and flew missions as required. Bad weather reduced much of the ETO air activity on the Continent and in England, but on 8 November the US Third Army, supported by XIX TAC units, began Operation 'Madison', an effort to break the German-held line centred on forts at Metz and to push through to the Rhine.

Attacking throughout the day, the fighter-bombers flew 389 effective sorties which included the elimination of German

Above: A blown nosewheel tyre could cause a P-38 to nose-over suddenly, although the oleo was strong, allowing take-offs from surprisingly rough airfields. This J model of the 429th Squadron, 474th Group, would be quickly repaired. *Imperial War Museum*

Right: Tucking up its wheels at the start of another ground-attack mission, this P-47D of the 361st Squadron, 356th Group, also carried a 'flat' belly tank. It was being flown by Lt George Yocum. *J. Lambert*

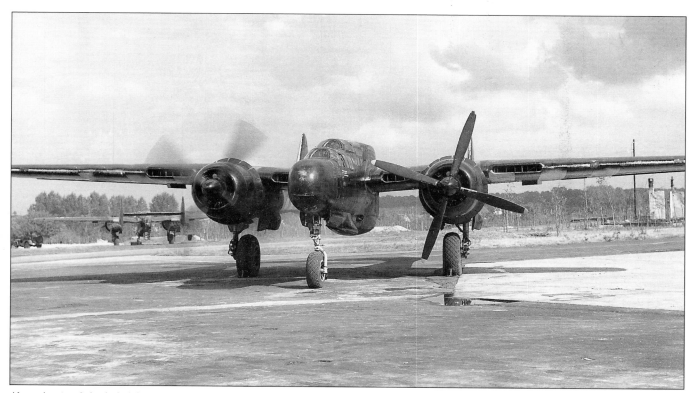

Above: An aircraft that looked dramatic and deadly from any angle, the P-61 gave the USAAF valuable data on nocturnal interception by radar. This one was warming up for a mission from its French base on 27 September 1944. *USAF*

Above: 'Touch of Texas' was a strikingly marked P-47D from the 510th Squadron, 405th Group. *J. Lambert*

Army command posts by the P-47s of the 405th Group. The result was that part of the Third Army was able to ford the Seille river at three points. Among the air casualties was Captain Edward E. Hunt, a P-51 ace with the 354th Group, whose aircraft went into the ground near Mericourt for reasons unknown.

While the TAC fighters flew their support sorties, those of the Eighth escorted the bombers and for the first time in days, found some action. By shooting down 12 enemy fighters the American pilots kept bomber losses down to a modest three, although 11 of their own were listed as missing in action. Among the pilots whose victories that day put them into the ranks of the aces or increased their scores were Captain Richard A. Peterson of the 357th, whose single Bf109 kill gave him a total of 15.5 confirmed, and Lieutenant Joseph Z. Matte of the 362nd who shot down an Fw190 and probably two others for his total of five.

On 9 November 'Madison' had the support of the heavy bombers which pounded the defences around Metz. The mediums joined in as well, but their sorties were curtailed by bad weather which, although also something of a hazard to low altitude attacks, did not prevent the XIX TAC from sending out P-47s to complete 162 effective sorties in the Metz area.

More indirect support for the troops in the front line was provided by attacks on marshalling yards at Düren in Germany.

Thanks to these timely air support sorties, 'Madison' was deemed a success when the Third Army was able to make further crossings of the Moselle and to capture several forts, towns and villages in the German defensive area.

Whenever the weather allowed, the Eighth invariably maintained the pressure on Germany by sending out heavy bomber missions and a fighter escort, usually one with a high ratio of fighters to bombers. Such operations were flown on 9, 10 and 11 November and on each of the three days, losses were acceptably low, those aircraft that were listed as MIA being more often than not the victims of flak rather than enemy fighters.

The weather then began to get progressively worse and all air forces were at near total stand-down for four days. Not until 16 November did air operations pick up again, when the tactical fighters, trying to maintain the momentum of the advance by the US First and Ninth Armies, attacked German positions around Aachen as part of Operation 'Queen'. This operation drew heavily on the groups which sent out 212 and 137 fighters from

IX and XXIX TACs respectively. Having proved that saturation bombing could work well in the previous Operation 'Cobra', 'Queen' could not achieve as much and would drag on for four weeks when other events forced it to be curtailed.

Such support for the army continued on the 18th and 19th while strategic strikes on Germany brought the Luftwaffe up to battle. Enemy opposition to heavy bomber missions now held the additional threat of a sudden attack by jet fighters and to help neutralise that danger, VIII FC fighters strafed their airfields and destroyed 14 Me262s on 18 November. About 70 fighters were noted attempting to attack the bombers, and the US pilots claimed 24 shot down in return for seven of their own. Captain Dale E. Shafer, Jr, of the 339th Group's 503rd Squadron got the better of a Bf109 to become an ace, as did Captain Evan M. Johnson of the 505th. Captain Michael J. Jackson of the 56th also brought his score to five, his victim being an Fw190.

During attacks in Germany the Ninth's fighters destroyed 11 enemy fighters on the 19th, continuing as they had on several previous occasions, to beat the daily scores of their colleagues primarily engaged on escort duty. Opposition by the

Right:
'Put it there!' Celebrating pilots of the 353rd Group at Raydon. *J. V. Crow*

Below:
Late-war flamboyance in the 353rd Group was to extend the black and yellow nose checks on its Mustangs, as this example at Raydon also shows. *J. V. Crow*

Luftwaffe to USAAF sorties was uneven, for a number of reasons. There was increased fighter action on 21 November when the heavies bombed synthetic oil targets in various locations. The output from such plants was now of vital importance to the German war effort and, although fighter reaction could rarely be accurately predicted, the AAF had previous experience of how violently this vital industry could be defended. Much more reliable was the flak which usually gave the bombers a hot reception at most targets but more particularly those associated with the lifeblood of the German war machine.

Patrolling over one of the plants at Merseburg, Lieutenant Claude J. Crenshaw of the 359th Group became an ace when he shot down four Fw190s. In the same general area were Mustangs of the 352nd Group. Captain William T. Whisner, who already had 4.5 kills to his name, became an ace in a day with a score of at least five Focke-Wulfs and a couple of probables for good measure.

After limited air action, mainly as a result of bad weather on 22, 23 and 24 November, the Ninth recorded some

reaction by the Luftwaffe to its fighter-bomber strikes on the 25th, during which the Americans claimed another 12 enemy aircraft destroyed. These were invariably interceptor fighters bent on driving the AAF aircraft away from their own hard-pressed ground forces — which they usually failed to do. The Eighth sent out a relatively modest number of heavy bombers that day, but a new screening force comprising aircraft of the 36th BS was included. Carrying equipment designed to jam German ground radars, the squadron completed a successful combat debut to become an integral part of future bomber missions. Fighter-bombers continued to harry German defensive positions and, despite the weather, which was definitely getting worse, there seemed little question that the Allies could dictate the future progress of the war in the West on their terms.

An oil plant at Misburg was the main objective for the Eighth's B-24s on 26 November, although the larger part of the bomber force was briefed for tactical targets in a day of large scale action that included numerous US fighter sorties. The Luftwaffe was also up in force and the

Eighth's pilots reported 123 enemy fighters downed as well as an He111. New aces were from two units: Captain Frederick R. Haviland, Jr, and Lieutenant Royce W. Priest of the 355th Group, and Lieutenants Lester C. March and J. S. Daniell, both of the 339th.

More combat success came on the night of 26/27 November when the 422nd NFS sent 11 P-61s to attack a V-weapon site. During the intruder mission one of the crews also shot down an enemy aircraft while returning to base — but a dearth of airborne targets on most nights led to a gradual but increasing deployment of the Black Widow in a nocturnal attack role. Able to carry a useful weight of ordnance including bombs and rockets, the big twins also adopted the practice of strafing drop tanks released on targets to douse them in gasoline. Napalm bombs were also being manufactured and these came into service shortly after the P-61 made its debut in Europe.

For some time the fighter-bombers had been attacking more strategic targets and on 27 November VIII Fighter Command sent 460 of them to four oil centres in northern and central Germany. Dive-

Above: Parked on a steel mat hardstand a P-47D of the 366th Group with a portrait of the pilot's lady on the cowl awaits the next call to arms. *Robert Brulle*

bombing and strafing such heavily defended areas was even more hazardous for fighters than it was for the heavies, and 12 of them were lost in this attack. While the Ninth's fighters hit ground objectives in western Germany, other US fighters roved across the Reich and shot down 95 enemy aircraft including an He111. Captain Walter E. Starck of the 352nd Group had only a brief moment of glory: having destroyed three Bf109s to bring his score to seven, he was shot down and captured.

Better luck attended Lieutenant Charles J. Cesky flying a 353rd Group P-51. His single Bf109 made him an ace and he returned home to celebrate. Lieutenant Frank L. Gailer, Jr, of the 357th got two Fw190s to elevate himself to the ranks of aces, while Captain 'Chuck' Yeager ran his score up to a final tally of 11.5 by shooting down four Fw190s in the vicinity of Magdeburg. Captain Edward H. Beavers, Jr, of the 339th who had become an ace

only the day before, was shot down and killed by the Berlin flak.

Two pilots of the 359th Group had an amazing experience. After the rest of the group had abandoned the mission due to the bad weather Captain Ray S. Wetmore and Lieutenant Robert M. York continued into Germany. At around 13.00 hours they came upon a formation of enemy fighters. There seemed to be a great many of them but the two Mustangs went into action. Dogfighting with the Germans, Wetmore and York realised that the odds were a little stacked against them — two to 200! Despite this the intrepid pair fired off all their ammunition before beating it back to England. In the course of the combat Wetmore claimed three Bf109s to bring his score to 13.25 so far, while York's tally was three plus a probable.

After this hectic day of action there was little further contact with the Luftwaffe before the end of November; despite the heavy bombers attacking German oil targets

on the 29th and 30th under heavy escort, the enemy reaction was limited. One pilot who found combat was Lieutenant-Colonel Willie O. Jackson, Jr, CO of the 352nd Group, who made ace by shooting down a Bf109 near Chemnitz on the 30th.

For some time the Eighth had been sending out P-51s in a scouting role. Forming part of the regular escort, the pilots of these aircraft had the responsibility of checking weather conditions along the routes taken by the bombers. Experienced pilots drawn from the fighter groups — and flying Mustangs borrowed from their inventories — became an important part of the increasingly sophisticated tactics of the long-range war. That there were eventually three scouting forces in the Eighth is indicative of how important their work was, so it was unfortunate that a number of these Mustangs and their experienced pilots went down during some of the missions in November, according to AAF records.

Above: Throughout the gruelling European air-ground campaign, tactical reconnaissance was vital and the F-6 version of the P-51 made the ideal combination of camera platform and fighter. Capt V. J. Gentzler (*left*) shows his aircraft to P/O Robert Hicks, RAF, and recon Lightning pilot Commandant Rene Savoille of the First French Air Corps during the winter of 1944/5. *Imperial War Museum*

Above: With a light-coloured nose incorporating a thin (barely visible) sharkmouth, a P-38J (coded 9D-F) from the 401st Squadron, 370th Group about to touch down at Florennes with a dead engine following a strafing mission. The SHAEF Field Press Censor released the photo on 4 December 1944.
Imperial War Museum

December 1944

On 1 December the 354th Fighter Group moved to A-98 Rosières while other tactical sorties were flown in support of ground forces. A heavy bomber mission on the 2nd resulted in air combat, during which Major Paul A. Conger, CO of the 63rd FS, 56th Group, became an ace by destroying two Bf109s. Tactical fighters, plus the VIII FC groups, assisted the US Army's thrust into Hürtgen Forest by bombing and strafing various enemy-held areas.

It was not until 5 December that large scale air combat again took place over Germany and on that occasion the USAAF fighter pilots claimed 91 enemy machines destroyed. This was not an untypical one-sided score at that stage of the war: having lost the initiative, the Germans continued doggedly to attempt interceptions with too few aircraft, and these were flown in the main by inexperienced pilots. This was an arena where enthusiasm and nationalistic pride were no substitute for a few thousand hours at the controls of a Bf109 or Fw190, but Germany's war situation had deteriorated far beyond offering young men anything like an ideal training period before they were committed to battle.

The day began at 00.40 hours with a P-61 of the 422nd NFS shooting down an He111. When the night-fighters returned the morning's multiple bomber mission by 541 B-17s and B-24s was well advanced; their targets included the Berlin/Tegel tank factory, marshalling yards at Münster and a long list of T/Os. On the fighter bases similar activity was evident as 796 escorts were fuelled and armed.

Reaction by the Luftwaffe came as the bombers crossed the German border and a running battle covering a vast area developed as the enemy attacked the bomber boxes at various times, heights and directions. The first encounters took place shortly before 10.30 hours, Captain Merle M. Coons of the 55th Group shooting down an Fw190 and Bf109 near Berlin at 10.45 hours to become an ace with the baseline score of five.

Captain Clarence 'Bud' Anderson of the 357th brought his final tally to 16.25, confirmed with an Fw190 near Berlin, and Major William J. Hovde of the 355th

brought his score to 10.5 with a Bf109 and four Fw190s to also make him an ace in a day. To complete his day, Hovde shared in finishing off a fifth Fw190 over Berlin.

Another German pilot who went down over the big city was the victim of Captain William F. Wilson of the 364th Group, the kill making him an ace with five. Captain William R. Scheible, a staff officer with the 356th Group, more than proved he was as adept at the controls of a P-51 as he was behind a desk with two Fw190s destroyed. He, too, thus became an ace. Another pilot in the 356th, Captain Don Strait, duplicated other pilots with a pair of Fw190s to raise his own score to five.

The 4th's 'Deacon' Hively, then a major, also claimed a Focke-Wulf to add to his previous kills and came back with a total of 12, his final score. He went home in January 1945. Lieutenant-Colonel John H. Lowell, then commanding the 384th Squadron of the 364th Group, shot down three Fw190s, while Captain William F.

Tanner of the 353rd Group got one. Both pilots became aces on 5 December.

With the winter weather biting there was little Allied air activity on the Western Front for three days, but on 9 December the conditions allowed 381 B-17s and their escort of 247 fighters to attack targets in the Stuttgart area. The fighters also went out to strafe T/Os. A larger scale effort on the 10th saw 173 Liberators and 277 B-17s attacking marshalling yards at Bingen and Koblenz with a strong escort numbering 535 fighters. Little reaction by the Luftwaffe was observed.

The bombers were able to hit German targets almost with impunity on the 11th and 12th as, apart from the ever-present flak which invariably claimed aircraft and a percentage of the crews, enemy interceptors failed to materialise. In this period the tactical fighters were far from idle; used now to terrible weather, poor servicing facilities and living quarters best described as primitive, the men of the Ninth Air Force did not let such hardships stand in the way of their primary mission. Dividing their time between ground support to American troops and targets of a more strategic nature, the fighter-bomber pilots also continued their war of attrition against the Luftwaffe. They destroyed another 13 enemy fighters on 12 December.

But while the appalling weather on some winter days in 1944 defeated even the rugged fighter groups of the Ninth, there was rarely if ever a 24-hour period when absolutely nothing happened. One day when things got very close to that situation was 13 December, when virtually nothing was able to take off apart from the equally intrepid tactical medium bombers. To make matters even more difficult for the AAF in terms of maintaining pressure on the Germans in the West was the fact that the weather front often stretched right down through Italy, keeping the Fifteenth on the ground as well as the Eighth in England. If the 13th had been bad, the 14th was marginally worse, although on a day when the tactical bombers remained grounded, some TAC fighter sorties were possible.

On 15 December the skies cleared enough for a two-pronged attack comprising forces of 318 and 327 B-17s striking objectives at Kassel and Hanover respectively, although the 528 fighter pilots flying the escort were again under-employed. The Ninth Air Force meanwhile reduced the enemy's stocks of fuel, ammunition and supplies by bombing and strafing dumps in local 'defended areas'.

The Germans strike back

A quiet front line was suddenly shattered into life on 16 December when Gerd von Rundstedt's tanks came charging through the Ardennes quickly to overpower thinly defended US First Army positions. Overhead, the enemy fighter force seemed to have been given a new lease of life as numerous contacts were reported by Allied aircraft. This was not surprising as the Luftwaffe had marshalled 1,350 fighters and bombers to support the counter-attack. Exploiting the bad weather to the utmost, the enemy broke through the front line to drive a salient deep into what had been Allied-held territory for some time.

First reaction to the crisis was by Ninth Air Force fighter-bombers, which carried out the initial attacks on a variety of targets; the medium bombers were grounded and the Eighth was hampered by the conditions over Stuttgart where 81 B-17s (out of 236) bombed marshalling yards while another 33 attacked Bietigheim town.

Only slowly did the Allies become aware of the size of the threat which developed into a series of actions collectively known as the Battle of the Bulge. Air reconnaissance was hampered by the weather in much the same way as the rest of the tactical air forces and an early warning of the attack could not be given. During the night of 16/17 December the 422nd Squadron's P-61s found the enemy over eastern Belgium and western Germany. The night-fighters locked onto their targets and came home with claims of five enemy aircraft destroyed.

While IX and XIX TAC fighter-bombers did what they could with 647 effective sorties, few of these were flown into the most contested areas of the weathered-in Ardennes region. The pilots soon found unexpected opposition from the Luftwaffe fighter force. However, air combat brought not an aerial rout of the Americans but an impressive total of 80 victories. Among those who claimed was Captain John H. Hoefker of the 15th Recon Squadron, whose Fw190 kill made him an ace. Flying the F-6 version of the P-51, Hoefker would later emerge as the top recon ace in the ETO. The Ninth's efforts also saw the pilots claim the destruction of several hundred German Army vehicles, for a cost of 16 fighters.

It was two pilots of the 67th TacRecon Group carrying out a very hazardous mission on the 18th who enabled the US Army to counter a key part of the German advance. Flying through dense cloud with a very low ceiling, the F-6s brought back evidence of a strong enemy armoured column on a road near Stavelot. Reacting quickly, IX TAC sent the 365th and 368th Fighter Groups off to attack the column continuously to the point where it was rendered totally ineffective. Seven four-ship missions were flown until it was too dark for the pilots to see anything, during which the P-47s plunged into valleys, dodged flak and small arms fire, and released their bombs. They knocked out about 32 of the 60 tanks in the column, plus 56 out of 200 trucks.

Over Germany on the 18th, the Eighth continued to attack numerous objectives on its regular strategic list, although this would soon change almost entirely to tactical battlefield support strikes for the duration of the emergency in the Ardennes. There were no bomber losses but two of the 362 fighters comprising the escort failed to return. A sweep by the fighters from England also found relatively little action, although claims for 10 kills were filed. The unusual result was that all of them were credited to only two pilots; members of the 359th Group, they both became aces in a day. With five Fw190s apiece, Lieutenants David B. Archibald and Paul E. Olson of the 368th Squadron were unable to celebrate their new ace status together as Olson was shot down shortly afterwards and taken prisoner.

Flying as part of the day's heavy bomber escort were the P-38s of the 474th Group, and two pilots of the 429th Squadron also became aces: Lieutenants Robert C. Milliken and Lenton F. Kirkland, Jr got respectively one and two Bf109s to reach the five mark.

The tactical fighters had their hands full when, in the course of flying 500 sorties, the US pilots met slightly more than that number of German fighters, which was unprecedented. A series of dogfights resulted in 40 German aircraft going down, and although the quantity available to the Luftwaffe had apparently improved, the US pilots noted that their quality was still somewhat lacking.

With the Germans still advancing — and their weather ally still preventing a full response from Allied airpower — XXIX TAC took the precaution of pulling its headquarters out of Maastricht on the 19th and re-establishing it at St Trond. Whatever the weather brought, some elements of the Ninth Air Force's fighter strength made every effort to fly as on the 19th; if the pressure, however limited it was, could be maintained then the Germans would find their risky venture too costly.

Fifteen more enemy fighters were shot down by pilots of Eighth and Ninth Air Force groups, but otherwise the operational effort was severely limited by the conditions. Hardly any sorties were flown on the Western Front on 20 or 21

December — when IX and XXIX TACs were temporarily transferred to the control of the RAF's Second Tactical Air Force.

The break

Only a few sorties were possible on the 22nd and the Ardennes offensive rolled on, with the German troops keeping a watchful eye on the skies. They knew only too well what to expect if the skies cleared. For the entirely opposite reason, Allied air commanders studied the latest weather reports. And then — the weather did break for the first time in a week. Dawn on 23 December brought clear skies and immediately three XIX TAC fighter

groups were out, covering 260 C-47 Skytrains flying a mercy mission to deliver vital supplies to men of the 101st Airborne Division cut off at Bastogne.

Flying into Belgium from England that morning was the Eighth's 352nd Fighter Group, which took its P-51Ds to A-84 Chièvres. The three squadrons of 'blue-nose' P-51s that arrived from Bodney were followed by the three belonging to the 361st from Little Walden, which moved to France a short time later. The squadrons from England were to boost the air defence strength of the Ninth Air Force at a critical time. And nine days later this move was to pay dividends.

Echelon formation of the 61st Fighter Squadron showing the marked contrast between camouflage and natural metal finish (NMF) aircraft. From left to right, the pilots were: Steven Gerick, Robert J. Keen, Eugene Barnum and Robert J. Rankin — but don't assume they were all flying 'their' aircraft at the time of the photo!
Paul Conger

9 Jet Nemesis

The sheer scale of the air fighting over the Ardennes on 23 December led inevitably to Allied casualties: the 474th Fighter Group lost Lt Lenton Kirkland, the recent ace in the 429th Fighter Squadron, who was killed when his P-38 was downed by flak near Liège. With the weather clear, the Ninth sent out 696 effective sorties, most of them in direct support to US ground forces who were fighting desperately in the Bulge area to stop German tanks.

There was considerable reaction from the Luftwaffe to these sorties and 19 US fighters were lost to all causes during the day; the light flak, as ever, was deadly. But the Eighth and Ninth had an amazing run of aerial victories, combat culminating in claims for 133 enemy fighters shot down. While the Luftwaffe had managed to mount more sorties in one day than it had been able to for months, pilot skill had hardly had time to improve. Instances

where enemy pilots chose to abandon their aircraft at the very sight of US fighters increased during the last months of the war.

While the German single-seaters could be lethal in highly skilled hands, there were now far fewer of them and the Americans generally enjoyed a significant edge, not only in terms of equipment but also pilot experience and tactics. Numbers were not always the decisive factor, as the ratio of US kills to losses tends to show. The AAF also had the advantage of knowing within broad limits how rank and file German fighter pilots tended to react in combat, the limits of the aircraft they flew and the most effective tactics needed to beat them. On the ground, US Army AA units represented an additional hazard to the Luftwaffe.

The 23rd nevertheless saw the highest number of victories ever claimed by German fighters against US medium bombers, principally the B-26 Marauder.

Intercepting the unescorted mediums in the act of attacking several bridge targets, the Jagdflieger accounted for 16 aircraft out of 35 lost that day. German pilots flew an estimated 800 sorties, fighter and intruder patrols covering those areas of western Germany and eastern Belgium where their ground forces were advancing. Between 06.15 and 16.00 hours the skies were full of fighters and the occasional Ju88, several Gruppen of which flew pathfinder and nocturnal attack sorties during the period. One of the latter was included in the American combat claims for the day.

Colonel Dave Schilling, commanding the Wolfpack,' shot down three Bf109s and two Fw190s to become an ace in a day during a sweep over Euskirchen aerodrome. These claims brought his score to 22.5 which was to be his final total during the war. Another original member of the 56th was Major Harold E. Comstock, who then commanded the 63rd

Above: Billy Hovde's 355th Group Mustangs were all named 'Ole' and this was number six. The inscription below the exhausts is Hovde's name and rank in Russian. *Author's collection*

Squadron. He came home with two Fw190s to his credit and resulting ace status. This honour was shared by Captain Felix D. Williamson of the 62nd Squadron who destroyed a Bf109 and Fw190, also over Euskirchen.

Mustangs were now very much in the majority in Eighth Air Force groups and they, too, had an outstanding day. Four Bf109s shot down by Lieutenant James M. Fowle of the 384th Squadron, 364th Group, made him an ace, and Major George F. Ceullers, CO of the same group's 383rd Squadron, duplicated the feat with his four Bf109s. Flying the flag for the Ninth, Lieutenant David L. King of the 373rd Group shot down two Bf109s to become an ace.

Heavy bomber sorties amounted to 397 and, as their targets were way behind the new front lines, the skies were all but clear of enemy fighters, which were heavily occupied elsewhere. Eighth Fighter Command also sent out 163 fighter-bomber sorties in addition to covering the heavies with 592 more.

Although 23 December's 'maximum effort' by the Allied air forces did not stop the German advance, it significantly hampered progress, disrupted logistics and wreaked havoc on armoured columns wherever they were found. The aerial counter-offensive continued on the 24th as the weather again brought clear skies. Support sorties extended into Luxembourg, the Ninth Air Force reporting 1,157 effective fighter-bomber sorties throughout the day. These resulted in the destruction of 736 motor vehicles, 167 railway wagons, tanks and artillery pieces; numerous German troops were killed or wounded by relentless air attacks which had a demoralising effect on those who managed to survive.

Air combat began around 01.50 hours and continued until 19.35. In that time the Eighth and Ninth Air Force fighters accounted for 95 enemy aircraft, the groups involved including the Eighth's 55th, 357th, 359th and 364th, all of which had pilots who became aces. Lieutenant William J. Sykes of the 364th shot down a Bf109 for his fifth before himself being shot down and taken prisoner; Lieutenant Russel C. Haworth of the 55th also got a Bf109 for his fifth kill, while Lieutenant Otto D. Jenkins of the 357th became an ace when he shot down four Fw190s to add to his existing four, bringing him up to 8.5. Another

Above: Pilot — later author — Bob Brulle squatting on the wheel of a P-47 with a pair of HVARs at his shoulder. The launchers for these rockets had to be located directly below the ejection chutes for the shell casings and links of the gun ammunition. The rockets consequently had to be fired before the guns could be used. *Robert Brulle*

357th pilot, Lieutenant John A. Kirla, knocked down three Fw190s to raise his score to ace status, and Captain William R. Hodges of the 359th knocked down a single Fw190 for his fifth.

Clearer skies also enabled the Eighth to make maximum use of its B-17s and B-24s, there being 1,874 aircraft out over German targets. The Americans were joined by RAF Bomber Command which flew 800 sorties to make Christmas Eve 1944 the largest Allied heavy bomber operational day of the entire war. Escort was provided by 813 fighters and a wide range of tactical targets throughout western Germany were attacked to isolate the frontline troops from their supplies and reinforcements.

On the 25th a not entirely unknown hazard to tactical air operations was

brutally brought home to Eighth Fighter Command which had to report that George Preddy, leading fighter ace in the ETO still flying combat, had been shot down by 'friendly' ground fire. At 12.33 hours, moments after he shot down two Bf109s, Preddy was flying at low altitude chasing an Fw190 and happened to pass over several tracked US AA guns, which let fly at the Messerschmitts — and Preddy's pursuing P-51K. With mere seconds to sight and fire, the GIs were spot on target — the wrong one. Preddy, then CO of the 328th Squadron, received fatal wounds before the American gunners recognised their mistake and stopped firing. The Mustang came down in a field about 1,000 yards from the gun unit where rescuers found the ace to be dead in his seat. With his score frozen at 26.833,

Above: The last Eighth Air Force unit to convert from P-47s to Mustangs was the 78th, represented here by an 82nd Squadron P-51D model named 'Miss Pam'. *Author's collection*

Above: Bombs that inadvertently detached themselves from racks and detonated usually resulted in destruction of the carrier aircraft, as this 'after' view of Jim Kean's P-47D of the 354th Group's 353rd Squadron shows. *S. Blake*

George Preddy's victory tally was second only to that of Robert S. Johnson (27) who had returned home, and third after 'Gabby' Gabreski, the leading ETO ace then a PoW.

Despite this tragedy, the war had to go on and in air battles during the course of a day that would otherwise have been spent in vastly different activities, American pilots destroyed another 80 enemy aircraft in morning skirmishes above the Allied front line redrawn by von Rundstedt's Panzers. Another day of aces ensued, led by Captain William J. Stangel of the 352nd Group who had destroyed two 109s to reach that coveted position during a morning mission; Lieutenant Robert E. Welch of the 55th also got two Bf109s and Major Pierce McKennon of the 4th secured his twelfth and last kill by rounding up earlier percentage scores with a final half share in an Fw190. Lieutenant-Colonel Don Baccus of the 359th saw his fifth, a Bf109, fall near Bonn and Major Fred Glover's single Bf109 kill brought his score to 10.333, placing him among the leading aces of the 4th Group.

Heavy bombers continued their pounding of German targets west of the Rhine, and the Ninth's mediums, also taking advantage of the better weather, added their weight to the counter thrusts to contain what turned out to be the last major German offensive in the West. Even by the end of Christmas Day the effects of Allied air attack were being felt, with definite signs that the Ardennes operation was running out of impetus west of the Maas. No respite was given to the enemy and on the 26th the tactical and strategic bombers were out braving the weather which was once again closing in. Glider-borne supplies aided the US troops cut off at Bastogne and the 70 VIII Fighter Command P-51s of the 352nd and 361st, which were temporarily assigned to the Ninth, attacked targets in eastern Belgium, two Mustangs being lost.

As the 352nd was complying with the orders of the day, German fighters appeared and Lieutenant Duerr 'H' Schuh shot down three Bf109s to become another blue-nosers ace. Sharing the heavy bomber escort duty that day, the yellow-nosed Mustangs of the 361st Group included that flown by Lieutenant George A. Vanden Heuval. He lined up an Fw190 and shot it down near Merzig, followed shortly afterwards by a second 190 which George

shared with another pilot; he, too, was an ace subject to confirmation of the kill.

It was much later in the day, at around 22.10 hours, when Lieutenant Paul A. Smith brought his P-61 into a good firing position and destroyed a Ju188, which went down in the vicinity of St Vith. Continuing his patrol, Smith and his radar operator, Lieutenant Robert E. Tierney, stalked a second Ju188 and by 22.53 hours he had become an ace by also dispatching this second enemy bomber.

In another day of intense fighter activity over the continent, 27 December resulted in 73 more Luftwaffe losses at the hands of USAAF fighters. The record of AAF aces created during the Battle of the Bulge extended by a further five.

Captain Ernest E. Bankey, Jr, another of the Eighth's flying staff officers and assigned to the 364th Group, became an

ace in a day with his tally of four Fw190s and a Bf109, to bring his score to 7.5 confirmed. Captain Gilbert L. Jamison, also of the 364th, was only a half credit behind Bankey and achieved ace status with three Fw190s, to bring his total to a personal seven. Lieutenant Earl R. Lazear's single Bf109 made him an ace in the 352nd Group and Lieutenant Raymond H. Littge achieved his in rather more spectacular fashion with three Fw190s. The 352nd Group was also able to add the name of Major William T. Halton to the ace list. CO of the 352nd Squadron, he shot down three Bf109s and shared a fourth to bring his score to 7.5.

In a reshuffle designed to equalise the fighter forces available on both northern and southern sectors of the Bulge areas, the Ninth's 365th, 367th and 368th Groups flying P-47s were placed under the

Above: Bright identity markings were applied to most of the 354th Group's aircraft during its P-47D period, the 355th Squadron using a pattern of blue diamonds. *S. Blake*

operational control of XIX TAC in the south. This involved the 365th moving to Y-34 Metz/Frescati and the 368th to A-68 Juvincourt. To provide the necessary PR coverage for IX TAC, the 363rd TacR Group sent its 160th and 161st Squadrons to A-94 Conflans.

Freezing fog descended on the bases in England to frustrate numerous heavy bomber sorties, but 572 Fortresses and Liberators did manage to reach Germany and attack various targets. Of the 193 escort fighters, five were lost along with the two bombers. The fighters carried out a sweep in substantial strength.

On 28 December the bad weather really set in again to ground the entire Ninth Air Force, but England was relatively clear, enabling 1,124 heavies protected by 568 fighters to continue the pressure on rail targets, including the increasingly vital bridges and marshalling yards which made up the trains serving the German Army at the front. Two B-24s were lost from the force.

The Ninth got back into action on the 29th, there being several hundred sorties directly in support of the ground forces in the Ardennes region. A smaller Eighth Air Force bomber effort nevertheless

caused damage that the enemy was unable to sustain; the transport system was slowly and surely crumbling under the enormous weight of high explosive.

As usual, fighter escort to the bombers was solid, 587 aircraft being sent out from England. Among the P-51s were those marked with the black and white nose chequerboard of the 78th Group at Duxford, flying its first mission since converting from Thunderbolts. With this change the Eighth became an almost total Mustang force with only the 56th remaining on its trusty P-47s.

Weather groundings and recalls marred much of the air effort on 30 December, but the XIX and XXIX TAC sorties that were possible added to the woes of the German Army which was fast running out of irreplaceable tanks, vehicles and supplies, and particularly fuel. All across the critical sectors of the Western Front things began to look much brighter for the Allies. Even on a bad day the Ninth was able to get several hundred sorties into the air, a situation that prevailed into the last day of December. In addition, a massive heavy bomber strike indirectly supported the forward ground troops and Eighth and Ninth Air Force fighter pilots reduced

further the number of enemy fighters able to strafe and bomb friendly troops. Pilots from both air forces knocked down 64 German fighters on the 31st, the combats making aces of Major Samuel J. Wicker, CO of the 364th Group's 383rd Squadron, who nailed four Fw190s to make his total score seven, and Lieutenant Charles D. Hauver of the 355th Group, whose single Fw190 was enough to bring his score up to five.

January 1945

In a culmination of the much increased German fighter activity on the Western Front in December, Operation 'Bodenplatte', a mass strafing attack on Allied air bases in Holland and Belgium on 1 January, was hardly the disaster for the Allies that the Luftwaffe high command had intended. About 800 Bf109Gs and Fw190As and Ds hurled themselves at airfields hosting mainly RAF and USAAF fighter and bomber units, plus transports, causing widespread destruction at several of them. But overall the results were patchy. Rapid reaction to the raid by Allied fighter units and ground defences resulted in disproportionate numbers of German fighters being lost, added to

Above: To complete the 354th Group squadron trio was the 356th, which flew P-47Ds marked with white stars on a blue band. This mishap was caused by another pilot who borrowed Maj George 'Max' Lamb's aircraft for a sortie. *Shrader via S. Blake*

Above: Maj George Preddy of the 352nd indicating his six Bf109 victories on 6 August 1944. Such exploits helped make him the leading active ETO ace for a time. *Imperial War Museum*

which was the obsessive secrecy which surrounded the strike. This meant that German flak batteries were not pre-warned that a large force of their own fighters would be airborne — with some fatal consequences.

The two ends of the spectrum of what occurred during Operation 'Bodenplatte' were shown by events at two USAAF airfields, Asch and Metz.

At the first of these bases the P-47s of the 366th Group had taken off shortly before about 50 Bf109s and Fw190s of I., II. and III./JG 11 came screaming over the boundary just after 09.00 hours. Briefed to strafe enemy aircraft come what may, the bulk of the German pilots seemed not to have the experience to react fast enough when suddenly attacked by enemy fighters. The P-47s wheeled around, abandoned their intended ground-attack mission and came barrelling back to defend their base. Meanwhile the 352nd Fighter Group which was then sharing Asch with the

366th, had warmed up its Mustangs and began to take off at 09.10 hours; the 487th Squadron was first off and the wheels of the P-51s had barely tucked up when the base came under attack.

Even at this supposed disadvantage, the Americans rallied quickly and routed the German force without any losses to themselves. In a magnificent display of lightning-fast reactions, the blue-nosed Mustangs turned the attackers into the quarry. Lieutenant Sanford K. Moats became an ace within minutes with his bag of four Fw190s, Lieutenant Alexander F. Sears did the same by shooting down a Bf109 and Captain William T. Whisner got two Fw190s and two Bf109s to bring his score to a wartime peak of 15.5. The acting 487th Squadron commander, Lieutenant-Colonel John C. Meyer, shot down two to bring his score to a total of 24

— which made him the top ace in the ETO still on active service. The wrecks of enemy fighters scattered on and around Asch airfield attested to the ferocity of the air battle, which had been an amazing spectacle, particularly when seen from the ground. Among the most enthusiastic spectators were the AAF servicing crews, who rarely witnessed the performance of the fighters they repaired, refuelled and rearmed day after day. The P-47s and P-51s claimed 35 enemy aircraft shot down at Asch: JG 11 lost 21 pilots killed and four made prisoner, a virtual death sentence for the Geschwader at that time. The 487th FS got the only Distinguished Unit Citation awarded to a single VIII FC squadron for its work on 1 January.

Things went rather badly for the 365th at Metz/Frescaty. Attacked by the Bf109s of II., III. and IV./JG 53, 22 of the Hell

Above: Ice-covered airfields were hazardous even to heavy aircraft like the P-47D, which in any event had a steep ground angle to restrict the pilot's forward view. A man on the wing to act as a guide was often necessary, as this 358th Group flightline scene demonstrates. *Imperial War Museum*

Hawks' P-47s went up in flames as the Germans came in very low, spraying heavy cannon shells and machine gun bullets among the stationary Thunderbolts. The brunt of the attack was borne by the 386th Squadron which lost 12 aircraft out the total of 30 destroyed and damaged, being temporarily removed from the Allied order of battle until it could take delivery of fresh aircraft. It nevertheless managed to fly the next scheduled mission in P-47s borrowed from other squadrons, although even as the wrecks were still smouldering the Hell Hawks began to receive replacement aircraft.

Metz was the scene of the Germans' highest ground score against the US tactical force, although the RAF lost greater numbers of aircraft, including fighters, on its Dutch and Belgian airfields. It was a little ironic that the Luftwaffe high command did not count claims for ground kills, but in any event 'Bodenplatte' was a mere shadow of what it was originally meant to be. General Adolf Galland, the deposed General of Fighters, had envisaged a mass strike not on a ground target but American bombers; his plan was to concentrate a large force of fighters against an entire combat box of heavy bombers. They were to attack relentlessly, to the point where more B-17s or B-24s would have been destroyed than at any time previously. The disastrous losses of December 1944 and 1 January 1945 helped ensure that no such operation was

ever tried by the Jagdwaffe.

Combat on 1 January also came the way of the 359th Group's Lieutenant Robert M. York, who became an ace far away from the carnage of Operation 'Bodenplatte'. York was on escort duty, covering part of the force of 436 heavies making up 10 separate strike forces ranging in size from 99 down to 6 and covered by 626 fighters. He shot down an Fw190 for his fifth victory, and Lieutenant Van E. Chandler of the 4th Group did likewise when he destroyed a single Bf109.

On 2 January US pilots destroyed 14 enemy fighters over Germany, where a large force of heavies made more dents in the enemy's decimated transport system. Winter weather reduced the number of heavy bombers over Germany on the 3rd, a situation that prevailed into the 4th. On the 5th, when the 368th Fighter Group moved to Y-34 Metz/Frescaty, the bombers were back in force. They were also able to bomb various points in Germany on 7 January, but the ongoing bad weather meant that the number of effective sorties tended to vary considerably over the next week or so.

While the tactical fighters generally maintained some level of air support for the ground troops, there were January days when the entire Ninth was forced to remain

on the ground. A 'weather lull' that lasted from 9 to 13 January suddenly exploded into massive air action on the 14th when 847 heavy and 280 medium bombers blasted the German oil industry, enemy ground forces in the Ardennes and transport targets in general. Ably supporting the heavies, 645 VIII Fighter Command Mustangs had a field day when the Luftwaffe attempted to intercept the heavies, still the Jagdwaffe's primary target. For the loss of seven B-17s and eight of their own, the P-51 pilots reckoned on having destroyed 174 German fighters, the Eighth's best one-day aerial score of the war.

In a series of battles that ranged from Germany to The Netherlands, 14 January belonged to the 357th, which recorded a cumulative tally of 56 victories, the highest ever aerial score by a single USAAF unit on one mission. Among the victors were five pilots who became aces — and two who added further to their laurels to elevate them to the ranks of the Eighth's top scorers. The latter were Captain 'Kit' Carson, with two Fw190s and a Bf109 to give him 18.5, and Major John B. England, whose single Bf109 kill gave him 17.5. The 'first time' aces, all of whom brought themselves up to five, were: Lieutenant John L. Sublett, Lieutenant-Colonel Irwin H. Dregne, Lieutenant-

Above: Lt Victor Bast (centre) of the 61st Squadron describes his experiences to his ground crew, having just landed from a Berlin show on 3 February 1945. *Imperial War Museum*

Colonel Andrew J. Evans, Jr, Captain Chester K. Maxwell and Lieutenant Charles E. Weaver.

Lieutenant Harley L. Brown became an ace in the 20th Group when he shot down two Bf109s over Perleberg, while the 355th Group had another when Major Gordon M. Graham accounted for two Fw190s, to bring his total to five. Yet another 352nd ace was made on 14 January when Lieutenant Ernest O. Bostrom shot down an Fw190 to, also bring his score to five.

Lieutenant Robert P. Winks of the 357th did well on 15 January, his Me262 kill over Schöngau aerodrome not only bringing him ace status but entry to the select band of fighter pilots who had claimed kills over the German jets. On a day when tactical air activity over the Continent was limited, there were 619 heavy bomber sorties with a comfortable escort ratio of 611 fighters. In a separate mission, VIII Fighter Command dispatched 62 P-51s to bomb a marshalling yard.

On 16 January the Ninth Air Force further reorganised its fighter force, as follows:

IX TAC
48th, 366th, 370th, 404th and 474th Fighter Groups
XIX TAC
354th, 362nd, 365th, 367th, 368th, 405th and 406th Fighter Groups
XXIX TAC
36th and 373rd Fighter Groups

The above grouping shifted the focus more towards the most active US field armies, while XXIX TAC-assigned groups covered frontline sectors that were less active at that time.

After a return to more strategic oil industry targets on 16 January, the Eighth was obliged to double up on tactical targets as the weather clamped down again until the 19th, when IX TAC was returned to Ninth Air Force control after service under 2nd TAF. These moves reflected a stabilising of the front and a virtual end to further German offensive operations on the ground — from then on, the initiative would remain almost entirely in Allied hands.

No strangers to the terrible weather Europe could generate to hamper air operations, the Allied air forces were still surprised at how bad the conditions could get in the winter of 1944/45, one of the worst for decades. Britain was still the main supply centre for US aircraft deliveries from the US, and replacements for the frontline groups began to pile up when ferry pilots were unable to fly in the terrible conditions.

Strategic operations continued on 20 January when the escort included P-51s of the 357th Group. Lieutenant Dale E. Karger, then days short of his 20th birthday, spotted Me262s coming in on the bombers. Giving chase to one of them, he caught and shot it down near Munich to become the youngest USAAF ace of the war.

With the remnants of the German Army retreating by 22 January, the Ninth's mediums attacked bridges and roads to create an enormous traffic jam at the Our river near Dasburg that contained an estimated 1,500 vehicles. This was a signal for IX and XIX TAC to unleash its fighters to bomb and strafe half the concentration to destruction. In addition, the fighters helped US artillery to range in on the target.

A further result of the widespread destruction of bridges was another jam of 1,500 vehicles spotted by 362nd Group pilots bottled up near Prum. These were duly smashed by air attack and another 750 or so vehicles were denied to the enemy. Six IX and seven XIX TAC aircraft respectively were lost in these devastating attacks.

The gutted German Army was massively punished on 23 January, 600 effective sorties being mounted by the tactical fighters against the vehicles bogged down at Dasburg and Prum. Over 1,000 motor vehicles, tanks and horse-drawn vehicles were wrecked in a grim catalogue of destruction. There were also 159 effective sorties against the railways, and six locomotives and 150 wagons as well as 65 buildings were blasted at Düren which also had its rail lines and roads severed in nearly a dozen locations.

The fighters kept up the pressure on the 24th, making more attacks on the stalled German transport at Dasburg and Prum which were rapidly becoming graveyards. Official estimates gave 12 tanks, 30 other-type AFVs, 359 motor vehicles and 47 gun emplacements destroyed, losses that were both unsustainable and irreplaceable. The weather finally halted the attacks on these targets after a final round on 25 January. TAC's cumulative figures for the four-day campaign were: 61 tanks, 125 other AFVs, 3,627 motor vehicles, 149 gun emplacements, 35 locomotives, 1,157

Above: On 26 December 1944 Lt Paul A. Smith (left) and Lt Robert A. Tierney became the first Black Widow crew to obtain five confirmed kills in the ETO. Their P-61A-5 (42-5544) was named 'Lady Gen'. *Imperial War Museum*

Above: Yellow-nosed P-51D named 'Virginia' of the 361st Group taxying out at Bottisham. *J. V. Crow*

railway wagons and an unknown number of horse-drawn vehicles.

More fighter group movements at the end of January saw the 370th at Y-29 Asch by the 26th and the 365th at A-78 Florennes by the 29th. That day the tactical fighter forces were again reorganised as follows:

IX TAC
36th, 48th, 365th, 373rd, 404th and 474th Fighter Groups

XIX TAC
354th, 362nd, 367th, 368th, 405th and 406th Fighter Groups

XXIX TAC
366th and 370th Fighter Groups

January 1945 rounded out with 1,001 B-17s and B-24s attacking rail targets and industry at Kassel, escorted by 638 fighters. Ninth Air Force fighters were forced to remain on the ground due to the weather until 1 February. The two Eighth Air Force groups, the 352nd and 361st, remained on the Continent; the 352nd which had been under Ninth control since 23 December 1944 remained at A-84 Chièvres and was joined there by the 361st, which had been under XIX TAC control since 25 December.

Above: Keeping it in the family: Angie Laterza and Roy Berridge updating Maj Don Bochkay's score on his P-51D. Bochkay and Berridge were cousins. *J. V. Crow*

Above: Lt Rudolph L. Mark of the 397th Squadron, 368th Group, giving scale to a P-47D during the winter of 1944. *J. Lambert*

Above: Droop-snoot P-38s soldiered on until the end, although they were idle for periods when no suitable target could be found. Of course the number of P-38s also dwindled as the type was largely replaced and the 'lead ship' P-38s were not generally used in combination with other fighters. *USAF*

Above: Mustangs of the 355th Group's 358th Squadron with 'Lady Dana' in the background. *Author's collection*

Above: Belgian nationals were recruited into the Ninth Air Force as auxiliary military police in 1945 and Private Jean Martin of Brussels was one who guarded P-38s in Germany including an aircraft grandly named 'Rocky Mt Sweetheart II', possibly from the 474th Group. The location could have been R-2 Langensala. *Imperial War Museum*

10 Hunt to Extinction

Early in February there were more Ninth Air Force fighter group movements to airfields vacated by the Germans and more conveniently located to the front: the 367th went to A-64 St Dizier on the 1st and the 406th to Y-34 Metz on the 2nd. The latter date saw little activity apart from a sweep by the 56th on which Major Paul A. Conger, CO of the 63rd Squadron, brought his personal victory tally to 11.5 when he shot down an Fw190 and a Bf109 near Berlin.

The heavies were back over the 'big city' on the 3rd, and as well as bombs falling on Templehof marshalling yards, the 2nd Air Division's Liberators attacked a synthetic oil plant at Magdeburg. There was very heavy flak over Berlin and 23 B-17s were brought down, along with two B-24s. Of the 844-strong VIII Fighter Command escort, eight were lost including aircraft belonging to the scouting force.

In combat with German interceptors, the American pilots claimed 21 kills, these including several which added to personal scores to create more aces, among them Captain Cameron M. Hart of the 56th, who destroyed two Bf109s. An 'exotic' victory reported by Lieutenant Bernard H. Howes while flying a 55th Fighter Group P-51 near Boizenburg, was a Mistel combination, a manned Fw190 attached to an unmanned Ju88 'flying bomb'. Howes was one of the few pilots ever to catch an airborne Mistel and he quite legitimately claimed two victories by destroying it. Lieutenant-Colonel Elwyn G. Righetti, CO of the 55th, made ace when he also downed a Mistel and probably destroyed a second in the same area.

After a two-day bad weather stand-down which affected both the Eighth and Ninth Air Forces on 4/5 February, the 6th recorded the dispatch of 1,383 heavies and 829 fighters to various industrial targets in Germany, but the weather forced most of the crews to divert to T/Os. More recalls and complete stand-downs occurred on the 7th and on the 8th, when the 406th Fighter Group moved forward to Y-29 Asch.

Above: Tranquil scene at Bodney with P-51D 'Socky' at rest in the 487th Squadron dispersal. *Sam Sox*

Above: Capt Charles E. Weaver of the 362nd FS, 357th Group, had a novel way of recording personal victories on his P-51D and the artwork subject matter probably went down very well with observers! *J. V. Crow*

Another reshuffle of Ninth Air Force fighter groups took place on the 8th and the new distribution was:

IX TAC
36th, 48th, 365th, 404th and 474th Fighter Groups

XIX TAC
354th, 362nd, 367th and 368th Fighter Groups

XXIX TAC
366th, 370th, 405th and 406th Fighter Groups

In lieu of heavy bomber operations on the 8th, the Eighth sent 98 fighters on a sweep against rail lines, while the Ninth's bombers continued to pound junctions, a marshalling yard and T/Os.

Another multi-pronged heavy bomber strike took place on the 9th, VIII Fighter Command's escort force destroying 22 German fighters. Lieutenant William E. Whalen of the 2nd Scouting Force became an ace when he shot down two Bf109s and Captain George W. Gleason of the 479th brought his personal tally to 12 confirmed with a Bf109 and Fw190. Captain James E. Duffy of the 355th scored a single (an

Fw190) near Berlin to become an ace. On the debit side for the Americans, seven-victory ace Captain James W. Browning of the 357th was killed when he was shot down near Fulda.

Eighth Air Force heavy bomber missions were badly disrupted on 10 February and conditions barely improved on the 11th or the 12th as far as the tactical fighters were concerned. Not until 14 February could the Eighth put a sizeable force over German targets, when the escort downed 18 enemy fighters.

The 354th was out on tactical operations and enemy flak nailed the P-47 flown by Captain Kenneth H. Dahlberg of the 353rd Squadron, who was taken prisoner. To the 354th, it seemed that someone was making a mockery of its proud claim to be the Pioneer Mustang Group (which was hardly valid without qualification!) as its P-51s were replaced by Thunderbolts in the interests of standardisation by Ninth Fighter Command. Not everyone took to the mighty Republic fighter, but Dahlberg was among those who used it effectively. He had the group's bright markings applied to

his assigned Thunderbolt and the ground crew also faithfully reproduced his 14 Mustang victories on its flanks. As one of the top-scoring pilots in the group at that time, Dahlberg's experience was greatly missed when he became a prisoner.

On 15 February the 371st Group moved to Y-34 Metz and, although the heavies were out over Germany, there was relatively little action for the 433-strong fighter escort. The 371st Group was transferred to the Ninth Air Force from the 1st Tactical Air Force on the 16th to be assigned to XIX TAC, and the 367th Group, which had recently had a break from operations to transition from the P-38 to the P-47, returned to combat status. This change brought a negative reaction from the pilots similar to that felt by the 354th when its lost its Mustangs, but after a few missions the P-47 was accepted when its capabilities were appreciated.

Missions over Germany continued in the face of bad weather which continued to play havoc with planning, but there were always numerous targets of opportunity to be attacked and even a modest effort was rarely wasted. A fairly fluid front line meant that small army units often required the removal of an obstacle so that they could move forward with minimum casualties, and the tactical air cover invariably responded.

An offensive aimed at isolating the Ruhr in preparation for a major US Army drive into the region was begun on 18 February and the Eighth's fighters were back in action on the 20th. Protecting the heavies from the Luftwaffe cost 13 of the 476 fighters dispatched, for only 16 claims by American pilots. Lieutenant Clinton D. Burdick of the 356th Group made ace with victories over two Fi156 Storches and shared in downing a third near Bayreuth. Major Donald J. Strait, CO of the group's 361st Squadron, got three Storches to bring his score to 13.5. It was clearly a very bad day for the German unit flying the slow and vulnerable observation aircraft, probably with a number of senior officers on board.

The Ninth's fighters had been able to mount sorties against bridges, rail lines and ground defences on 20/21 February, their battlefield ground-attack missions often being on a day-to-day, hour-by-hour 'as required' basis as the ground forces fought their way towards the Rhine. Whenever their targets were visible, the fighter-bombers sent against specific objectives usually obtained highly satisfactory results

Above: Hardly able to believe that his P-47D managed to fly home after a flak hit had seriously weakened the rear fuselage, this 367th Group pilot surveys the near-terminal damage. The Thunderbolt was scrapped. *Author's collection*

from the viewpoint of the ground forces. If the target still impeded the advance, the tactical groups were based near enough for repeat strikes to be carried out, or for other units to be called in. While the USAAF had an ample number of fighter-bomber groups within range of most forward

targets, ground-attack operations were hardly risk-free. Local commanders were often quite unimpressed with the quality of training replacement pilots had received and a degree of local training was provided at unit level. But as this could interfere with operations, group commanders made it

Above: P-51D of the 357th FS, 355th Group, taken at Steeple Morden before its regular pilot, Lt Bill Cullerton, was shot down to become a PoW. *J. V. Crow*

known that they were not at all pleased with the situation. By all accounts, it did not completely improve before the war ended.

On 22 February the Eighth, Ninth and Fifteenth Air Forces embarked on Operation 'Clarion', which was intended as a final, decisive assault on the German transport system. Escort losses were generally far less than 5% of the force sent out from England and there was every sign that the enemy, while not completely out, was staying down. The Allied air forces brought about this situation without resort to unconventional weapons, in sharp contrast to the Germans who were frantically attempting to bring turbojet and rocket interceptors into service in sufficient numbers to turn the tide of war in their favour. Instead hundreds of Thunderbolts, Mustangs and Lightnings armed in the main with 0.50in machine guns, a range of bombs and unguided air-to-ground rockets were able to destroy all types of ground target from tanks to blockhouses. Newer

weapons were the exception rather than the rule, but napalm was being used to a limited extent, as were high velocity aircraft rockets (HVAR) attached to 'zero length' wing launchers which were an improvement over the cumbersome M-10 triple-tube launchers used mainly by P-47s.

'Clarion' would see a widening of the swathe of devastation already visited on strategic and tactical targets in Germany, and on the 22nd the heavy bombers went in low at 10,000 feet to attack industrial areas that were known not to be defended by flak. Again the Luftwaffe rose to do battle and again it lost heavily in fighters. Building fighters was the main focus of the German aircraft industry and the Luftwaffe's training programme — such as it was — to the detriment of virtually every other category of aircraft. Despite Allied bombing, the production rate of types such as the Me262, Fw190 and the later Bf109s rose; dispersal of vital components and a network of sub-assembly suppliers

succeeded in ensuring that the Luftwaffe invariably had aircraft to fly: its increasing problem was skilled pilots to man them. Combat victories on the 22nd included the destruction of an Me262 by Major Wayne K. Blickenstaff of the 353rd Group, who thus became an ace.

On 23 February the US First Army made its bid to cross the Roer river as a first phase of an assault which it was hoped would carry it to the Rhine. The heavies, mediums and fighters pounded targets behind the front line, making it increasingly difficult for the Germans to reinforce or supply critical areas.

It was to the Allies' great relief that the German jet threat had not materialised; pilots of the Me262 (the only truly practical jet fighter the Germans managed to bring into service) had met their match, not so much in terms of straight fighter-versus-fighter combat in which they invariably enjoyed a performance edge over piston-engined fighters, but in tactics.

Above: Well-posed portrait of a 383rd FS, 364th Group, P-51D at the unit's base at Honington. *USAF*

Above: P-47Ds of the 411th (foreground) and 412th Squadrons of the 373rd Group pictured on a Continental airfield. The tactical war took many of the groups into three or four countries by war's end. *Campbell*

Quickly realising when the Me262 was at its most vulnerable, the AAF used a degree of cunning and stealth and set about destroying as many as possible on the ground. By pounding known centres of turbojet production, fuel storage, the transport system and airfields, every phase of the delivery to frontline units was disrupted. Jets still managed to reach the remaining airfields and when they achieved operational status, they could still be destroyed by conventional fighters if they were caught on take-off and landing at typically low speeds.

Finally it was found that the relatively few Me262s that managed to get into the air could also be dealt with through sound fighter tactics — but it was freely admitted by the Allies that in combat the Me262 was superior to anything else, and numerous eye-witnesses had seen what its main armament, a quartet of 30mm cannon, could do to a B-17 or B-24. Dogged, however, by technical unreliability, the Me262, unlike US piston-engined fighters, also lacked endurance. If the German pilot experienced a flame-out, fuel starvation or airframe damage, the odds were quickly narrowed to give pursuing American fighters an even chance of a kill. More than one German pilot also opted for self-

preservation rather than last-ditch glory and abandoned his machine as soon as technical malfunction struck or American fighters were chasing him. Consequently, the number of AAF fighter pilots with confirmed Me262 victories rose steadily.

The best day the Eighth Air Force had against the enemy jet fighters came on 25 January when eight different assaults were made by the heavies on a wide variety of targets. Although the number of German fighters downed by the escort was only about 30, these included no fewer than seven Me262s, brought down during a running battle across northern Germany. All the jets were claimed by Mustang pilots of the 55th Fighter Group, which thus set a record in terms of jet kills by one group in one day, a distinction that remained unchallenged. In addition, two pilots of the 364th Group claimed what was believed to be the first confirmed kills of the Arado 234 jet bomber, while Captain Charles H. Cole of the 20th Group became an ace with claims for four Fw190s. Inevitably the USAAF ran the risk of losing a percentage of its best pilots on these late-war missions, even though overall casualties were modest. One pilot

who went down on 25 February was Captain Kendall E. Carlson, a six-victory ace of the 4th, who was captured after his P-51 hit the ground during a very low level strafing run.

In more than 1,000 sorties the Eighth maintained the pressure on Germany on 26 February, there being 687 fighters making up the escort. The Ninth Air Force managed but 50 effective sorties when the weather interrupted the day's planned operations.

A Do217 was a relatively unusual combat victim for Captain James N. McElroy on 27 February. Having been almost totally eclipsed in terms of frontline effectiveness, the remnants of the German conventional bomber force remained operational for a number of specialised duties including pathfinding. And of course the night-fighter arm deployed numerous Do217s in both training and first-line roles. Finding the Dornier near Plauen at 13.40 hours McElroy destroyed it, to add his name to the list of 355th Group aces.

February ended with nearly 1,000 Eighth Air Force heavy bomber sorties, but, on this as on other operations during

Above: A touch of humour crept into the markings of the 358th Group, the 'Orange Tails', near the end of the war with a small kicking mule painted on the cowl flaps of this 367th Squadron P-47D. *J. Lambert*

the period, German fighter reaction was virtually nil and not untypically it was the flak that was largely responsible for bringing down eight bombers and two fighters.

March 1945

March began with a major Eighth Air Force bomber strike, a pattern that was to continue, weather permitting, for the next few weeks. Fighter escort kills jumped from 17 on 1 March to 71 on the 2nd when the Ninth also sent off more than 1,700 sorties, mainly in support of a US Third Army offensive. Escort fighters covering the heavies numbered 713 and scored most of the kills, the day beginning with the 422nd NFS which shot down two Ju87s over the Rhine between 04.47 and 05.06 hours, making Lieutenant Herman E. Ernst and his radar operator Lieutenant Edward H. Kopsel joint P-61 aces.

More 357th pilots achieved ace status, but any elation was short-lived for Captain Alva C. Murphy and Lieutenant Raymond M. Bank, as both were shot down by flak soon afterwards. While Bank was made a prisoner, Murphy was killed. A third 357th pilot, Captain Robert G. Schimanski of the 352nd Squadron, got a Bf109 and shared a second to return home an ace, as did Major William H. Julien, CO of the 83rd Squadron of the 78th

Group, whose two Bf109s brought his score to five. Lieutenant Arthur C. Cundy of the 353rd Group shot down a Bf109 and two Fw190s, a feat he shared with another member of the group's 352nd Squadron, Lieutenant Horace Q. Waggoner, who got two Fw190s and a Bf109.

Captain Edwin L. Heller's Fw190 kill brought him the mantle of ace in the 482nd Squadron, 352nd Group. Before the weather curtailed operations on 4 March, the heavies carried out a massive, largely unopposed series of missions on the 3rd.

Grounding orders drastically reduced air operations planned for the 5th, the weather front extending down to Italy and also hampering the Fifteenth Air Force. IX and XIX TAC operations were cancelled on 6 March and although XXIX TAC was able to fly on the 7th, the rest of the Ninth Air Force was grounded.

Neither were the tactical fighters able to fly many sorties on 8 March, although the heavies were out over Germany. Standardisation of fighters continued with the 370th Fighter Group relinquishing its P-38s for P-47s and flying the first Thunderbolt mission on the 9th. While protecting medium

bombers that day, the Ninth Air Force fighters destroyed 11 enemy interceptors which, displaying a rare show of force, attacked a formation of medium bombers and shot down three of them.

Elements of the US First Army captured Bonn on the 9th, while heavy and medium bombers smashed a range of tactical targets; on the 10th Lieutenant Arthur Cundy of the 353rd Group, who had been an ace only since 2 March, ditched in the North Sea and was killed.

On 11 March the 373rd Fighter and 373rd Tactical Reconnaissance Groups moved to Y-55 Venlo while heavy bomber missions went to such locations as Swinemünde to bomb the marshalling yards. The following day the weather prevented any bomber or fighter sorties from England, but 13 March proved lucky for tactical fighter groups as they claimed 15 kills over Germany. P-38 pilot Captain Joseph E. Miller, Jr, of the 474th Group became an ace with a single Fw190 kill, this following four earlier victories he had accumulated in the MTO. Major Lowell K. Brueland, CO of the 355th Squadron of the 354th Group, brought his victory total to a final 12.5 confirmed with a Bf109.

Remagen

By 14 March American troops were at the Ludendorff bridge spanning the Rhine at Remagen, which soon became the scene of bitter fighting as the Germans tried desperately to demolish this one remaining intact crossing point. Patrolling Ninth Air Force P-47s of the 36th Group spotted more than 50 German bombers preparing to take off from Lippe aerodrome. This force was bound for Remagen, but the timely intervention by the AAF fighters all but ruined the strike. Making strafing, rocket and bombing runs across the airfield, the P-47s sent 23 Ju87s up in smoke. Minutes later a dozen P-47s of the 404th Group joined in to destroy 21 of the remaining Junkers dive-bombers. Two pilots collided and were lost, although the attacks on Remagen bridge thereafter dropped off, the Germans having thrown 372 sorties against it between 7 and 14 March.

Meanwhile the Eighth and Ninth fighter groups had disposed of another 26 German aircraft, among them an Ar234. This was claimed by Captain Donald S. Bryan of the 352nd Group. The Arado bomber kill — over Remagen incidentally — brought Bryan's personal total to 13.333 confirmed. Lieutenant-Colonel Paul P. Douglas, CO of the 368th Group, shot down three Fw190s near Frankfurt-am-Main at 15.45 hours to become another Ninth Air Force P-47 ace.

With Allied troops pounding on the West Wall of the Reich by 15 March, the Ninth was heavily committed to support the US Army push into Germany, codenamed Operation 'Undertone'. Medium bomber groups had their hands full and helping out was Captain Ray S. Wetmore of the 359th Group who warded off enemy fighters and brought his final tally of victories to 21.25 confirmed with a rare victory over an

Me163 rocket fighter at Wittenberg. The 365th Fighter Group moved into Y-46 Aachen on the 15th.

The most intensive single day of action ever recorded by the 362nd Fighter Group took place on 16 March when it mounted 173 effective sorties against ground targets. The P-47s accounted for 403 motor vehicles, 40 horse-drawn vehicles, three tanks, six other AFVs, six locomotives and 28 railway wagons, six gun emplacements and eight 'defended buildings'. To round off the score, three enemy fighters were shot down at a cost of a single P-47.

An historic base move was made by the 354th Fighter Group on 17 March when it occupied Y-64 Ober Olm aerodrome to become the first USAAF tactical unit to operate from German soil.

Operations began on 18 March to prepare the ground for the US Third, Seventh and Ninth Armies to cross the Rhine; it was estimated it would take five

Above: Lt-Col Robert D. Johnston of the 50th Group made ace quite late, on 9 April 1945. His P-47D-30 (44-33315) carried the 81st Squadron code '2N'. *Robert Johnston*

Above: P-51D 'Ensign Babs' was the personal mount of Lt Robert J. Ramer, who flew with the 355th Squadron, 354th Group. The Mustang was pictured in Germany in 1945 at the end of the war. *J. V. Crow*

Above: They also serve: a P-51B of the 55th Fighter Group's 'Clobber College', the ETO theatre introduction school run by combat units for freshman pilots. This and other War Weary school aircraft had their individual code letters replaced by numbers, for example a Mustang coded 'CY-10' served with the 338th Squadron. *Author's collection*

Headquarters strike

While the heavy and medium bombers continued to pound a variety of strategic and tactical targets on 19 March, XIX TAC sent the P-47s of the 367th Fighter Group against a German headquarters at Ziegenburg. This was an 'extreme precision' mission and the pilots succeeded in placing bombs accurately (including lobbing them through the windows) on the fortress-like building in an attempt to wipe out key members of the staff of the German C-in-C West. Allied intelligence was apparently unaware that Albert Speer, Reich Armaments Minister, was on a flying visit to the HQ recently vacated by von Rundstedt. Speer was uninjured in the attack.

In the meantime, another 44 German aircraft went down in air battles with the Eighth and Ninth Air Force bomber escort over Germany. Among the victors was Major Niven K. Cranfill, CO of the 359th Group's 369th Squadron, who became an ace with an Me262 kill near Leipzig. Lieutenant Joe W. Wattas, an F-6 Mustang pilot of the 363rd TacR Group, also became an ace with a Bf109 and Major Louis H. Norley of the 4th also shot down a Bf109 for his final victory, giving him a total of 10.333.

With part of Patton's Third Army having secured Koblenz the day before, the 20th was relatively quiet in terms of tactical sorties, although air combat again took place on 21 March. The day's run of American victories started in the early hours with a P-61 of the 422nd NFS catching up with a Do217. Guided by Lieutenant Robert F. Graham, who became a 'radar ace', the pilot dispatched the bomber (or possibly a Do217 night fighter) in the vicinity of the Rhine between 00.45 and 01.05 hours.

Lieutenant Dudley M. Amoss of the 55th Group got three Fw190s to become an ace in dramatic style near Münster, but was himself shot down by flak to become a prisoner — similar incidents had happened before — it was almost as though the German gunners had followed the combat and deliberately locked on to the new ace!

Patton was on the Rhine by 21 March and the following day saw an enormous tactical air effort against German army bases and installations, aerodromes and rail communications; fighter combat resulted in 22 enemy aircraft claims and a new crop of aces. Among them was

days to soften up the defences in about 600 effective sorties. Tactical air strikes began the operation with fighters striking communications centres, marshalling yards and targets in several towns.

Another first occurred over Berlin that day when P-51 pilots of the 359th Group observed Red Air Force aircraft over the German capital, the first known instance when missions from the Western and Eastern Fronts had overlapped. Unfortunately Soviet aircraft recognition was not of the highest order and a 353rd Group P-51 was shot down in the first of a number of similar incidents. Eighth and Ninth Air Force fighters destroyed 22 enemy aircraft and Captain Ralph L. Cox of the 359th became an ace when he shot down an Fw190 over Joachimsthal.

Lieutenant-Colonel Sidney S. Woods, executive officer of the 4th Group, who became an ace in a day with a score of five Fw190s, these bringing his tally to seven by adding the German victories to two Japanese aircraft claimed while flying P-38s in the Pacific.

Another new 354th Group ace on 22 March was Lieutenant Franklin Rose, Jr, whose two Fw190s fell near Mannheim. In another base change, the Ninth's 474th Group moved into Y-59 Stassfeld that day.

Bf109s were again attempting to disrupt heavy bomber operations on 23 March. The German fighters clashed with the 354th Group and Lieutenant Colonel Jack T. Bradley, CO of the 353rd Squadron, made short work of a Bf109 to raise his score to 15. That victories were not invariably fighters was shown by Captain George A. Doersch of the 359th Group who dispatched an Arado Ar96 trainer near Salzwedel at 14.45 hours. His score thus rose to 10.5 confirmed.

Across the Rhine

The previous days' ground operations culminated in Operation 'Varsity', the mass Anglo-American airborne assault on the Rhine. Heavy bomber sorties kept the Germans cowed under carpets of high explosive rolling across their airfields in north and northwestern Germany, while there were 1,297 tactical sorties by VIII Fighter Command. Clearing attacks by fighter-bombers attempted to wipe out all opposition to the Allied paratroop drop, numerous ground targets coming under attack in order to divert attention away from the vulnerable gliders and parachute troops. In total there were 2,039 effective fighter sorties on that first day of 'Varsity'. Despite casualties, the objectives were seized by the ground forces, their task being greatly aided by relays of fighter-bombers running a shuttle service above

Above: Representing the 357th, the Eighth Air Force group with more aerial victories than any other, this P-51D (C5-Q) of the 364th Squadron was flown by ace Irwin H. Dregne. *J. V. Crow*

Above: Another 357th Group Mustang was P-51D (44-64051) of the 362nd Squadron. *Olmsted*

them. The Germans fully appreciated the significance of 'Varsity' and threw in aircraft to beat back Allied troops as they established a bridgehead; some of these sorties appeared to border on the desperate, as when Allied fighter pilots found a formation of Ju87s at Eisenach. Making short work of two of them was Captain Clyde B. East, an F-6 pilot of the 15th PRS, 10th RG (Reconnaissance Group), who became an ace. Just over double the baseline score — 10.5 — was the tally of Lieutenant-Colonel John A. Storch of the 357th Group after he had shot down a Bf109.

The 357th's Captain Paul R. Hatala became an ace with two Bf109s and Major Robert Foy, the group operations officer, got a 109 to bring his score to a final 15. Major Robert A. Elder, CO of the 354th's 353rd Squadron, became an ace in a day with a score of four Fw190s and a Bf109, while Captain Raymond E. Hartley, Jr, of the 353rd Group also returned home an ace, his two Fw190s and a Bf109 being added to two victories he had scored with the Fifteenth Air Force. Lieutenant-Colonel Wayne Blickenstaff, 350th Squadron CO, brought his tally to 10 with victories over three Fw190s and a Bf109.

Even on a day when the weather deteriorated to the point where the majority of the heavy bomber sorties had to be aborted, 25 March did record air combat,

Above: Chequer-tailed F-6 Mustang of the 15th Tactical Reconnaissance Squadron photographed in Germany in 1945. *J. V. Crow*

albeit on a reduced scale. Ten enemy fighters were claimed destroyed over Germany. Major Glenn T. Eagleston of the 354th, who was already a triple ace, added a Bf109 to his tally to give him 18.3 confirmed, to lead the table of Ninth Air Force aces, a position he retained until the end of the war.

Reduced to 12 effective sorties to bomb their primary oil target on the 26th, the bulk of the 1st Air Division's B-17s diverted to their secondary, a tank factory

at Plauen. Other formations had Plauen as their primary, so the target was duly plastered. The weather clamped down to ground the entire Ninth Air Force the following day and, although conditions improved somewhat on 28 March, the air support effort still had to be curtailed. The 36th Fighter Group moved to Y-46 Aachen, although there was little activity at the front. This situation prevailed through to the 30th, although missions were flown in strength on the last day of March. A

Above: The 370th Group was an original Ninth Air Force P-38 outfit which in common with all but one of its contemporaries converted to the P-51 before the end. A vertical blue stripe identified aircraft of the 485th Squadron. *Author's collection*

Above: The last Mustang group in the Eighth was the 479th, which also converted from the P-38. A P-51D of the 434th FS, 'American Maid' flown by Eugene Sears, warms up its engine as gliders and tugs fly overhead. *T. R. Bennett*

typically heavy force comprising five separate raids was accompanied by 847 fighters and in combat some of these were responsible for the loss figure of 14 suffered by the enemy.

Armies push ahead

April opened with the tactical air forces in northwest Europe all but grounded by the weather while the US First Army captured Paderborn and elements of the Third began clearing Kassel of German troops. The Eighth's heavies experienced many recalls on 2 April and while XXIX TAC was grounded, XIX TAC fighters went out and shot down 17 enemy aircraft. Lieutenant Henry S. Rudolph of the 354th destroyed two Fw190s near Bayreuth to become an ace.

A German defensive position known as the Ruhr Pocket temporarily held up the US First and Third Armies from the 2nd, while the Eighth Air Force turned its attention to German shipyards and U-boat construction on the 3rd and 4th, the latter date recording air combat on a larger scale than previously; 34 German aircraft were destroyed by pilots of the Eighth and

Ninth Air Forces, Lieutenant Colonel George F. Ceullers, CO of the 364th Group's 383rd Squadron, shooting down an Me262 over Leipzig to bring his score to 10.5.

Lieutenant William J. Cullerton of the 355th Group also achieved ace status with his single Fw190, but in terms of numbers destroyed on the ground, the 339th began to overshadow all other groups by amassing a phenomenal score during a series of strafing attacks, starting with 105 on 4 April. That day, XXIX TAC was returned to Ninth Air Force control after completing its duty under 2nd TAF.

As the US Ninth Army crossed the Weser river on 5 April, US fighters destroyed 14 of the enemy in aerial combat. The First Army was across the river by the following day.

In something approaching a crescendo of fire, the Eighth Air Force launched 1,261 bombers against German targets on 7 April — and the Germans made a

sterling effort to make them pay a heavy price. It was the virtual swan-song of the Jagdwaffe which was resorting to desperate measures including ramming the US bombers. Of the 17 B-17s destroyed, at least five were believed to have gone down as a result of deliberately being rammed. It was also felt that five of the 830-strong escort had been sent down in this fashion. The Germans had a high number of volunteers for what amounted to suicide missions (although each pilot was issued with a parachute) but to fulfil a pledge to bring down a bomber they first had to reach their quarry and evade the escort. For many individuals this proved impossible.

Well used to dishing out punishment far worse than it took, the US fighter force exacted a toll of 82 of the enemy, and some of the last aces were made at a time when the Germans were unquestionably on the ropes. Few believed that the Germans could continue to resist — but it wasn't over until it was over and Major Robin

Above: Kaufburen breaking. Surplus P-51s of all three squadrons of the 55th Fighter Group awaiting the scrapper's torch in Germany after the war. Many aircraft have the red and yellow Allied occupation stripes around the fuselage. *Flugzeug/Rick Chapman*

Olds, commanding the 434rd Squadron of the 479th Fighter Group, waded unto the German fighters milling around the bombers and shot down a Bf109. This kill brought his score to 13 and, in the event, he was unable to add further to it before the war ended.

Lieutenant Richard G. Candelaria, also of the 479th, shot down four Bf109s and claimed an Me262 as a probable, to become an ace. The 353rd's Captain Gene E. Markham also brought his score to five with a Bf109, as did Captain Harrison B. Tordoff of the same group, also with a Bf109. Captain Donald M. Cummings of the 55th got two Bf109s which made him an ace with a total of 6.5, while Captain Valentine S. Radar, an F-6 pilot with the 67th TRS, also joined the ranks of the aces.

Another 1,103 heavy bomber sorties were flown on 8 April and again the Luftwaffe fighters put in an appearance, although there were fewer in number than the day before; hereafter their numbers would finally dwindle. Pilots from the 763-strong escort force shot down 38 enemy aircraft and Lieutenant Leland A. Larson of the 10th TRS became an ace by dispatching a Ju87 and sharing in the demise of an He111 with another pilot. Having enjoyed something of a respite in

terms of losing aces in combat, the Eighth had to strike Lieutenant William J. Cullerton of the 355th Group from its roster when his P-51 was shot down by flak and he was taken prisoner.

The Ninth was moving its fighters ever deeper into Germany and such strongholds as Frankfurt/Rhein Main now supported aeroplanes marked with white stars rather than black crosses. In this and other areas the locals could only marvel at how events could have brought about such changes.

Other AAF transfers included the return of the 361st Fighter Group to the Eighth's control on 9 April, following the unit's stint in Belgium with the Ninth. In the meantime the Eighth laid on a 1,215-strong bomber mission to tactical targets, including 10 airfields. Riding shotgun were 812 fighters, five of which were lost along with seven bombers. The day's cumulative total of victories by the Eighth, Ninth and 1st TAF fighters was 27, two Fw190s falling to the guns of Lieutenant-Colonel Robert D. Johnston, CO of the 81st Squadron of the 50th Fighter Group, who became an ace.

The toll of German fighters on 10 April was 43, the AAF escort covering the

heavies attacking mainly tactical targets. Among the fighter aces of the day were two more pilots from the 353rd Group, Captain Gordon B. Compton and Captain Robert W. Abernathy, both of whom downed an Me262 apiece near Dessau.

On 11 April Major Gilbert F. Talbot, CO of the 354th Group's 355th Squadron, made ace when he destroyed a Bf109 near Mulhausen. That day 1,270 heavy bombers attacked tactical targets in Germany for the loss of only one B-17. The Germans again came off worse in combat with AAF fighters, 47 aircraft being claimed. Lieutenant Edward B. Edwards became a P-47 ace in the 373rd Group when he shot down four Fw190s over Sachau aerodrome.

A steady toll of enemy aircraft was also accruing to the P-61 night fighters of the Ninth, and on 11/12 April Lieutenant Eugene D. Axtell of the 422nd NFS became an ace when he found and destroyed a Ju52 on each of two separate missions, at 23.07 and 01.08 hours.

With the US Ninth Army in Magdeburg, the 366th Group moved into Y-94 Münster/Handorf and the 404th occupied Y-86 Fritzlar; with bad weather forecast, the 12th was marked for the AAF tactical fighters by victories on the ground rather than in the air. It was the 36th Fighter Group that did the damage when 11 pilots shot up 14 He111s and three Do217s on Scheuditz aerodrome. Coming off the target they spotted a huge mass of enemy aircraft — estimated at about 300 — on another aerodrome at Leipzig/Mockau. Proceeding to make continuous strafing runs on this plum target, the 11 P-47s accounted for 16 Ju88s, nine Fw190s, eight Bf109s, six He111s and five Me410s. Along with single examples of the Me262 and Ju87, several trainers and a captured P-47 were also shot up for a score of about 60 aircraft at both airfields.

On 13 April bad weather again limited the number of heavy bomber sorties, but IX TAC P-47s carried out a raid on the headquarters of the German Army Group B located inside the Ruhr Pocket. Captain Clyde East secured his place as the leading PR ace of the AAF with a final score of 13 when he shot down a Bf109 near Hof,

but Lieutenant Richard Candelaria of the 479th was shot down by flak and taken prisoner. The Ninth Army meanwhile crossed the Elbe and the 366th Group moved its P-47s into Y-86 Fritzlar.

Combat on 14 April saw 14 enemy fighters downed by Ninth and First TAF pilots and on bomber escort duty, Lieutenant Lloyd Overfield of the 354th Group shot down an Me262 and an He111 to bring his score to 11 confirmed. On the ground, the advance of the US First and Third Armies split the Ruhr Pocket in half.

In a series of clearing operations that began on the 14th, the Eighth's heavies concentrated on those French Atlantic coastal areas still in German hands including Bordeaux and Royan. The latter target was the first and only one subjected to napalm attack by Eighth Air Force bombers; the results were disappointing. Fighters ranged over Germany and gained 10 victories in air combat, Captain Richard W. Ashbury of the 354th becoming another group ace when he

shared in the demise of an He111. Lieutenant Bruce W. Carr from the same group brought his score to a final total of 15, also by adding an He111, and Captain Gerald Brown of the 55th Group made ace by destroying an Fw190 and yet another He111 near Münster.

That territory still in German hands was shrinking fast was shown on 16 April when P-47 pilots of the 368th Fighter Group shot down three enemy fighters over Czechoslovakia. That event was overshadowed by the destruction of no less than 747 enemy aircraft on the ground as all 15 Eighth Air Force fighter groups went hunting the grounded Luftwaffe across Germany and into Czech territory. The 339th, which had set a record on 4 April with over 100 ground kills in a day, claimed another 118 and became the only USAAF unit to accomplish such a feat on two occasions. Light flak and small arms fire, the most deadly to low flying aircraft, claimed 34 VIII FC aircraft. One of the P-51s was flown by Lieutenant-Colonel

Above: Flying for fun late in 1945 was P-51D-20 of the 363rd FS, 357th Group, previously the mount of Don Bochkay. *J. V. Crow*

Above: Peace meant just that! After years of aeroplane noise the citizens of Europe apparently wanted no more 'buzzing'; highly readable underwing codes were applied so that people could report transgressions. This P-51D of the 356th Group was the 360th Squadron's 'PI-Z' alias 'Audrey 4th'. *Herb Rutland*

Sidney Woods, executive officer of the 4th, who was captured when he went down over Prague/Kbely aerodrome.

During the course of the day Ninth and First TAF aircraft also shot down 30 enemy fighters in aerial combat over Germany and widespread strafing of airfields netted another 215, the highest ever one-day tally credited to the Ninth, which also claimed 190 aircraft damaged. The US Army overran the Ruhr Pocket and 16 April saw the Red Army begin its final drive on Berlin, launching from positions on the River Oder and advancing on a 200-mile front.

Two pilots of the 366th and 354th Groups became aces on 17 April, their personal claims being among the total of 28 credited to Ninth and First TAC fighter pilots that day. Lieutenant Donald O. Scherer of the 366th and Captain Jack A. Warner of the 356th claimed an Me108 and an Me262 respectively for their fifth victories.

Joining the increasing number of pilots with higher than average scores who were seeing their final actions in April 1945, was Major Donald H. Bochkay, CO of the 357th Group's 363rd Squadron. A confirmed Me262 destroyed on a sweep of the Prague area on 18 April brought his score to 13.833. In the event Bochkay would not, in common with numerous other aces, have any further chances to add to this total, at least in the air.

The enormous destruction meted out by American fighters at the remaining German airfields produced new ground aces, although, as mentioned earlier, the Ninth Air Force did not recognise these. And not all pilots bothered to count their ground kills, despite official credit being given by Eighth Fighter Command.

Heavy bomber sorties were to the German-Czech border on 19 April, escort being provided by 532 VIII Fighter Command aircraft; 16 enemy fighters were shot down over Germany. The small price paid by the Americans in terms of numbers (two fighters and five B-17s) was actually high in personnel terms, for one of the fighter pilots lost was Lieutenant Colonel Elwyn G. Righetti, CO of the 55th Group. Skilled and daring, 'Eager Al' as he was nicknamed had few peers when it came to wreaking havoc on German airfields. Righetti's cool-headed strafing was awesome to behold and the circumstances of his subsequent demise were never completely explained. After crash-landing near Dresden he was seen to be alive when his P-51 came to rest — but he was never heard from again.

Mob rule

The assumption was that Righetti had been killed by an angry mob, a grim aspect of the war which was the subject of warnings to bomber crews and fighter pilots in the event of their being shot down. As order in Germany increasingly broke down, the rule that enemy flyers should be placed in Luftwaffe custody for interrogation prior to moving to a PoW camp was occasionally ignored. Aircrew were most at risk when they could not be secured quickly by a Luftwaffe field unit, but in general captured flyers were not deliberately harmed.

With the US Army in Halle and Leipzig, the end was only a matter of time. Surrender moves were being made behind the scenes but little changed in the front line. With all Germany their hunting ground, the USAAF fighters, mediums and heavies became almost a daily sight above industrial areas and cities, as predictable as the passing of the hours. Only bad weather stopped them coming.

On 20 April a small force of B-24s bombed Klatovy in Czechoslovakia, while both Liberators and Fortresses attacked targets in the Berlin area. Lieutenant Andrew J. Ritchey of the 354th Group became an ace by shooting down two Bf109s near Kladno whilst escorting the Libs, as did Major Henry S. Bille, CO of the 357th Squadron, 355th Group. He also dispatched two Bf109s to receive the accolade of ace. For the Ninth, Lieutenant Melvyn R. Paisley of the 366th became an ace with an Fw190 shared with a second pilot.

More tactical fighter units made base moves in mid-April, the 370th arriving at Y-99 Gütersloh and the 373rd at Y-98 Lippstadt.

The ground forces' momentum had carried elements of the US Army beyond the German border and into Czech territory and the racing tanks were given air support on 21 April. Behind them the Eighth's heavies attacked German targets with 408 fighters to protect them from a now all but exhausted Luftwaffe; there were fewer targets remaining for the air forces as Allied troops had most of the Third Reich in a vice. On the 21st the 55th, 56th and 339th Fighter Group were stood down after flying their last missions from England, while the 36th Group moved to R-12 Kassel/Rothwesten. On 22 April XXIX TAC moved its headquarters forward to Brunswick and the 363rd TRG occupied R-37 Brunswick, one of the airfields in that area. The 474th meanwhile went to R-2 Langensalza.

A day of inclement weather on 23 April saw only XIX TAC aircraft maintaining the pressure on the Germans, as the Red Army entered the suburbs of Berlin. The Eighth flew some of its longest missions of the war into Czechoslovakia, but on the 25th even these ceased after a final mission to rail targets and a transformer station in Bavaria by 278 B-24s, and a run to a munitions factory at Pilsen by 279 B-17s, escorted by 539 fighters. Ever alert, the flak gunners brought down six bombers and one fighter. During the escort phase of the mission, Lieutenant Hilton O. Thompson of the 479th Group shot down an Ar234 near Berchtesgaden — which turned out to be the last aerial combat claim by VIII Fighter Command in World War 2.

The 78th Fighter Group came home on the deck with guns blazing, its Mustang strafing attacks sending 135 enemy aircraft up in smoke to set a new Eighth Air Force record of ground destruction in one day. US First Army and Red Army troops met on the Elbe river at Torgau that day.

The final missions for Eighth Bomber Command rounded out one of the most significant campaigns of the war; the shutting down of one of the most decisive instruments in the final defeat of Hitler's Germany was a further indication that the latter event was only a matter of days away.

On 26 April the tactical fighters again made the air above Germany their own hunting ground and shot down 22 enemy aircraft. Lieutenant Edward F. Bickford of the 354th became an ace with two Fw190s. Under a last wartime reshuffle of fighter-bomber units, the 405th Fighter Group was transferred from XXIX to XIX TAC on the 26th, the latter command flying 125 effective sorties the following day. On 28 April the 48th Group was transferred from IX to XIX TAC.

The 387 sorties flown on the 29th were less than were planned; the bad weather that had lasted for some days kept many aircraft on the ground. The Ninth's fighters nevertheless shot up 191 motor vehicles, one tank, four locomotives, 52 railway wagons and 397 horse-drawn vehicles still serving the German Army. The 48th Group moved again, to occupy R-10 Illesheim and on 30 April, the day Hitler committed suicide in Berlin, the 362nd Fighter Group flew its last missions of the war. The Ninth's bombers continued to pound tactical targets during late April and into May, by which time the 354th Group was based at R-45 Ansbach, the 362nd at R-30 Fürth and the 405th at R-6 Kitzingen.

On 1 May the Ninth laid on a dive-bombing mission to Hitler's mountain retreat at Berchtesgaden while the weather continued to interrupt the final missions of the war; grounding orders saved numerous targets from further destruction as 3 May brought the last medium bomber sorties of the war.

For its last wartime mission the 366th Group went after a relatively rare target for Ninth Air Force tactical fighters: shipping and harbour installations at Kiel and Lübeck. Concurrently 19 P-47s of the 406th attacked a large cargo vessel in Lübeck harbour. With these final missions against specific targets, the Ninth's fighters finished their war; further armed reconnaissance flights were made on 4 May, 356 effective sorties completing this operation which ranged over areas still occupied by elements of the Luftwaffe. The AAF fighters destroyed aircraft that

might have constituted a further threat, particularly jet fighters, 29 of which were claimed in strafing attacks. Several ships and U-boats were also attacked in the approaches to Kiel and Flensburg. In the air, the US fighters knocked down 16 enemy aircraft, including the last Me262 credited to the Ninth Air Force.

The German surrender in the West became effective at 08.00 hours on 5 May and on the 6th the 373rd Group's P-47s flew what were termed 'demonstration' missions over the Klotze region. German resistance had not completely ended as on 7 May the Ninth's P-47s swept the area between Chemnitz and Prague while PR flights were intercepted by four die-hard German pilots flying Fw190s, one of which was shot down near the Czech capital.

As President Harry S. Truman proclaimed VE-Day on 8 May 1945 the fighter units of the Ninth flew several hundred sorties over German-occupied areas. They found enemy aircraft and destroyed nine of them in return for an F-6 loss. Lieutenant Leland A. Larson of the 15th TRS became the last ace in the ETO when he shot down an Fw190 near Radnitz at 20.00 hours.

With the German surrender now formally signed, the Allied high command ordered all Luftwaffe aircraft to be rendered unfit to fly (usually by removal of propellers) and abandoned. The tactical reconnaissance squadrons indulged in a bizarre aerial 'round up' in their part of Germany centred on Fürth. In the manner of cowboys, they flew their F-6 Mustangs to guide numerous German aircraft to put down at Fürth to surrender. There were one or two incidents, but in the main the erstwhile enemy airmen accepted the situation with as much dignity as they could muster in the circumstances.

There remains the definitive claim for the last German aircraft destroyed during hostilities by a US fighter pilot, as against one operating in a reconnaissance role (which may be taking qualification a bit too far). The devil was in the detail: Leland Larson, flying an aircraft almost identical to a standard P-51D apart from the fact that the F-6 carried cameras for its dual PR role, was given credit but a counter claim for the final kill — five minutes later — went into the records as that apparently made by Lieutenant Kenneth L. Swift of the 429th FS, 474th Group. Flying a P-38J at 20.05 hours he

Above: Also painted with underwing codes was P-51D (44-14692) 'My Rosie' of the 77th Squadron, 20th Fighter Group, pictured at St Trond, Belgium, in 1945. *J. V. Crow*

was understood to have shot down a courier aircraft. It appears, however, that the 474th made no such claim, but two German aircraft (an Fi156 and an He111) were forced down by a section of the group's P-38s on 8 May although neither was destroyed. The records incidentally counted the aircraft destroyed on 8 May as the 7,504th victory credited to a USAAF pilot in the war against Germany and the 11,268th Axis aircraft downed by an AAF pilot since 2nd Lieutenant Samuel F. Junkin of the 31st Fighter Group destroyed an Fw190 over Dieppe on 19 August 1942.

In any event, the USAAF fighter forces had finally completed their task when all hostilities in Europe ceased at 00.01 hours on 9 May 1945.

Aftermath

With peace, selected USAAF fighter groups were designated to remain in Germany on occupation duty. Unit

personnel changed quite rapidly during this period as combat veterans were released from duty to return home. Training in the US and the transfer of troops to Europe could not be switched off overnight, and numerous individuals arrived in the former combat zone of the ETO to find that they became members of units that had lost most, if not all, of their ground officers, pilots and maintenance crews who, like ghosts, had faded away, taking the traditions, the records and often the very flavour of the old squadron or group with them.

Other newcomers, *en route* when the surrender occurred, found the quite bewildering sight of German workers busily engaged in breaking up the very combat aircraft that they had fully expected to fly, as peace brought about a giant slimming-down process. In the

early summer of 1945 the USAAF suddenly had thousands of surplus aircraft in Europe and many of these had to be struck from new, leaner inventories as the awesome process of clearing up and reconstruction began. And it was not too long before a defeated Germany became a bulwark against Russian communism, which completely turned the situation around; American forces were now pledged to defend much of the territory they had so recently conquered and to do that adequately they still needed airpower. While maintaining an increasingly uneasy peace, the number of US personnel, aircraft and units in Germany gradually reduced until the first examples of turbojet types were available and a slow expansion took place.

Appendices

Appendix One

The Top 100 USAAF Aces, Eighth/Ninth Air Forces (ETO only)

	NAME	SCORE	UNIT(S)	FATE
1	Gabreski, Francis S.*	28	56th	PoW flak 20 July 44
2	Johnson, Robert S.	27	56th	
3	Preddy , George E.+	26.833	352nd	KIA ff 25 Dec 44
4	Meyer, John C.	24	352nd	
5	Schilling, David C.	22.5	56th	
6	Gentile, Dominic S.	21.833	4th	
7	Christensen, Frederick J., Jr	21.5	56th	
8	Wetmore, Raymond S.	21.25	359th	
9	Mahurin, Walker M.*	19.75	56th	ev flak 27 Mar 44
10	Duncan, Glenn E.*	19.5	353rd	ev flak 7 July 44
11	Eagleston, Glenn T.	18.5	354th	
12	Carson, Leonard K.	18.5	357th	
13	Gladych, Boleslaw M.	18	56th	
14	Beckham, Walter C.*	18	353rd	PoW flak 22 Feb 44
15	Zemke, Hubert A.*	17.75	56th/479th	PoW acc 30 Oct 44
16	England, John B.	17.5	357th	
17	Beeson, Duane W.*	17.333	4th	PoW flak 5 Apr 44
18	Garrison, Vermont*	17.333	4th	PoW flak 3 Mar 44
19	Thornell, John F., Jr	17.25	352nd	
20	Johnson, Gerald W.*	16.5	56th	PoW flak 27 Mar 44
21	Anderson, Clarence E., Jr	16.25	357th	
22	Godfrey, John T.*	16.333	4th	PoW flak 24 Aug 44
23	Beerbower, Don M.+	15.5	354th	KIA flak 9 Aug 44
24	Peterson, Richard A.	15.5	357th	
25	Whisner, William T.	15.5	352nd	
26	Bradley, Jack T.	15	354th	
27	Carr, Bruce W.	15	363rd/354th	
28	Foy, Robert W.	15	357th	
29	Hofer, Ralph K.+	15	4th	KIA e/a 2 July 44
30	Blakeslee, Donald J. M.	14.5	4th	
31	Landers, John D.	14.5	55th/357th/78th	
32	Powers, Joe H., Jr	14.5	56th	
33	Brown, Henry W.*	14.25	355th	PoW flak 3 Oct 44
34	Goodson, James A.*	14	4th	PoW flak 20 June 44
35	Dahlberg, Kenneth H.*	14	354th	PoW flak 14 Feb 45
36	Emmer, Wallace N.*	14	354th	PoW flak 9 Aug 44
37	Jeffrey, Arthur F.	14	479th	
38	Bochkay, Donald H.	13.833	357th	
39	Carpenter, George W.*	13.833	4th	PoW e/a 18 Apr 44

	NAME	SCORE	UNIT(S)	FATE
40	Strait, Donald J.	13.5	356th	
41	Bryan, Donald S.	13.333	352nd	
42	East, Clyde B.	13	10th TRG	
43	Millikan, Willard W.*	13	4th	PoW coll 30 May 44
44	Moran, Glennon T.	13	357th	
45	Olds, Robin	13	479th	
46	Stephens, Robert W.	13	354th	
47	Williamson, Felix D.	13	56th	
48	Brueland, Lowell K.	12.5	354th	
49	Brown, Quince L.**	12.333	78th	flak 6 Sept 44
50	Gleason, George W.	12	479th	
51	Hively, Howard D.	12	4th	
52	Schreiber, Leroy A.+	12	56th	KIA flak 15 April 44
53	Megura, Nicholas*	11.833	4th	int flak 22 May 44
54	Conger, Paul A.	11.5	56th	
55	Kirla, John A.	11.5	357th	
56	Stewart, James C.	11.5	56th	
57	Yeager, Charles E.*	11.5	357th	ev flak 5 Mar 44
58	Frantz, Carl M.	11	354th	
59	McKennon, Pierce W.*	11	4th	ev flak 7 Aug 44
60	Quirk, Michael J.*	11	56th	PoW flak 10 Sept 44
61	Overfield, Lloyd J.*	11	354th	ev flak 7 Aug 44
62	Turner, Richard E.	11	354th	
63	O'Connor, Frank Q.*	10.75	354th	PoW flak 5 Nov 44
64	Clark, James A., Jr	10.5	4th	
65	Hovde, William J.	10.5	355th	
66	Ceullers, George F.	10.5	364th	
67	Doersch, George A.	10.5	359th	
68	Halton, William T.	10.5	352nd	
69	Littge, Raymond H.	10.5	352nd	
70	Storch, John A.	10.5	357th	
71	Glover, Fred W.*	10.333	4th	ev flak 30 Apr 44
72	Norley, Louis H.	10.333	4th	
73	Anderson, Charles F. Jr+	10	4th	KIA 19 Apr 44
74	Blickenstaff, Wayne K.	10	353rd	
75	Lines, Edward E.	10	4th	
76	Rankin, Robert J.	10	56th	
77	Bankey, Ernest E., Jr	9.5	364th	
78	Spencer, Dale F.	9.5	361st	
79	Adams, Fletcher E.+	9	357th	KIA e/a 30 May 44
80	Andrew, Stephen W.*	9	352nd	PoW 2 July 44
81	Beyer, Willam R.	9	352nd	
82	Dalglish, James B.	9	361st	
83	Elder, Robert A.	9	355th	
84	Fiebelkorn, Ernest C.	9	20th	
85	Gallup, Kenneth W.	9	353rd	
86	Juchheim, Aldwin M., Jr*	9	78th	PoW coll 28 May 44

NAME	SCORE	UNIT(S)	FATE
87 Meroney, Virgil K.*	9	352nd	PoW flak 8 Apr 44
88 Morrill, Stanley B.+	9	56th	KIA acc 29 Mar 44
89 Roberts, Eugene P.	9	78th	
90 Bennett Joseph H.*	8.5	56th/4th	PoW coll 25 Apr 44
91 Cesky, Charles J.	8.5	357th	
92 Hayes, Thomas L., Jr	8.5	357th	
93 Hoefker, John H.	8.5	10th TRG	
94 Jenkins, Otto D.+	8.5	357th	KIFA 24 Mar 45
95 Luksic, Carl J.*	8.5	352nd	PoW 24 May 44
96 McDowell, Donald +	8.5	354th	MIA 28 May 44
97 McGrattan, Bernard J.+	8.5	4th	KIA e/a 6 June 44
98 Moats, Sanford K.	8.5	352nd	
99 Schlegel, Albert L.+	8.5	4th	KIA flak 28 Aug 44
100 Booth, Robert J.*	8	359th	PoW flak 8 June 44

KEY:
* lost – cause as noted   coll – collision   + KIA – killed in action   PoW – prisoner of war
acc – accident   ff – friendly fire   KIFA – killed in flying accident
e/a – enemy aircraft   flak – AA fire   MIA – missing in action
ev – evaded   fint – interned   ** – murdered

NB: In some case, early victories were achieved with RAF squadrons and boosted in later wars. These latter have not been included.

Appendix Two

Combat Statistics: Principal Fighters, Eighth/Ninth Air Forces

AIRCRAFT	SORTIES	VICTORIES (AIR)	(GROUND)	LOSSES
P-47 Thunderbolt	423,435	3,082	3,202	3,077
P-38 Lightning	129,849	1,771	749	1,758
P-51 Mustang	213,873	4,950	4,131	2,520
Totals:	767,157	9,803	8,082	7,355

Appendix Three

Fighter Units and Squadron Codes, Eighth/Ninth Air Forces

UNIT	CODE	AIRCRAFT	AIR FORCE	UNIT	CODE	AIRCRAFT	AIR FORCE
4th Fighter Group		Spitfire;P-47;	Eighth	**36th Fighter Group**		P-47	Ninth
334th FS	QF	P-51		22nd FS	3T		
335th FS	WD			23rd FS	7U		
336th FS	VF			53rd FS	6V		
20th Fighter Group		P-38; P-51	Eighth	**48th Fighter Group**		P-47	Ninth
55th FS	KI			492nd FS	F4		
77th FS	LC			493rd FS	I7		
79th FS	MC			494th FS	6M		

UNIT	CODE	AIRCRAFT	AIR FORCE	UNIT	CODE	AIRCRAFT	AIR FORCE
50th Fighter Group		P-47	Ninth	**357th Fighter Group**		P-51	Eighth
10th FS	T5			362nd FS	G4		
81st FS	2N			363rd FS	B6		
313th FS	W3			364th FS	C5		
55th Fighter Group		P-38; P-51	Eighth	**358th Fighter Group**		P-47	Eighth/Ninth
38th FS	CG			365th FS	CH		
338th FS	CL			366th FS	IA		
343rd FS	CY			367th FS	CP		
56th Fighter Group		P-47	Eighth	**359th Fighter Group**		P-47; P-51	Eighth
61st FS	HV			368th FS	CV		
62nd FS	LM			369th FS	IV		
63rd FS	UN			370th FS	CS		
78th Fighter Group		P-47; P-51	Eighth	**361st Fighter Group**		P-47; P-51	Eighth
82nd FS	MX			374th FS	B7		
83rd FS	HL			375th FS	E2		
84th FS	WZ			376th FS	E9		
339th Fighter Group		P-51	Eighth	**362nd Fighter Group**		P-47	Ninth
503rd FS	D7			377th FS	E4		
504th FS	5Q			378th FS	G8		
505th FS	6N			379th FS	B8		
352nd Fighter Group		P-47; P-51	Eighth	**363rd Fighter Group**		P-51	Ninth
328thFS	PE			380th FS	A9		
486thFS	PZ			381st FS	B3		
487thFS	HO			382nd FS	C3		
353rd Fighter Group		P-47; P-51	Eighth	**364th Fighter Group**		P-38; P-51	Eighth
350th FS	LH			383rd FS	N2		
351st FS	YJ			384th FS	5Y		
352nd FS	SX			385th FS	5E		
354th Fighter Group		P-47; P-51	Eighth/Ninth	**365th Fighter Group**		P-47	Ninth
353rd FS	FT			386th FS	D5		
355th FS	GQ			387th FS	B4		
356th FS	AJ			388th FS	C4		
355th Fighter Group		P-47; P-51	Eighth	**366th Fighter Group**		P-47	Ninth
354th FS	WR			389th FS	A6		
357th FS	OS			390th FS	B2		
358th FS	YF			391st FS	A8		
356th Fighter Group		P-47; P-51	Eighth	**367th Fighter Group**		P-38; P-47	Ninth
359th FS	OC			392nd FS	H5		
360th FS	PI			393rd FS	8L		
361st FS	QI			394th FS	4N		

UNIT	CODE	AIRCRAFT	AIR FORCE	UNIT	CODE	AIRCRAFT	AIR FORCE
368th Fighter Group		P-47	Ninth	**405th Fighter Group**		P-47	Ninth
395th FS	A7			509th FS	G9		
396th FS	C2			510th FS	2Z		
397th FS	D3			511th FS	K4		
370th Fighter Group		P-38; P-51	Ninth	**406th Fighter Group**		P-47	Ninth
401st FS	9D			512th FS	L3		
402nd FS	E6			513th FS	4F		
485th FS	7F			514th FS	O7		
371st Fighter Group		P-47	Ninth	**474th Fighter Group**		P-38	Ninth
404th FS	9Q			428th FS	F5		
405th FS	8N			429th FS	7Y		
406th FS	4W			430th FS	K6		
373rd Fighter Group		P-47	Ninth	**479th Fighter Group**		P-38; P-51	Eighth
410th FS	R3			434th FS	L2		
411th FS	U9			435th FS	J2		
412th FS	V5			436th FS	9B		
404th Fighter Group		P-47	Ninth				
506th FS	4K						
507th FS	Y8						
508th FS	7J						

Index

NB: Ranks shown in index are generally the
highest attained by the individual